TEXAS LONGHORNS
FOOTBALL HISTORY A TO Z

TEXAS LONGHORNS
FOOTBALL HISTORY A TO Z

Richard Pennington

MAPLE STREET PRESS
Hingham, MA

Maple Street Press LLC is in no way affiliated with the University of Texas or the NCAA. The opinions expressed in this book are those of the author and not necessarily those of Maple Street Press.

Jacket design: Garrett Cullen

Front cover photos, clockwise from top left: Herb Scharfman//Time Life Pictures/Getty Images; AP/Time & Life Pictures/Getty Images; Ronald Martinez/Getty Images Sport; Stephen Dunn/Getty Images; Harry How/Getty Images

Chapter opening photography provided by the University of Texas Athletic Department. All rights reserved.

Interior design: Bryan Davidson

Richard Pennington. *Texas Longhorns Football History A to Z*
ISBN 978-1-934186-13-8

Library of Congress Control Number: 2007938334

Maple Street Press LLC
11 Leavitt Street
Hingham, MA 02043
www.maplestreetpress.com

Printed in the United States of America
07 7 6 5 4 3 2 First Edition

Contents

Preface

It is an honor as well as a major responsibility to write the history of football at the University of Texas. Credit must be given to so many people who have built UT's great football tradition: Men long dead and men still very much alive; players, coaches, and athletic directors; students, alumni, and garden-variety fans of the Longhorns. I acknowledge them and all their contributions. This book, which aims to document 114 years of football at my alma mater, has been a genuine labor of love.

As a Dallas native, I first saw the Longhorns play in the Cotton Bowl, both against SMU and in the New Year's Day game. After my inauspicious arrival in Austin in 1971, I began to soak up the history, culture, and vibe of UT football. A person does not get his orange blood overnight. It's a gradual thing, one that takes root and grows with the wins and losses, the ups and downs that are the nature of intercollegiate sports. I was a history major during those long-ago days, with many classes in Garrison Hall, right in the shadow of the Tower. Few, if any, professors were dazzled with my academic and intellectual brilliance, but I am grateful that they taught me to look for context, nuance, and varying perspectives.

Although it's not easy to strike a balance between being a true believer and engaging in objective analysis, I ask the reader to make the attempt along with me. We can be passionate as well as critical, engaged but honest. This book contains lots of football statistics: touchdowns, yards gained, all-conference honors, and so forth. But it is most assuredly not of the rah-rah, cheerleading variety. I find such books of little interest. I hope the reader will be informed and amused, occasionally challenged and perplexed because this is not a simple, linear story.

OK, let me wave the flag just a bit. I know about other schools' cherished traditions—Notre Dame has Touchdown Jesus, Texas A&M has the 12th man, Ohio State dots the "i," Southern California has Traveler, Oklahoma has "Boomer Sooner," Nebraska has the tunnel walk, Clemson players rub Howard's rock, Florida State has the flaming spear, Alabama has Bear Bryant's hound's-tooth hat, Colorado has Ralphie, and Tennessee has "Rocky Top." That's fine. I will take Bevo, Smokey, Big Bertha, the Longhorn Band, "The Eyes of Texas," the best-looking helmet in college football, Clyde Littlefield, Bobby Layne, DKR, Earl, Ricky, and Vince. I can't help it—I love the Horns.

Finally, I wish to dedicate *Texas Longhorns Football History from A to Z* to my fiancée, Helen Litrada. She has been a blessing and an inspiration to me since before this project began.

Richard Pennington
Austin, Texas

Foreword

Many people consider Lou Maysel's two-part classic *Here Come the Texas Longhorns* (1970 and 1978) the definitive read on the history of Texas football. Now, by highlighting 114 years of UT football, Richard Pennington brings Maysel's concept up to the present day. Decade by decade, he chronicles the program's evolution from its ad hoc beginning in the early 1890s to a modern-day football and marketing powerhouse.

When most of you read the pages that follow, you will find that specific players, games, stories, and moments will trigger thoughts—both good and bad. But when I think of the history of Texas football and my very small part in it, I realize I lived a dream.

At age 10, I walked down the tunnel at the Cotton Bowl just behind my father's officiating crew. I was on the sidelines when Russell Erxleben kicked a 64-yard field goal against Rice that seemed to hang in the air forever. I sat in the "knothole section" of Memorial Stadium for Darrell Royal's last game. I was in the stands as a high school recruit when Robert Brewer and the explosive 1982 Horns blew out Texas A&M. And in September 1983, I walked onto the field at Jordan-Hare Stadium in Auburn, Alabama as a puffy-haired freshman ready to take on Bo Jackson and Auburn in a nationally televised game.

Probably every player who has ever put on a Longhorns jersey has a moment when he realizes what the uniform stands for. For me, that moment wasn't tied up in game-winning field goals, or championships won, or those that got away (and some of them did). It came from a knock on the locker-room door.

Having watched as a boy as my father and the other officials went to each locker room to call for the respective team captains, I dreamed of what it would be like to walk ahead of everyone while representing the state of Texas, the university, and all of the players who would come pouring out of that tunnel after me.

We were huge underdogs to Oklahoma in 1986, and admittedly we were outmanned. But as much as the loss that day would sting forever, when the officials pounded on the door on that October Saturday and yelled, "Texas captains, it's time," I was first out to soak in every moment, knowing full well what that walk meant.

Richard Pennington's *Texas Longhorns Football History from A to Z* is not just about games, players, and controversial moments. Rather, it's a telling of the larger-than-life storylines of UT football. As you read, you will come to understand that the college sports landscape has the Longhorns' hoofprints all over it. Few fans know that Texas athletics actually embraced pro football for a time in the 1950s. And Pennington points out that at one time Texas officials were terrified of television's impact on the future of college football (an idea that is comical in this day and age).

Pennington even highlights a great motivational slogan created by one of the most feared and respected men in UT history. Legendary trainer Frank Medina once posted a locker-room sign that read, "Hats off to the past, roll up your sleeves for the future."

Not far behind Medina's inspirational slogan was a great pre-game speech, courtesy of my head coach, Fred Akers. It took place in New Jersey in September of 1984 when we were No. 2 in the polls before our game with Penn State.

As we gathered in the spacious locker room, Fred parted a group of kneeling players, took off his hat, and jumped up on a bench. He stood there for a few moments and then calmly told us, "Men, the Meadowlands is sold out for the first time for a college game."

He then paused and looked around the room before yelling out, "and do you know why the Meadowlands is sold out for the first time for a college game?"

By now, the room was dead silent. He quietly finished, "it is sold out today because Texas is here."

We beat Penn State that day, 31–3.

From the early days of Clark Field, to the hiring of Darrell Royal, to the firing of John Mackovic, to the night Vince Young crossed the goal line to beat Southern Cal in the Rose Bowl and clinch the 2005 national title, Pennington will take you through the incredible history of Longhorns football. He reminds us all of the great players, the big games, the championships, and the men who have guided Texas athletics through the years. While many pages will be filled with burnt-orange successes, he never hides from pointing out the failures and stormy periods that make Texas football a compelling story.

Page after page, you will read about one of the great programs in the history of the game, and for a few lucky ones like me, it was a dream come true to play a part.

Hook 'em!

Jeff Ward

McLANE

MORRISON

MYER

McLANE

MOORE

MAN

McLEAN

CRAWFORD

UT 93

It was the start of something big. The 1893 University of Texas football team went 4–0 and fancied itself the state champion. (Photo courtesy of the University of Texas.)

In the early 1890s, football came to Texas from the East and Midwest by a process that began slowly before picking up speed. Its arrival was unannounced, unsponsored, almost completely unnoticed, and sometimes unwelcome. But this new game with so much body contact and spirit fit the mood of the young men of the region, which was just emerging from a rugged frontier life. College campuses in the Lone Star State were receptive, as were the hubs of YMCAs and high schools. Loosely organized teams soon arose, claiming to represent Houston, Dallas, San Antonio, and other cities. What those first experiments lacked in polish, they made up for in vigor because the climate in Texas was just right for football.

The rules of the game were treated lightly, if they were known at all. Organization was random, team rosters changed from day to day, and coaching was ad hoc. Players knew only that the motive was clear—to carry, kick, bump, and push forward to get that touchdown. Those on defense used much the same methods to prevent it. Although some got hurt, the bloody nose, black eye, and split lip were badges of the day.

This new semi-organized mass mayhem won collegiate sanction at the University of Texas in 1893, and other schools followed quickly. The records from those early years must be taken with a proverbial grain of salt. Few who lived then would have taken a solemn oath that the scores and performances, not to mention the real names of the players, were handed down accurately and faithfully. Sometimes the wish was father to the results as reported, and an alias provided flexibility to rovers who played here, there, and yonder from one year to the next. "Varsity" as UT called its team early on, was not immune to such problems. The chroniclers of the day were rather generous, too. From a modern perspective, sportswriters then shamelessly doubled as cheerleaders.

The enrollment of three students at UT in the fall of 1893 is where it all began. The McLane brothers, Paul and Ray, sons of a Laredo district judge, are said to have attended Cornell or Columbia or both, but documentation is lacking. The third of the three originators of Longhorns football was James Morrison. A native of Virginia, he had played at Hampden-Sydney College before coming to Austin primarily to care for an elderly uncle who was on the UT faculty. Although there was no coach the first year, Paul McLane, the most knowledgeable about the sport, in effect served that role on the budding Texas team. He gave instructions in the crude techniques of football after classes at a spot on the northwest corner of the 10-year-old campus.

By the Numbers

4   Points given up by the 1898 Texas team in six games.

15 Students who participated in UT's first game in 1893, against the Dallas football club.

19 Members of the Southern Intercollegiate Athletic Association, which Texas joined in 1895.

30 Dollars for tuition, good enough for a student's entire course of study at UT.

50 Cents admission to the final game of 1893, a rematch with Dallas.

88 Other colleges fielding football teams in 1893.

100 Dollars given by Austin haberdashery Harrell & Wilcox to cover the team's food and lodging in Dallas for the initial game.

150 Dollars in red the UT football program was after the 1899 season.

162 Pounds in average weight of the 1893 team members.

200 Students and other fans who accompanied the UT team to play San Antonio on February 3, 1894.

355 Student enrollment (including coeds) in 1893.

Archive

Home games in **bold**

1893 Record: 4–0 Coach: None
Texas 18, Dallas 16

Texas 30, San Antonio 0

Texas 34, San Antonio 0

Texas 16, Dallas 0

1894 Record: 6–1 Coach: Reginald Wentworth
Texas 38, Texas A&M 0

Texas 12, Tulane 0

Texas 6, Austin YMCA 0

Texas 24, Austin YMCA 0

Texas 54, Arkansas 0

Texas 57, San Antonio 0

Missouri 28, Texas 0

1895 Record: 5–0 Coach: Frank Crawford
Texas 10, Dallas 0

Texas 24, Austin YMCA 0

Texas 16, Tulane 0

3

Varsity Athletic Field/Clark Field

Texas played its first home game down along the Colorado River, followed by 10 more in Hyde Park before actually having one on campus. Football practice had been held from time to time at the northwest corner of 24th and Guadalupe streets, but that was not actually UT property. Nor was a five-acre field at the southeast corner of 24th Street and Speedway, on the other side of the Forty Acres. It was a sparsely settled area, covered with cedar trees and mesquite bushes. Chemistry professor and stalwart fan Edgar Everhart urged that UT football move operations there, and so it happened in 1897.

Texas' new football field belonged to an absentee owner, a Mr. de Cordova, who permitted the students to use it for three years and then demanded that they either buy or vacate. Responding to de Cordova's ultimatum, Dean of Engineering T. U. Taylor and Judge R. L. Batts negotiated a price of $3,000, to be paid in three installments. The students' refunded library deposits paid for the first, Taylor got money from the faculty and alumni for the second, and the Board of Regents took care of the third in 1901. Thus was the campus first expanded and Texas football put on more solid footing.

A wooden fence was erected around the perimeter of the field for $350, and a few bleachers were soon built on the west side. That was the extent of improvements for the first 10 years. Varsity Athletic Field, as it had been known rather generically since 1897, was renamed 7 years later in honor of James B. Clark. A supporter of UT athletics, Clark had been one of the original members of the Board of Regents, proctor, librarian, secretary of the faculty, buildings and grounds manager, dean of students, registrar, business manager, and admissions officer. Clark, a graduate of Franklin College in Tennessee, had studied law at Harvard and served in the Confederate army during the Civil War.

After the Longhorns played at the University of Missouri in 1907, students were impressed by what their counterparts in Columbia had done in build-

(Continued in sidebar on next page)

Texas 38, San Antonio 0
Texas 8, Galveston 0

1896   Record: 4–2–1   Coach: Harry Robinson
Texas 42, Galveston 0
Texas 0, Dallas 0
Texas 12, San Antonio 4
Texas 12, Tulane 4
LSU 14, Texas 0
Texas 22, Dallas 4
Missouri 10, Texas 0

1897   Record: 6–2   Coach: Walter "Mike" Kelly
Texas 10, San Antonio 0
Dallas 18, Texas 4
Fort Worth 6, Texas 0
Texas 18, Add-Ran 10
Texas 42, Houston 6
Texas 12, San Antonio 0
Texas 38, Fort Worth 0
Texas 20, Dallas 16

1898   Record: 5–1   Coach: Dave Edwards
Texas 16, Add-Ran 0
Texas 48, Texas A&M 0
Texas 17, Galveston 0
Texas 29, Add-Ran 0
Sewanee 4, Texas 0
Texas 26, Dallas 0

1899   Record: 6–2   Coach: Maurice G. Clarke
Texas 11, Dallas 6
Texas 28, San Antonio 0
Texas 6, Texas A&M 0 (in San Antonio)

Sewanee 12, Texas 0

Vanderbilt 6, Texas 0

Texas 11, Tulane 0

Texas 32, Tulane 0

Texas 29, LSU 0

10 Big Games

Texas 18, Dallas 16 / November 30, 1893 / Fairgrounds Park (Dallas, Texas)

James Morrison and the McLane brothers lead a band of students to Dallas and upset a previously unbeaten team before 2,000 spectators.

ing bleachers around their football field. So they came home and embarked on a campaign to raise money to buy the materials. With help from local laborers, they got at it with hammers and saws, finishing the job in less than a week—bringing seating capacity to 2,000. More piecemeal changes took place over the next decade, making room for 15,000, although it overflowed with crowds in excess of 20,000 when the Texas A&M Aggies came to town in the early 1920s.

Clark Field was not just used for football. Varsity baseball, basketball (until the Men's Gym was built next door in 1916), and track and field events were contested there. And that does not include the multiplicity of intramurals, pageants, military marching in World War I, and graduation ceremonies hosted at Clark Field over a period of nearly 30 years.

Texas 38, Texas A&M 0 / October 19, 1894 / Hyde Park (Austin, Texas)

UT moves up and down the field with the greatest of ease as Ray McLane and James Morrison both score twice against A&M. The Farmers of A&M will eventually learn how the game is played.

Texas 54, Arkansas 0 / November 29, 1894 / Hyde Park (Austin, Texas)

The travel-weary Razorbacks (then the Arkansas Industrial University Cardinals) have been on the road for nearly a week. They take it on the chin in their first game against Texas.

Missouri 28, Texas 0 / December 14, 1894 / Hyde Park (Austin, Texas)

A sobering defeat by Missouri concludes the 1894 season. The Tigers employ a much different style of football than what coach Reginald Wentworth's players (who had until then scored 191 points and not given up one) are accustomed to.

Texas 16, Tulane 0 / November 23, 1895 / Hyde Park (Austin, Texas)

In a game played in a sea of mud, Texas posts a win over its visitors from Louisiana; fullback John Maverick scores two touchdowns.

Texas 8, Galveston 0 / December 6, 1895 / (Galveston, Texas)
Another game is played amid rain and mud, but this time down on the island. Jim Caperton and J. S. "Snaky" Jones both score for UT.

Texas 12, Tulane 4 / November 14, 1896 / (New Orleans, Louisiana)
In the first trip out of state, Coach Harry Robinson's team edges Tulane. But two days later in Baton Rouge, it's a different story as LSU wins, 14–0.

Texas 20, Dallas 16 / December 11, 1897 / Varsity Athletic Field (Austin, Texas)
Kid Bethea and Otto Pfeiffer lead UT in a disputed win over the Dallas Tigers, winners of a game earlier in the season. Coach Mike Kelly's team will finish with a 6–2 record.

Texas 6, Texas A&M 0 / November 4, 1899 / (San Antonio, Texas)
The Alamo City is a neutral site for the game, as A&M really tests UT for the first time. Semp Russ' 50-yard run with a double lateral is the only score of the day.

Texas 29, LSU 0 / November 30, 1899 / Varsity Athletic Field (Austin, Texas)
This Thanksgiving Day game with the Tigers is a victory despite injuries to key players. Fullback C. C. Cole has two touchdowns.

All-Decade Team

Back	Jim Caperton (1895–1896)
Back	Cade "Kid" Bethea (1897–1899)
Back	Semp Russ (1898–1900)
Lineman	Dan Parker (1894–1897)
Lineman	Andrew Denmark (1895–1897)
Lineman	James Clarke (1895–1897)
Lineman	Richard "Chub" Wortham (1895–1898)
Lineman	Lamar Bethea (1896–1898)
Lineman	Ed Overshiner (1898–1899)
End	Walter Schreiner (1896–1900)
End	Jim Hart (1897–1900)
Kicker	Addison Day (1893–1894)

Q & A

Q. When did University of Texas students begin playing football?

A. The year was 1883. The university had opened its doors just a few weeks before some students challenged Bickler's German and English Academy to an informal game. It was played at a spot east of Congress Avenue and north of the Capitol. The Bickler's boys, who scored two goals, were declared winners. Other such pickup games were held on or near the Forty Acres in the years to follow, but there is little to document the teams, the players, or the games. There were at least three football clubs on campus in 1891. Only in 1893 (24 years after the first football game, played by Rutgers and Princeton) did a team purport to represent UT, and so we recognize this as the true beginning. James Morrison and brothers Paul and Ray McLane organized a group of students who played an exhibition game against a team from the Austin Athletic Club (AAC) on November 11. Almost every aspect of the game was helter-skelter, including the final score, which was either a 6–6 tie or a 10–2 win by the AAC. The first real game in UT history came 19 days later against the Dallas football club at Fairgrounds Park. About 100 of their classmates joined them on the nine-hour train ride up from Austin. The Dallas team fancied itself the state champion, but Texas fullback Addison Day scored two touchdowns and kicked a pair of field goals in a two-point upset, after which UT players bought big cigars and strutted down Main Street.

Q. And where was the first home game played?

A. Off campus, at Dam Baseball Park near the banks of the Colorado River. There, on December 16, 1893, a team from San Antonio took a 30–0 licking before 600 fans (including Governor Jim Hogg), most of whom moved up and down the sidelines with the action when they weren't huddled around bonfires to stay warm. Texas beat San Antonio, 34–0, in the Alamo City on February 3. Nineteen days later, the final game of the season took place in Hyde Park, in the middle of an erstwhile horseracing track. Morrison, the McLanes, and their teammates won again, finishing UT's first football season with a 4–0 record. They celebrated with a tour of downtown.

Q. There had been no coach, per se, in 1893. Who was hired for that position before the 1894 season?

A. Reginald Wentworth, an alumnus of Williams College. He was given a salary of $325, and another $100 to buy uniforms and other equipment. Wentworth's hiring was brought on by the action of two recent law graduates, A. S. Walker and Thomas W. Gregory. Gregory later embarked on a marathon fundraising project to build a big gymnasium that bore his name.

Q. What happened to the UT football team that lost to Missouri at the end of the 1894 season?

A. They felt so dishonored that some quit football, some went to other schools, and Wentworth left town entirely. He returned to the East and later went into the marine insurance business.

Q. After that beating by Mizzou in 1894 and Wentworth's departure, Texas had some trouble finding a new coach. Who replaced him?

A. Frank "Little" Crawford, a New Hampshire native who had been at Nebraska the previous two seasons. He did not arrive in Austin until mid-October, so the season was a bit delayed. Crawford, who stressed physical conditioning, often had his players run from campus to the Hyde Park practice field and back. Crawford rode a bicycle to watch out for laggards.

Q. How did the team do under Crawford?

A. They won all five games and did not give up a single point.

Q. Identify the predecessor of the Southwest Conference.

A. UT belonged to two: The Southern Intercollegiate Athletic Association, and one of its spin-offs, the Texas Intercollegiate Athletic Association (TIAA). The TIAA was formed by Dr. Homer Curtiss, UT gymnasium director and assistant football coach from 1900 through 1905.

Q. Intercollegiate sports were, for the most part, a haphazard, student-run endeavor until when?

A. That began to change in 1895, at which time the Athletics Council was formed. This faculty committee was determined to bring things under its control.

Q. Who was the next of UT's one-year wonders?

A. Harry Robinson, a former lineman at Tufts, who had an electrical engineering degree and was reputedly a fine string musician. He had been the coach of the Missouri team that beat Texas so badly in 1894. Like Wentworth and Crawford before him, Robinson moved on after one season.

Jim Hart

Equally adept as a tackle, end, fullback, quarterback, or kicker, Jim Hart was one of the most versatile of Texas' early football players. This native of Austin was 6' 2", 165 pounds and served as captain of the 1899 team. For 26 years, he was the alumni representative to the Athletics Council, helped fund construction of a baseball facility (Clark Field II), and was inducted into the Longhorn Hall of Honor in 1968. Hart's son, James P. Hart, was a justice of the Texas Supreme Court and later the first chancellor of the UT System.

Q. Name the first time the Texas football team went out of state.

A. Twice in 1896. They traveled to New Orleans and beat Tulane, 12–4. And after a season-ending 10–0 loss to Missouri in Austin, a local entrepreneur arranged for the two teams to take a trip to Mexico and play a series of exhibition games. Mizzou won three of them, and there was a scoreless tie.

Q. Of whom was it said, "He cried like an infant and swore like a trooper from the first whistle to the last of every game"?

A. J. S. "Snaky" Jones, one of the captains of the 1896 Texas team.

Q. The 1897 schedule had eight games, seven of them with city teams. Who coached the Texas football team that year?

A. His name was Walter "Mike" Kelly, and he was another Yankee, having played collegiately at Dartmouth. Kelly was hired as physical director of men—a job that went beyond coaching football and that lasted the entire school year. He stepped down to be assistant coach (the first in school history) the next year when Dave Edwards led the team to a 5–1 record marred only by a tough loss to Sewanee at Varsity Athletic Field.

Q. What aesthetic monstrosity did Edwards come up with in his one year in Austin?

A. He shunned the traditional orange and white, and equipped his team in uniforms of orange and maroon. The natives did not take kindly to this move and pushed to make orange and white the official school colors soon thereafter. Like so many others, Edwards was soon on his way out of Austin, eventually entering the legal field in New Jersey.

Q. When did UT athletes first have a gymnasium, rudimentary showers, and a locker room?

A. Not until 1898, when the east wing of the Main Building was completed and used for that purpose.

Q. Texas' coach in 1899 was Maurice G. Clarke. Where did he learn his football?

A. For the previous three years, he had quarterbacked Amos Alonzo Stagg's University of Chicago team. Clarke, who had no assistant, won six games and lost two in his lone season at UT.

Q. What happened in the 1899 season opener?

A. It was against the Dallas Tigers at Fairgrounds Park. Spectators were crowded around the field, there was some rough play, and a minor brawl broke out. The game was called on account of darkness, with Texas up by a score of 11–6. The faculty and administration, already trying to move away from scheduling town teams, passed a resolution to that effect. Such teams "often had men who did not know the difference between a football game and a free-for-all fight," as one source put it.

Q. In the 1899 game with Texas A&M in San Antonio, an argument erupted after Texas scored the only touchdown of the day. Texas A&M Coach Bill Murray pulled his team off the field although 28 minutes of play remained. What wry poem soon appeared on the front page of the Battalion (A&M's student newspaper)?

A. "Our players proved they have grit/and played an honest game/The referee robbed us 6–0/We held the Varsity just the same."

Q. A big crowd of 2,000 gathered in Austin to witness the Texas–Sewanee game on Thursday, November 9, 1899. The superbly conditioned Sewanee Tigers won, 12–0. What made that so unique?

A. It was the first of five wins in six days—all shutouts, all on the road, and all against quality opponents. Billy Sutter's team jumped back on its special train for Houston, where they defeated A&M, 10–0 on Friday. Saturday in New Orleans, it was 23–0 over Tulane. Two days later in Baton Rouge, they whacked LSU, 34–0. Finally, on Tuesday in Memphis, Sewanee beat Mississippi, 12–0. The small Episcopalian college from the hills of Tennessee had pulled off what may have been the greatest road trip in the history of college football.

Q. He played five years, served as captain of the undefeated 1900 Texas team, and was later a member of the Board of Regents. Who was he?

A. Walter Schreiner.

CHAPTER 2
1900–1909

Lucian Parrish—captain of the 1906 Texas
football team, student body president, and future
member of the U.S. House of Representatives.
(Photo courtesy of the University of Texas.)

A new century had dawned. Football was still a crude game of short plunges into the line but it had begun to take root at the University of Texas. The financial situation was shaky—despite the increasing involvement of the faculty and administration—and the revolving door of coaches surely did not help. Although the growing pains continued for another quarter-century or so, it was a vibrant sport at colleges throughout the state. The emotional swirl of football sucked many students into a new campus experience, and the feelings lingered after graduation. At UT and elsewhere, the growing involvement of alumni and other boosters was an undeniable reality.

Coaching was becoming more scientific and better disciplined. Although faculty members lent their hand as assistant and head coaches, this was becoming less the norm. Many professors at colleges in the Southwest had studied and played the game (or at least followed it attentively), but how many really wanted to spend several afternoons a week to drill aspiring players on a practice field that often resembled a cow pasture?

Texas football, reared far from the sophisticated centers of the game, was usually a bit behind in adapting to the kaleidoscopic rule changes and styles of play. What it did share with the Harvards, Yales, Princetons, Michigans, and other top programs of the day was brutality and danger to participants. Concern had been growing before 1905, the year 18 players died nationally and 10 times that number were seriously injured. The flying wedge, mass formations, and gang tackling prompted many schools to discontinue the sport. Some urged that the game not just be reformed but abolished.

The University of Texas was not among the 13 schools that convened in New York in December 1905 to initiate changes in football playing rules. From these meetings came a number of innovations, the most significant of which were the formation of the National Collegiate Athletic Association (NCAA) and legalization of the forward pass. This seemingly simple stroke, more than any other milestone in football's evolution, opened up a whole new world. The forward pass allowed all sorts of innovations and shifted the emphasis from brawn to brains, from sheer size to agility, from destruction to deception. Schools in Texas did not master it immediately, but they did in time. The forward pass eventually allowed slingshot specialists to shoot many a Goliath out of the saddle, both at home and abroad.

Sportswriters up North and back East frequently compiled all-America teams and awarded mythical national championships—usually on the basis of little hard data, but it made for fun reading. None of them bothered with the University of Texas, and for good reason: The Longhorns lost at least three games four times in this decade, and possibly their best chance for all-America honors, Fred Ramsdell, transferred to Penn after just two years.

By the Numbers

3 Perfect seasons in the first eight years of Texas football: 1893, 1895, and 1900.

40 Points UT scored against Texas A&M and Baylor in a four-day span in October 1901. The Aggies and Bears were blanked.

200 Yards gained by Fred Ramsdell in a 24–0 manhandling of Texas A&M in 1906.

700 Fans at the UT–A&M game on Thanksgiving Day 1900. The weather was awful, and the turf at Varsity Athletic Field was nothing but mud.

800 Dollars that had to be borrowed to pay for UT to undertake the Vanderbilt–Arkansas–Oklahoma road trip in the middle of the 1905 season.

Archive

Home games in **bold**

1900   Record: 6–0   Coach: Samuel H. Thompson
Texas 28, Oklahoma 2
Texas 22, Vanderbilt 0 (in Dallas)
Texas 5, Texas A&M 0 (in San Antonio)
Texas 17, Missouri 11
Texas 30, Kansas City Medics 0
Texas 11, Texas A&M 0

1901   Record: 8–2–1   Coach: Samuel H. Thompson
Texas 32, Houston 0
Texas 5, Nashville 5 (in Dallas)
Texas 12, Oklahoma 6
Texas 17, Texas A&M 0 (in San Antonio)
Texas 23, Baylor 0
Texas 10, Dallas 2

15

Texas 11, Missouri 0
Kirksville Osteopaths 48, Texas 0
Kansas 12, Texas 0
Texas 11, Oklahoma 0
Texas 32, Texas A&M 0

1902   Record: 6–3–1   Coach: John B. Hart
Texas 22, Oklahoma 6
Texas 11, Sewanee 0 (in Dallas)
LSU 5, Texas 0 (in San Antonio)
Texas 0, Texas A&M 0 (in San Antonio)
Texas 27, Trinity 0
Haskell 12, Texas 0
Texas 11, Nashville 5
Texas 10, Alabama 0
Texas 6, Tulane 0
Texas A&M 12, Texas 0

1903   Record: 5–1–2   Coach: Ralph Hutchinson
Texas 17, School for Deaf & Dumb 0
Haskell 6, Texas 0 (in Dallas)
Texas 6, Oklahoma 6
Texas 48, Baylor 0
Texas 15, Arkansas 0
Texas 5, Vanderbilt 5
Texas 11, Oklahoma 5 (in Oklahoma City)
Texas 29, Texas A&M 6

1904   Record: 6–2   Coach: Ralph Hutchinson
Texas 40, TCU 0
Texas 24, Trinity 0
Haskell 4, Texas 0
Texas 23, Washington of Missouri 0
Chicago 68, Texas 0
Texas 40, Oklahoma 10
Texas 58, Baylor 0
Texas 34, Texas A&M 6

1905 Record: 5–4 Coach: Ralph Hutchinson
Texas 11, TCU 0
Haskell 17, Texas 0
Texas 39, Baylor 0
Vanderbilt 33, Texas 0
Texas 4, Arkansas 0
Oklahoma 2, Texas 0
Transylvania 6, Texas 0
Texas 17, Sewanee 10
Texas 27, Texas A&M 0

1906 Record: 9–1 Coach: Henry Schenker
Texas 21, 26th Infantry 0
Texas 22, TCU 0
Texas 28, West Texas Academy 0
Vanderbilt 45, Texas 0
Texas 11, Arkansas 0
Texas 10, Oklahoma 9
Texas 28, Haskell 0
Texas 40, Daniel Baker 0
Texas 17, Washington of Missouri 6
Texas 24, Texas A&M 0

1907 Record: 6–1–1 Coach: W. E. Metzenthin
Texas 0, Texas A&M 0 (in Dallas)
Texas 12, LSU 5
Texas 45, Haskell 10
Texas 26, Arkansas 6
Missouri 5, Texas 4
Texas 27, Baylor 11
Texas 29, Oklahoma 10
Texas 11, Texas A&M 6

1908 Record: 5–4 Coach: W. E. Metzenthin
Texas 11, TCU 6
Texas 27, Baylor 5
Colorado College 15, Texas 0

17

Fred Ramsdell

He weighed 180 pounds and could run like the wind. Fred Ramsdell, a native of Salado, was a halfback on the UT football team in 1907 and 1908. But he was also the school's first real track and field star as a sprinter, high jumper, long jumper, and even a miler when the team needed that. In 1908, while competing in an intercollegiate meet in Virginia, Ramsdell tied 1904 Olympic silver medalist Nate Cartmell of the University of Pennsylvania in 9.45 seconds, not far off the world record. That June, the U.S. Olympic trials were held in Philadelphia. Ramsdell did not make the team, but he chose to stay at Penn rather than return to Austin. Nicknamed "Tex" while in Philly, he was just as great in both sports for the Quakers. In 1910, the football authority of the day, Walter Camp, listed Ramsdell as a third-team all-American.

Texas 21, Arkansas 0
Southwestern 11, Texas 9
Texas 24, Texas A&M 8 (in Houston)
Oklahoma 50, Texas 0
Tulane 28, Texas 15
Texas 28, Texas A&M 12

1909 Record: 4–3–1
Coach: Dexter Draper
Texas 12, Southwestern 0
Haskell 12, Texas 11 (in Dallas)
Texas 18, Trinity 0
Texas 24, TCU 0
Texas A&M 23, Texas 0 (in Houston)
Texas 10, Tulane 10
Texas 30, Oklahoma 0
Texas A&M 5, Texas 0

20 Big Games

Texas 22, Vanderbilt 0 / October 13, 1900 / Fairgrounds Park (Dallas, Texas)

All four backs—Jim Hart, Sam Leslie, Semp Russ, and John De Lesdernier—score touchdowns to help avenge the 1899 loss to the Commodores in Nashville.

Texas 17, Missouri 11 / November 17, 1900 / Varsity Athletic Field (Austin, Texas)

Leopold "Big" Sam, a guard-turned-halfback, carries for 83 yards (probably a school record, although statistics were not kept with any regularity), making up for the loss of injured quarterback Semp Russ. Memories of the shutout losses to the Tigers in 1894 and 1896 are wiped away.

Texas 5, Nashville 5 / October 12, 1901 / Fairgrounds Park (Dallas, Texas)

Nashville, coached by Charley Moran—a future nemesis at A&M—plays Texas to a stalemate. William McMahon scores a 65-yard TD in the first

18

four minutes, but the visitors from Tennessee come back with a 50-yard trick play, and there the score stands.

Texas 32, Texas A&M 0 / November 28, 1901 / Varsity Athletic Field (Austin, Texas)

Battered from having played four road games in 10 days, UT is missing Sam Leslie and Rembert Watson but still has no trouble with A&M. That concludes an 8–2–1 season.

Texas 11, Sewanee 0 / October 10, 1902 / Fairgrounds Park (Dallas, Texas)

Fullback John Jackson is the star this day, plowing over the goal line twice for scores in a bruising defeat of the Tigers. John Hart's team would suffer four shutouts in '02, definitely not up to the standards to which UT is accustomed.

Texas 6, Oklahoma 6 / October 17, 1903 / Varsity Athletic Field (Austin, Texas)

The Longhorns and Rough Riders—as OU's teams were then known— would meet twice in 1903. In this, the first game, Texas appears to have won but a fumbled punt on its five-yard line in the last minute is recovered. Oklahoma scores, kicks the extra point, and heads back to Norman happy to have secured a tie.

Texas 5, Vanderbilt 5 / November 6, 1903 / Varsity Athletic Field (Austin, Texas)

UT and Vandy play to a tie when the Commodores' kicker, Frank Kyle, misses an extra point at the end. J. R. Henry, the visitors' coach, would later charge Texas with excessively rough play, using 12 men at a time, and other improprieties. An editorial in the *Daily Texan* refutes all such allegations.

Chicago 68, Texas 0 / November 5, 1904 / Marshall Field (Chicago, Illinois)

Articles in the Chicago press have people convinced that a team of supermen is coming up from the Lone Star State. Those reports are soon proven inaccurate, as Amos Alonzo Stagg's team scores 11 times, including runs of 40, 25, 25, and 50 yards, and a field goal of 45 yards. A crowd of 10,000 sees what remains the worst defeat in University of Texas history.

Texas 58, Baylor 0 / November 19, 1904 / Carroll Field (Waco, Texas)
Bill Blocker, the lightest player on the squad at 131 pounds, has an 80-yard run against the Bears in a game that is over by halftime.

Texas 39, Baylor 0 / October 21, 1905 / Clark Field (Austin, Texas)
Bob Ramsdell, ordinarily a tackle, is moved into the backfield for this game against the Bears, and the experiment works brilliantly. He scores three touchdowns in another rout of BU.

Texas 4, Arkansas 0 / October 31, 1905 / (Fayetteville, Arkansas)
Such inhospitality. The Longhorns are kept waiting an hour in the cold, and fans shower them with rocks in UT's first trip to the Ozarks. Coach Ralph Hutchinson's team gets a field goal from Winston McMahon, and that is enough for a narrow victory.

Vanderbilt 45, Texas 0 / October 27, 1906 / Dudley Field (Nashville, Tennessee)
After breezing by three weak opponents, the Horns hardly know what hit them until it's over. Coach Dan McGugin's Commodores are superior in every aspect of the game.

Texas 28, Haskell 0 / November 9, 1906 / Clark Field (Austin, Texas)
QB Winston McMahon throws the first touchdown pass in school history to Bowie Duncan, and kicks four extra points and a field goal in a sweet defeat of the Indians, who had blanked Texas in four previous games.

Texas 12, LSU 5 / October 19, 1907 / Hyde Park (Austin, Texas)
Rainstorms cause the home opener to be moved off campus, but conditions are only marginally better in Hyde Park. Fullback Bill Krahl scores two second-half touchdowns; Doc Fenton has one for the losing Tigers.

Texas 11, Texas A&M 6 / November 28, 1907 / Clark Field (Austin, Texas)
The unofficial state championship is on the line as the Aggies and Horns meet before a crowd of 6,000 in Austin. UT captain Bowie Duncan makes a teary pre-game speech (he would do the same thing before next year's season finale against A&M), and Fred Ramsdell riddles the Ags with his kicking, defense, and offense. He wins the game with a late 40-yard touchdown run.

Oklahoma 50, Texas 0 / November 13, 1908 / Boyd Field (Norman, Oklahoma)
On a cold and windy day in Norman, the Longhorns suffer one of their most humiliating defeats. Sooners backs Willard Douglas and Ralph Campbell break run after run in a game that is called because of darkness and perhaps a measure of good sportsmanship. OU claims to have almost 800 yards in total offense.

Texas 28, Texas A&M 12 / November 29, 1908 / Clark Field (Austin, Texas)
Bowie Duncan and Ed Slaughter have Texas up, 14–0, at halftime; 1,200 students start their customary snake dance, carrying brooms. Some incensed Ags tear into the prancing Longhorns, and a melee ensues. UT beats A&M for the second time that season.

Texas 24, TCU 0 / October 30, 1909 / Clark Field (Austin, Texas)
Quarterback Arnold Kirkpatrick and end Ben Dyer both have long touchdown runs in a defeat of the visiting Horned Frogs.

Texas A&M 23, Texas 0 / November 8, 1909 / West End Park (Houston, Texas)
Louie Hamilton has a 90-yard TD run in the Aggies' victory in Houston. The new A&M Coach, Charley Moran, makes no secret of his intention to win—but at what cost? The ease with which his team dispatches Texas in this game only adds fuel to the rumor fires. The A&M administration issues a public denial that any of its players are nonstudents or have been paid.

Texas 30, Oklahoma 0 / November 19, 1909 / Clark Field (Austin, Texas)
Ben Dyer leads something of a player revolt and Coach Dexter Draper, to his credit, follows the captain's suggestions. Two of the men Dyer champions, Marshall Ramsdell and Bart Moore, are moved into the starting lineup. They are the key figures in a skunking of OU in Austin.

All-Decade Team

Back	Rembert Watson (1901–1904)
Back	Don Robinson (1903–1905)
Back	Fred Ramsdell (1906, 1907)

Lineman	Marshall McMahon (1898–1901)
Lineman	Leopold Sam (1899–1900)
Lineman	Dave Prendergrast (1901, 1902, 1904)
Lineman	Lucian Parrish (1903–1906)
Lineman	Lawrence "Fuzzy" Feldhake (1906–1909)
Lineman	Emil Stieler (1907–1909)
End	Bowie Duncan (1905–1908)
End	Ben Dyer (1906–1909)
Kicker	Winston McMahon (1905, 1906)

Q & A

Q. How were orange and white chosen as the school colors?

A. They were first used in the spring of 1884 when some students took a train to Georgetown for a baseball game with Southwestern. Other combinations (such as gold and white, yellow and white, and orange and maroon) had been used intermittently, and there was a vote over the matter between students at the flagship institution in Austin, the UT Medical Branch in Galveston, and the alumni. After considerable debate, votes were cast, and orange and white were officially adopted as UT's colors on May 10, 1900. The same year, what would become the Longhorn Band was formed and first played at Texas home games.

Q. What was Brackenridge Hall?

A. It was the primary men's dormitory for years, close by the football field. From the windows of B Hall, freeloaders would watch games and offer many a lusty cheer.

Q. Name the halfback on the 1900 and 1901 Texas teams who later played five years of pro baseball.

A. Sam Leslie.

Q. Who was Texas' first coach of the 20th century?

A. His name was Samuel Huston Thompson, and he was known to friends as "Shy." Thompson studied law in New York City and was living in Denver when hired by UT. He had some coaching experience, having been at Oberlin in 1897, and Lehigh in 1898 and 1899. His assistant both of his seasons in Austin was Homer Curtiss, who was also the new gymnasium director. Thompson had played at Princeton, and his hiring was orchestrated by C. C. Cresson of San Antonio, another Princeton grad who had officiated at early Texas games. A strict disciplinarian and self-styled martinet, Thompson forbade his players to drink water during practice or games.

Q. Identify the first game between Texas and Oklahoma.

A. This storied series had a rather inauspicious beginning. It was in 1900, a 28–2 defeat of the Rough Riders. Because UT would be facing Vanderbilt (perceived then as a much tougher opponent; the Commodores won seven of their first nine games with UT) in Dallas three days later, Thompson used few of his key players.

Q. Thompson took his team on a 1,500-mile trip north in November 1901 that would include four games in 10 days. How did it go?

Ben Dyer

Ben Dyer, a native of Houston, was right in the middle of everything pertaining to UT football. Of ex-coach Ralph Hutchinson, Dyer commented, "He could talk and cuss and shame as much fight into a man as any living human. A player was usually so mad when Hutch finished with him, he was prepared to practice any villainy from simple assault to mayhem." Dyer, captain of the 1909 team, essentially forced Coach Dexter Draper to change his tactics. Dyer would later serve as sports editor of the *Dallas Morning News*.

Before that, however, he was editor of the alumni magazine, *Alcalde*. Soon after the 1916 UT–A&M game—during which a longhorn steer was presented to the school as a living mascot—Dyer was in his campus office, preparing the next issue of the magazine. He wrote about the game and halftime proceedings in which the rambunctious and frightened animal made his debut before 15,000 fans. Perhaps Dyer had an epiphany, but he stated simply, "His name is Bevo. Long may he reign!" In February 1917, a band of Texas A&M students broke into the south Austin stockyard where Bevo was comporting. After a struggle, the Aggies managed to put a crude "13–0" brand on his left side—the score by which A&M had beaten UT in 1915. When the big bovine's Texas handlers discovered the dastardly deed, they made alterations to have it read "Bevo." The story of how UT's famous mascot was named is full of legends and half-truths, but it originated with Dyer.

A. They had beaten Missouri, but then disaster struck. A team representing the American School of Osteopathy of Kirksville, Missouri, purportedly composed of pickups from all over the country, took a 48–0 win during which the UT team was humiliated on and off the field. Texas lost to Kansas (12–0) three days later in Lawrence but beat Oklahoma in Norman, keyed by a 55-yard punt return by Rembert Watson. The 1901 team recorded a school-record eight wins.

Q. Thompson quit coaching after the 1901 season with a 14–2–1 mark. What did he do later?

A. He went on to serve as assistant U.S. attorney general under President Woodrow Wilson from 1913 to 1918 and on the Federal Trade Commission from 1919 to 1927.

Q. What player on the 1901 Texas team was hired to coach the University of Oklahoma in 1902?

A. Marshall "Big" McMahon, whose brother, William ("Little") was a half-back for UT at the same time.

Q. Who, in UT sports history, was D. A. Frank?

A. For a person who never played a down of football, Frank had a huge impact. He was sports editor of the *Daily Texan* in 1903 when he took it upon himself to begin referring to the school's athletic teams as the "Longhorns," although there is some evidence of it being used intermittently a few years earlier. At any rate, Frank did so systematically, and the monicker stuck. And in 1904, Frank used what might be considered a dubious journalistic ploy to have Varsity Athletic Field renamed in honor of James B. Clark. He wrote and printed several anonymous letters, signed "A Senior Law," "A Senior Engineer," and "A Football Player," extolling Clark and urging that he be honored in this way. Just like "Longhorns" as UT's mascot, the name of Clark Field was adopted, and it has been part of the Forty Acres ever since—in three versions.

Q. Who took Thompson's place as UT coach?

A. John B. Hart, and there was some skepticism when he arrived. First, he was young, having just graduated from Yale. He was also rather small (5' 5" and 130 pounds) so he had to prove himself. But he suited up for one scrimmage and showed his players why he had earned his letter with the Bulldogs. Hart's team ended the 1902 season with a 12–0 defeat at the hands of rival Texas A&M, its first-ever win over UT. He departed following the loss to the Aggies.

Q. Hart took his team on a southern excursion in 1902, playing Nash-ville, Alabama, and Tulane in the span of a week. How did they do?

A. They won all three games, the latter two by shutouts. The Tulane game was especially rough, as fighting among players halted the proceedings several times. UT halfback Ed Crane alleged that Tulane was employing some non-students. A New Orleans newspaper, though, saw it differently, with a headline that read, "Chivalry of Louisiana Goes Down Before Texas Muckers."

Q. What team shut out UT every year from 1902 to 1905?

A. The Haskell Indian Institute, then a football powerhouse. Based in Law-rence, Kansas, the undersized Indians were coached by former Penn all-American John Outland and were fan favorites because of the spirited and daring way they played the game. They had picturesque names like Bobtail Bull, Thunderbolt, and Red Water. The last game in the Texas–Haskell series would come in 1919.

Q. Who was the captain of the 1903 and 1904 Texas teams?

A. Rembert Watson, who played quarterback and halfback.

Q. Another Princeton man coached the Longhorns for three seasons (1903–1905) and compiled a record of 16–7–2. Who was he?

A. Ralph Hutchinson. The faculty and administration, gradually taking con-trol of the emerging UT sports program, created the post of outdoor athletic director (AD), a job that would include coaching football, baseball, and track. The AD's salary, instead of coming from ticket sales as before, would be paid by the university. Before coming to Austin, Hutchinson had coached at his alma mater and at Dickinson College.

Q. Halfback Don "Mogul" Robinson (1903–1905) was something of a football dynamo. And what else?

A. He was a vagabond, having traveled all over the western U.S. and Alaska, and played at Drury College, Montana State, Colorado State, and Stanford before coming to Austin. He later spent five decades as a coconut tycoon in the Philippines.

Q. What is the origin of UT's song, "The Eyes of Texas?"

A. It was born in 1903 when John Lang Sinclair parodied "I've Been Working on the Railroad." A quartet of students sang it at an opera house on West Sixth Street at the direction of Dr. Daniel Penick, the long-time tennis coach. Within a few years, it had been officially adopted as the school song. A knockoff of a frivolous old minstrel song, "The Eyes" has been sung at virtually all UT sporting events for more than a century.

Q. Who enlivened halftime of the 1904 A&M game in Austin?

A. Carrie Nation, as part of her one-woman campaign against alcohol consumption, spoke to the crowd at Clark Field.

Q. Who played quarterback in a postseason game against a team from Fort Sam Houston on December 11, 1905?

A. The coach, Ralph Hutchinson.

Q. The flying wedge was outlawed and the forward pass legalized after the 1905 season. Who were the Longhorns' primary passers the next year?

A. Winston McMahon, who tended to hurl the ball sidearm, and Ben Dyer.

Q. After going 5–4 in 1905 and enduring a bit too much criticism from the Texas athletic family, Hutchinson quit as coach. The man chosen to replace him, Henry Schenker, would last but a single season. What is known about him?

A. Schenker had recently graduated from Yale, but it is unclear whether he ever played football there. He claimed to have a recommendation from the football authority of the day, Walter Camp, and thus Schenker got the job. It soon became clear, however, that he knew little about the game. It was a mystery why Schenker was hired. And as captain Lucian Parrish said in a players-only confab, "Men, we will have to face the fact that our coach is incompetent. It is true he should be taking lessons from us, rather than we from him. But the fact remains that he is employed to handle the team and is certainly the head of the football organization. I want to earnestly urge you to keep your mouths shut and follow the directions of the coach every day you are on the field. If you are instructed to do something that you know to be bad football, do the thing willingly and promptly at the time, and then come to me about it. I will see that all mistakes are remedied."

Q. So how did the 1906 Longhorns do with such a woeful coach?

A. Fortunately, Schenker had help from two professors, W. E. Metzenthin and A. Caswell Ellis. He leaned on them throughout the season for matters both strategic and intricate. The team flourished in spite of Schenker, finishing 9–1.

Q. This 6' 3", 190-pound guard on the 1906 team was elected student body president, and 13 years later he joined the U.S. House of Representatives. Who was he?

A. Lucian Parrish.

Q. He was a guard on the 1905 and 1906 teams and was responsible for starting varsity basketball at UT. Name him.

A. Magnus Mainland, a native of the Orkney Islands off the coast of Scotland.

Q. Identify Henry "Doc" Reeves.

A. It's a tender subject. Reeves, born in Tennessee, was the son of freed slaves and in an era in which Jim Crow ruled throughout the South, he managed to find a niche as UT's team trainer, masseur, and water-carrier from 1895 until 1915. During a time when it was unthinkable that black people would be part of the student body—much less the football team—Reeves was a beloved figure, whether that love was paternalistic or not. He took care of the players, encouraged them, and traveled with them to out-of-town games. When the train pulled into the station, he would, without a word of complaint or explanation, disappear into that city's black neighborhoods and fend for himself. At game time, he was right there at the gridiron with the Longhorns.

Q. Has Texas ever had a head coach who was born in a foreign country?

A. Just one: Waldemar Eric Metzenthin, a native of Berlin, Germany. The ineffectual Schenker had been sent on his way, and Metzenthin's work as an assistant in 1906 was so appreciated that he was called upon to take the top job for the next two seasons—at no additional pay. He had played quarterback at Franklin & Marshall and Columbia, so he had the qualifications. Metzenthin's first season went well (6–1–1) and the football program cleared more than $1,000. His team struggled in 1908, and he'd had enough. Metzenthin was still on campus two decades later when he served briefly as AD.

Q. Who, then, took Metzenthin's place as UT football coach?

A. Dexter Draper was hired immediately. Before he got to Austin for the 1909 season, he had received his medical degree. Draper, who had been an all-America tackle at the University of Pennsylvania, was an old-style, hard-nosed football coach. He very emphatically did not believe in the forward pass and wasn't popular among the Texas players.

Q. Two shutout losses to Texas A&M had Draper on the hot seat, but he could have returned in 1910 had he wanted. What did he do?

A. Draper chose to go back East, later coaching at Franklin & Marshall and William & Mary before more fully applying his medical education as a pediatrician and medical examiner in Lancaster, Pennsylvania.

Clark Field, where the Longhorns played
football from 1897 until the opening of Texas
Memorial Stadium in November 1924.
(Photo courtesy of the University of Texas.)

Football games at the University of Texas in the second decade of the 20th century featured teams doing battle on a weed-choked field laid out north–south between tilted wooden goalposts. Clark Field's hand-operated scoreboard gave spectators the score of the game and no more. Concessions left much to be desired, as young boys walked about with baskets full of apples, selling them for a nickel apiece. Inevitably, many a visiting team got pelted with apple cores. Cheerleaders and their megaphones were the sole system of public address; organized cheers and yells formed a much bigger part of the spectacle than they do today. A pistol shot usually signaled game's end.

The rules continued to evolve. The game was divided into 15-minute quarters, and seven players were required on the line of scrimmage. Interlocking interference was banned, as was pushing, pulling, and throwing the ball carrier. Touchdowns, previously valued at five points, were now worth six. Some players wore crude leather helmets, but they were rare and would not be mandatory for another two decades. UT co-eds, formerly rather prim at games, had begun to catch football fever. Some broke with tradition in 1913 and marched without dates to seats reserved for them in the stands. A few years later, a hundred or so bold young women went out onto the field at halftime to join their male counterparts in the snake dance. Texas did not have female cheerleaders until 1939. Numbers first appeared on the backs of the Longhorns' jerseys in 1916.

One Longhorn who stands out in this period is Clyde Littlefield, a man of many legends and one who could do it all. Whether he was best in football, basketball, or track (he won four letters in each sport, which no one else in school history has ever done) can be debated, but our focus here is on his pigskin proclivities. He was big, he was fast, and he was one of the first truly talented forward passers to emerge—certainly in the Southwest, perhaps in the country as a whole. Littlefield could fling the long ball, although it was still more of a fat spheroid than what is seen today.

The decade featured two undefeated teams (1914 and 1918), but it was clear that the Longhorns' country cousins in College Station had become their match and more. The dominant figure in college football in the state of Texas was Dana X. Bible, who was turning Texas A&M into a national power. Whereas earlier, it was widely assumed that Charley Moran made the Aggies competitive by using ringers and employing other ungentlemanly methods, no such charge was ever made against Bible. The short, bald man with the baritone voice would, of course, later come to Austin and re-make UT athletics.

Football had been grunting and groaning in the Southwest for 20 years. There was a crying need for more orderly administration of common objectives, standards of practice, behavior, and regulation both on and off the gridiron. Many institutions of higher learning found themselves unintentionally breeding tramp athletes, talented mercenaries who took a dim view of academia. Matters such as this prompted Texas' new athletic director, L. Theo Bellmont, to assert control over college football in the region. Bellmont gathered representatives of the main state and denominational schools in a pair of meetings at the Oriental Hotel in Dallas and the Rice Hotel in Houston in May and December 1914, respectively. They got down to the business of forming the Southwest Conference.

Issues of membership, scheduling, rules, and eligibility were agreed upon, and play began the next year. Charter members of the SWC were the University of Texas, the University of Oklahoma, the University of Arkansas, Texas A&M College, Oklahoma A&M College, Southwestern University, Baylor University, and Rice Institute. Louisiana

Henry J. Lutcher Stark

He came from one of the richest families in southeast Texas, its fortune having been made primarily in lumber, steel, oil, and rice farming. After Henry J. Lutcher Stark—known to both friends and enemies as "Lutch"—got to UT in 1905, he became the first student to own a car, an orange roadster. Stark was no athlete himself, being pampered from birth and rather chubby. His sports thrills were of a vicarious nature. As the student manager of the Texas football team in 1910, he arranged the schedule and took care of the Longhorns as no one had ever done before. It was then that he began his long practice of sitting on the team's bench, rather than up in the stands—whether at Clark Field or on the road.

After graduating, he took a strong hand in running the family's businesses especially while his father served on the UT Board of Regents from 1911 to 1915. Stark himself became a regent in 1919, and except for a two-year hiatus in the early 1930s, remained on the board until 1945. During most of his four decades on the Forty Acres, Stark was a towering figure, a man who made decisions, sometimes unilaterally. Team equipment, band uniforms and instruments, watches, trophies, first-class travel, summer jobs, and loans—there was virtually nothing he was unwilling to do for the greater glory of his alma mater. Stark subsidized countless athletes at UT, although to be fair, he helped out many rank-and-file students too.

Perhaps his most lasting contribution was in leading the drive to build Memorial Stadium in 1924. He could easily have paid for the whole thing himself, but he did not want any part of a Lutcher Stark Stadium. He shamelessly suggested plays or other strategy to coaches who knew far more about the game than he did. Stark got some guys fired and also called the shots on hiring Dana X. Bible away from the University of Nebraska in 1937. One of Bible's conditions for accepting the job was that Stark would have to sit up in the stands with the other fans. He was a rich and powerful fan, but a fan nonetheless.

L. Theo Bellmont

A native of Rochester, New York, L. Theo Bell-mont graduated from the University of Tennessee in 1908. He continued his southwesterly movement, landing in Houston, where he served as secretary of the YMCA from 1909 until 1913. Although Stark was not yet a regent, it is safe to assume he assented to the hiring of Bellmont as the university's first bona fide athletic director. That post included supervising intercollegiate athletics, physical training, and intramural sports. Bellmont left quite a legacy during his 15 years as AD, pulling the athletic program out of debt, organizing the Southwest Conference, coaching the Longhorns basketball team to a 44-game winning streak, founding (along with track coach Clyde Littlefield) the Texas Relays, organizing the T Association to honor former UT athletes, and working with Stark to fund and build Texas Memorial Stadium.

He was gone for two years during the war, serving as a flight instructor in San Antonio. In that capacity, Bellmont survived a crash that almost took his life. He had returned to his duties at UT in the fall of 1919. What was surely the biggest disappointment of his life came in 1928 when he was removed from his job as AD. Bellmont had run a tight ship and may have stepped on a few toes along the way. A simmering conflict went far beyond the athletic department, involving alumni, faculty, and the administration. Stark backed Bellmont, but he did not prevail this time, and "the Chief" lost his primary post. To his credit, he refused to publicly criticize any of those who had brought him down and stayed on at the university for another 30 years as director of physical training for men. Bellmont Hall, the building supporting the west-side upper deck of Memorial Stadium, was named for him in 1972. It is indicative of his stature in UT athletic history that Bellmont was one of the first four men named to the Longhorn Hall of Honor in 1957.

State University attended the confabs but declined to join. Southwestern and Rice left in 1916 (but the Owls were back for good in 1918), OU in 1919, and Oklahoma A&M in 1925. Southern Methodist University joined in 1918, Phillips University for one season in 1920, Texas Christian University in 1923, Texas Tech University in 1960, and the University of Houston in 1976.

Under the guardianship of a new kind of custodian, football in the region grew and flourished. The founding fathers of the SWC were flexible in their approach, rolling with the punch and sitting loose in the saddle. This group of academic realists and their descendants would have their share of internecine battles over the next 81 years, but they were in accord on the spirit and letter of the main issues facing them.

By the Numbers

0 Texas players on the 1918 all-SWC team.

1 Point for Texas, none for Baylor in a forfeit victory of the 1910 game played in Waco. BU archives have it as a 6–6 tie, which was the score when Coach Ralph Glaze took his team off the field after disagreeing with an official's call.

3 Year hiatus of athletic relations between UT and Texas A&M (1912–1914).

5 Dollars for a 1912 season ticket, which enabled a student to attend 36 events throughout the school year; the charge was $7.50 for others.

20 Victories out of 21 games for the Longhorns, entering the 1915 season.

92 Points scored against Daniel Baker College in the second game of the 1915 season, still a school record.

121 Points scored by Len Barrell (14 touchdowns, 34 extra points, and 1 field goal) in 1914, a record that lasted until broken by Ricky Williams in 1997.

200 Deaths in Austin caused by the 1918 flu epidemic. One Longhorns football player—lineman Joe Spence—was among them.

2,500 Dollars in salary paid to Coach Gene Van Gent in 1916.

19,030 Dollars in receipts for Texas' 1913 football season, against expenses of $16,731.

Archive

Home games in **bold**

1910   Record: 6–2   Coach: Billy Wasmund
Texas 11, Southwestern 6
Texas 68, Haskell 3
Texas 48, Transylvania 0
Texas 9, Auburn 0
Texas 1, Baylor 0 (forfeit)
Texas A&M 14, Texas 8
Texas 12, LSU 0
Oklahoma 3, Texas 0

1911   Record: 5–2   Coach: Dave Allerdice
Texas 11, Southwestern 2
Texas 11, Baylor 0
Texas 12, Arkansas 0
Sewanee 6, Texas 5
Texas 6, Texas A&M 0 (in Houston)
Texas 18, Auburn 5
Oklahoma 6, Texas 3

1912   Record: 7–1   Coach: Dave Allerdice
Texas 30, TCU 10
Texas 3, Austin College 0
Oklahoma 21, Texas 6 (in Dallas)

Texas 14, Haskell 7
Texas 19, Baylor 7
Texas 53, Mississippi 14 (in Houston)
Texas 28, Southwestern 3
Texas 48, Arkansas 0

1913 Record: 7–1 Coach: Dave Allerdice
Texas 14, Fort Worth Poly 7
Texas 27, Austin College 6
Texas 77, Baylor 0
Texas 13, Sewanee 7 (in Dallas)
Texas 52, Southwestern 0
Texas 14, Oklahoma 6 (in Houston)
Texas 46, Kansas A&M 0
Notre Dame 30, Texas 7

1914 Record: 8–0 Coach: Dave Allerdice
Texas 30, Trinity 0
Texas 57, Baylor 0
Texas 41, Rice 0
Texas 32, Oklahoma 7 (in Dallas)
Texas 70, Southwestern 0
Texas 23, Haskell 7 (in Houston)
Texas 66, Mississippi 7
Texas 39, Wabash 0

1915 Record: 6–3 Coach: Dave Allerdice
Texas 72, TCU 0
Texas 92, Daniel Baker 0
Texas 59, Rice 0
Oklahoma 14, Texas 13 (in Dallas)
Texas 45, Southwestern 0
Texas 27, Sewanee 6 (in Houston)
Texas 20, Alabama 0
Texas A&M 13, Texas 0
Notre Dame 36, Texas 7

1916 Record: 7–2 (Southwest Conference co-champions)
Coach: Gene Van Gent

Texas 74, SMU 0

Texas 16, Rice 2

Texas 14, Oklahoma A&M 6 (in San Antonio)

Texas 21, Oklahoma 7 (in Dallas)

Baylor 7, Texas 3

Missouri 3, Texas 0

Texas 52, Arkansas 0

Texas 17, Southwestern 3

Texas 21, Texas A&M 7

1917 Record: 4–4 Coach: Bill Juneau

Texas 27, Trinity 0

Texas 35, Southwestern 0

Oklahoma 14, Texas 0 (in Dallas)

Rice 13, Texas 0

Baylor 3, Texas 0

Texas 7, Oklahoma A&M 3

Texas A&M 7, Texas 0

Texas 20, Arkansas 0

1918 Record: 9–0 (Southwest Conference co-champions)
Coach: Bill Juneau

Texas 19, TCU 0

Texas 25, Penn Radio School 0

Texas 22, Penn Radio School 7

Texas 26, Ream Flying Field 2

Texas 27, Oklahoma A&M 5

Texas 22, Camp Mabry Auto Mechanics 0

Texas 14, Rice 0

Texas 32, SMU 0

Texas 7, Texas A&M 0

1919   Record: 6–3   Coach: Bill Juneau
Texas 26, Howard Payne 0
Texas 39, Southwestern 0
Phillips 10, Texas 0
Oklahoma 12, Texas 0 (in Dallas)
Texas 29, Baylor 13
Texas 32, Rice 7
Texas 35, Arkansas 7
Texas 13, Haskell 7
Texas A&M 7, Texas 0

20 Big Games

Texas 9, Auburn 0 / October 29, 1910 / Clark Field (Austin, Texas)
Auburn (then known as Alabama Polytechnic Institute) comes to Austin and engages in a bruising game with Billy Wasmund's Longhorns. The Tigers' big fullback, Brad Streit, is held in check. Joe Estill picks up a fumbled punt and scampers 40 yards for a score.

Oklahoma 3, Texas 0 / November 24, 1910 / Clark Field (Austin, Texas)
An even battle between the Sooners and Horns. Three times UT is close to the goal line but never gets in. The kicking game prevails for OU as Claude Reeds booms a 107-yard punt and Trim Capshaw kicks a field goal in the third quarter that suffices. Arnold Kirkpatrick's long field goal try at the end hits the crossbar and bounces back.

Texas 6, Texas A&M 0 / November 13, 1911 / West End Park (Houston, Texas)
Charley Moran's Aggies have won three straight over Texas and are highly favored to make it four as a partisan crowd of 12,000 roars. In the second quarter, Kirkpatrick picks up A. R. Bateman's fumble and runs it in for the only score of the day. Aggies fans are convinced they have been robbed and behave menacingly toward anyone wearing orange on the streets of downtown Houston that night. Dr. W. T. Mather, chairman of the UT Athletics Council, will soon announce that the school has chosen to halt athletic relations with A&M.

Texas 18, Auburn 5 / November 18, 1911 / Clark Field (Austin, Texas)

The Tigers leave some of their best players back home in Alabama with typhoid fever. Arnold Kirkpatrick is at it again, scoring two touchdowns, and kicking two extra points and two field goals—all in the first half, before he is injured.

Texas 3, Austin College 0 / October 12, 1912 / Clark Field (Austin, Texas)

The Kangaroos of little Austin College give the Horns a battle behind quarterback Cecil Grigg, who would later win three pro titles with the Canton Bulldogs and coach at his alma mater. Texas wins only with a long punt return by Nelson Puett, Sr. and a drop-kick field goal by Len Barrell.

Bibb Falk

Austin native Bibb Falk had quite a career in the amateur and professional sports ranks. He played baseball and football at UT before signing with the Chicago White Sox in 1920. He did little with the Sox until the 1919 Black Sox scandal broke and eight players were suspended for throwing games; Falk replaced Shoeless Joe Jackson in left field. Falk was a consistent hitter, ending his career after 12 seasons with a .314 career batting average. He was known as "Jockey" due to his merciless riding of opponents. Traded to Cleveland in 1929, Falk enjoyed three more productive seasons with the Indians before retiring as a player.

Falk succeeded UT's long-time baseball coach Billy Disch in 1940 and was there until 1967 (minus three years as an Army Air Force sergeant during World War II). Aggressive, blunt, and witty, his Longhorns baseball teams went 468–176, and won 20 SWC titles and two national championships. He and Disch were honored in 1975 when Disch-Falk Field was built and named after them.

Texas 53, Mississippi 14 / November 13, 1912 / West End Park (Houston, Texas)

In a game that replaces the annual match with A&M, the Longhorns lead the Rebels by just 7 at the half. They pour it on with 20 in the third quarter and 26 in the fourth, despite an injury to their quarterback, Puett.

Texas 13, Sewanee 7 / October 25, 1913 / Fairgrounds Park (Dallas, Texas)

A crowd of 10,000 overflows the grandstands of a horse racing oval at the State Fair as the Longhorns and Tigers play a thrilling game on the infield. Sewanee is up by one until Milton Daniel takes an interception back 69 yards to win.

Notre Dame 30, Texas 7 / November 27, 1913 / Clark Field (Austin, Texas)

The Longhorns have won 12 straight games, but they have never seen anything like what happens to them at Clark Field on this Thanksgiving Day. New athletic director L. Theo Bellmont's $4,000 fee to bring Notre Dame down pays off with a historic game, albeit a loss for the Horns. The Ramblers (as they were then called) have quarterback Gus Dorais, end Knute Rockne, and 210-pound fullback Ray Eichenlaub, and they drub their hosts. The provincial Longhorns learn a lot about football on this sultry day.

Texas 32, Oklahoma 7 / October 24, 1914 / Gaston Field (Dallas, Texas)

Dave Allerdice's team comes into the OU game with three big shutouts of Trinity, Baylor, and Rice. After the Sooners' Hap Johnson runs back the opening kickoff 85 yards for a score, Texas captain Louis Jordan calls his mates together for a little encouragement. Then they proceed to score the next 32. The same 11 Longhorns play the whole game.

Oklahoma 14, Texas 13 / October 23, 1915 / Fairgrounds Park (Dallas, Texas)

In the first year of the Southwest Conference, charter members Texas and Oklahoma tangle in Dallas. A crowd of 11,000, then the biggest ever to witness a football game in the state, see an entertaining passing duel between UT's Clyde Littlefield and OU's Spot Geyer; they combine for 71 passes (some of which serve the same purpose as punts, according to the rules of the day). Geyer's extra point with three minutes left wins it.

Texas A&M 13, Texas 0 / November 19, 1915 / Kyle Field (College Station, Texas)

The Longhorns and Farmers have kissed and made up—almost—by resuming athletic relations after a three-year hiatus. A&M pulls a monumental upset with great kicking by Rip Collins and some key plays by end Johnny Garrity. UT is just 3-for-23 passing.

Notre Dame 36, Texas 7 / November 25, 1915 / Clark Field (Austin, Texas)

UT plays host to Notre Dame for the second time in three years, and the result is much the same although Rockne has graduated and is now serving as an assistant coach. Littlefield is sick and is sorely missed, as the Ramblers batter the Horns with 462 yards rushing. Allerdice, whose team makes just three first downs, coaches his last game before retiring.

Baylor 7, Texas 3 / October 28, 1916 / Clark Field (Austin, Texas)

The Bears and Longhorns have met 11 times, and all have been UT wins—seven of them by shutout. But that comes to an end when the green and gold take a close one in Austin. Yank Wilson throws an 80-yard TD pass to John Reed in the first quarter, and Texas can only counter with a field goal by Sam Harwell.

Texas 52, Arkansas 0 / November 14, 1916 / Clark Field (Austin, Texas)

It is a bitter cold day in Austin, but the Longhorns are hot throughout in this destruction of the Hogs. Billy Trabue has the most memorable play, returning a punt 75 yards for a score.

Texas 21, Texas A&M 7 / November 30, 1916 / Clark Field (Austin, Texas)

Thanksgiving Day brings E. H. Harlan's Farmers back to Austin for the first time since 1909, and Clark Field is overrun with more than 15,000 football fanatics; the gate receipts exceed $20,000. The lighter Horns achieve a 21–7 upset, thanks in large part to another long punt return by Trabue and some fine kicking by William "Rip" Lang.

Texas A&M 7, Texas 0 / November 20, 1917 / Kyle Field (College Station, Texas)

Bill Juneau's Longhorns, who had earlier been skunked by OU, Rice, and Baylor, seemingly have no chance against an undefeated A&M team that is aided by the presence of military trainees on campus. It is scoreless until late in the game when hulking Dunny McMurrey goes over for a score.

Texas 14, Rice 0 / November 16, 1918 / Rice Field (Houston, Texas)

Shortly after announcement of the Armistice ending World War I, the Longhorns travel to Houston to engage the Rice Owls. In the only road game of the 1918 season, one played in the mud, UT gets a clinching touchdown when Louis Smyth takes it 30 yards.

Louis Jordan

He was known as "the Big Swede" on campus. Louis Jordan, born and raised in Fredericksburg, majored in electrical engineering. He was a four-year starter on the football team and was probably the best lineman yet to play at Texas. The Horns went 27–4 during his career, and he served as captain of the 1914 team. Walter Camp chose Jordan as a second-team all-American (no UT player would be a first-teamer until 1941 when guard Chal Daniel was so honored) after his senior year.

Jordan finished third in the hammer throw at the inaugural SWC track meet, not long before his graduation. He volunteered for military service in 1917 and was commissioned a first lieutenant. Soon after his arrival in France, he was in the midst of combat and trench warfare. Jordan was killed during an attack near Lorraine on March 5, 1918, and buried with full military honors two days later. He was awarded the Croix de Guerre posthumously, and both houses of the Texas Legislature passed resolutions in his honor. He was reinterred in Fredericksburg in 1921. The American Legion post there was dedicated to him, as was a flagpole in the south end of Memorial Stadium when it opened in 1924. Like Bellmont, he was in the first class of inductees of the Longhorn Hall of Honor in 1957. In his life and in his death, Louis Jordan brought nothing but honor to the University of Texas.

Texas 7, Texas A&M 0 / November 28, 1918 / Clark Field (Austin, Texas)

Clark Field is denuded of grass because of so much military marching, compounded by a hard rain the day before Texas and Texas A&M meet. Both teams are undefeated (albeit with schedules featuring several ill-prepared service squads), but it is UT's turn to take a tight one. Dave Pena rules line play, and Joe Ellis caps an early 55-yard drive with the day's only score for the Southwest Conference co-champs.

Phillips 10, Texas 0 / October 11, 1919 / Clark Field (Austin, Texas)

The Longhorns are shocked when Phillips, a small school from Oklahoma, beats them at home. The Haymakers, coached by John Maulbetsch and starring future pros Steve Owen and Dutch Strauss, would join the SWC in 1920 before dropping out.

Texas A&M 7, Texas 0 / November 27, 1919 / Kyle Field (College Station, Texas)

Dana X. Bible is back coaching the Aggies after missing one season for military service. His team has scored 268 points and not given up one, but the Horns make it a game over in the Brazos Valley. The inside-outside backfield tandem of Jack Mahan and Roswell Higginbotham is too much for UT, but freshman Oscar Eckhardt gives reason to hope for brighter days ahead.

All-Decade Team

Back	Len Barrell (1911–1914)
Back	Clyde Littlefield (1912–1915)
Back	Billy Trabue (1915–1917)
Lineman	Louis Jordan (1911–1914)
Lineman	K. L. Berry (1912, 1914, 1915, 1924)
Lineman	Gus "Pig" Dittmar (1913–1916)
Lineman	Alva "Fats" Carlton (1913–1916)
Lineman	Albert "Grip" Penn (1916, 1917, 1919)
Lineman	Bibb Falk (1918, 1919)
End	Pete Edmond (1913–1915)
End	Maxey Hart (1916, 1919, 1920)
Kicker	Arnold Kirkpatrick (1909–1911)

Q & A

Q. How did Clark Field get its first press box?

A. Reporters, long accustomed to roaming the sidelines, were ordered off the field by Stark in 1910. So a bench with a long writing board was installed above the top row at the 50-yard line.

Q. All of Texas' first coaches (Wentworth, Crawford, Robinson, Kelly, Edwards, Clarke, Thompson, Hart, Hutchinson, Schenker, Metzenthin, and Draper) had come out of the East. Who broke that pattern?

A. William S. "Billy" Wasmund, who had been a quarterback at Michigan. He coached the Longhorns to a 6–2 record in 1910, with the losses being to A&M and OU.

Q. Wasmund was the first UT coach to hold a pre-season training camp, leaving campus for a site near Marble Falls. There they engaged in vigorous swimming and hiking, although it is unclear how much actual football work took place. His team was ready for the 1911 season opener, but what tragedy then occurred?

A. He died as the result of a sleepwalking accident. Wasmund was replaced by another Michigan alumnus, Dave Allerdice. A protégé of Fielding "Hurry Up" Yost, his teams would go 33–7 over the next five years. Allerdice was perhaps the most successful coach of the early era of Longhorns football.

Q. Who were Allerdice's assistants in 1911 and 1912?

A. Billy Disch, who coached the UT baseball team for 30 years, and J. Burton Rix, who ran the track and basketball programs.

Q. Feelings were running high between fans of the Longhorns and Aggies in 1911. What did some UT students chant at their counterparts in that year's game in Houston?

A. "To hell, to hell with Charley Moran and all his dirty crew. And if you don't like the words of this song, to hell, to hell with you."

Q. Some early UT–A&M games were played in Houston as part of what festival?

A. No-Tsu-Oh ("Houston" spelled backwards).

Q. The Longhorns had crossed paths with Amos Alonzo Stagg when they played his University of Chicago team (UC) in 1904, and they did so again in 1912. Under what circumstances?

A. As a favor to Hugo Bezdek (one of his big stars at UC), Stagg agreed to officiate the Texas–Arkansas game in Austin. He even stopped in Fayetteville on his way down to offer some pointers. They didn't help much, however, because Bezdek's Razorbacks lost, 48–0.

Q. This lineman played every minute of every game of the 1912 season. Who was he?

A. William Murray, who earned a law degree in 1914 and was a public official for nearly half a century.

Q. Where and when was the Longhorns' Clyde Littlefield born?

A. Oil City, Pennsylvania, in 1892.

Q. Can his athletic career be summarized?

A. Not easily. As mentioned earlier, Littlefield remains the only man to earn 12 letters at UT—four each in football, basketball, and track from 1912 to 1916. He was head track coach for 41 years, with his teams winning 25 SWC titles, and he produced many all-Americans and Olympians. Co-founder of the Texas Relays, he was also an assistant coach for the United States in the 1952 Olympics in Helsinki. And let's not forget that he coached the UT football team from 1927 to 1933, winning two SWC championships.

Q. He was a halfback on the Texas football team from 1910 to 1913 and a catcher on the baseball team. Identify him.

A. Wesley "Little" Brown.

Q. This native of Denton was a lineman for the Longhorns in 1912 and 1913. He went on to establish the athletic department at Sam Houston Teachers College. Who was he?

A. Eugene R. Berry, brother of K. L. Berry.

Q. What halfback on the 1913 team had a most unusual way of avoiding tacklers?

A. Paul Simmons. With the dexterity of a gymnast, he would perform a diving somersault, holding the ball in one hand and springing off the ground with the other. Sometimes it worked, sometimes not. At any rate, Simmons' spectacular move did not set a trend. There is no record of other players attempting it, if for no other reason than its inherent danger.

Q. Allerdice's 1914 team was surely the best yet at Texas. They won all eight games and allowed their opponents to score but 21 points. Seven members of that team were later inducted into the Longhorn Hall of Honor. Who were they?

A. Littlefield, guard Louis Jordan, center Gus "Pig" Dittmar, end Pete Edmond, tackle K. L. Berry, guard Alva "Fats" Carlton, and halfback Len Barrell.

Q. The Rice Owls were playing just their third season of football in 1914 when they encountered the Longhorns. How did they do?

A. Better than might be expected, losing by a score of 41–0. Hey, it was 57–0 for Baylor, 70–0 for Southwestern, and 66–7 for Ole Miss.

Q. There was discussion of setting up a postseason game in 1914 to support the Belgian War Relief Fund. Did that idea bear fruit?

A. No. Tennessee and other schools declined. And anyway, the UT administration was strongly opposed to the Longhorns playing in postseason games, for charity or otherwise.

Q. As for Bevo, who was responsible for bringing this beautiful bovine to Austin?

A. Steve Pinckney, manager of the 1911 football team. But the costs of Bevo's upkeep were such that Bellmont had him butchered and barbecued prior to a UT–A&M confab at the Men's Gym in 1920. His hide, head, and horns were the subject of many an adventure in the years to come. Bevo II arrived on the scene in 1936, his successor in 1945, and there has been one ever since. Now tended by the Silver Spurs, Bevo is a major part of UT lore.

Q. This early-day UT great is best known for football, but he also captained the baseball and basketball teams. Who was he?

A. Pete Edmond, who died fighting in World War I and was awarded the Silver Star for gallantry in action.

Q. One of Edmond's teammates led Texas to a pair of Southwest Conference basketball titles. Identify him.

A. Gus "Pig" Dittmar.

Q. Allerdice had confided to friends during the 1915 season that he would be leaving because of the overly critical nature of Texas fans. So Bellmont took a trip north in January 1916 to find a replacement. Who did he bring back?

A. Gene Van Gent. At 6' 3" and 200 pounds, he looked the part of a football coach. Reared in Ottumwa, Iowa, Van Gent had played football, basketball, and track at the University of Wisconsin. He had spent two years on the University of Missouri staff, and the people in Columbia did not want to see him go, so Bellmont was forced to raise his offer to get Van Gent to come to Texas. Van Gent led the 1916 team to a 7–2 record and a share of the SWC title.

Q. What did Van Gent do soon after that season?

A. He, along with more than 500 students, left Austin when the United States declared war on Germany. The UT coach reported to officers' training camp in San Antonio and served in field artillery during the war.

Q. Van Gent came back in one piece, but his job had been taken—by a person he knew very well. Who?

A. Bill Juneau, his former coach at the University of Wisconsin. Like Van Gent, he had played multiple sports while a student at UW. He had also been the head man at South Dakota State and Marquette. Juneau was hired largely on the recommendation of baseball coach (and assistant football coach) Billy Disch, with whom he had played high school sports in Milwaukee. Van Gent had been given a leave of absence and was less than pleased when he returned to Austin in 1919 only to find his job taken. He served that season as line coach, and Juneau was recognized as the head coach.

Q. Both Van Gent and Juneau had coaching gigs after leaving UT. Where, and how did they do?

A. Van Gent was at Stanford in 1922, where his Indians went 4–4–2. Juneau coached at Kentucky from 1920 to 1922, and his Wildcats won 13, lost 10, and tied 1.

Q. This UT math professor served as an assistant coach from 1913 to 1919 and was among those who led a revolt against athletic director L. Theo Bellmont in 1928. Who was he?

A. H. J. Ettlinger.

Q. Name four ex-Longhorns who died fighting in World War I.

A. Louis Jordan, Bothwell Kane, Pete Edmond, and James Higginbotham.

Q. Louis Smyth, a fullback, was one of the first ex-Horns to play pro football. For what teams did he play?

A. The Canton Bulldogs, Rochester Jeffersons, Frankford Yellow Jackets, Providence Steam Roller, and Hartford Blues, from 1920 to 1926.

Q. Who was Texas' only representative on the 1917 all-SWC team?

A. Freshman guard Dewey Bradford.

Q. Ettlinger was the coach of an unusually strong 1919 Shorthorns team, composed of freshmen and ineligibles. How did they do in a game at Clark Field against West Texas Academy?

A. UT won, and the final score was 103–0.

Q. He ran Arkansas ragged in 1919 and was three times all-SWC as a centerfielder for Billy Disch's baseball team. Who was this native of Crockett, Texas?

A. David "Bobby" Cannon, who later coached high school sports for 34 years.

Q. Who captained the 1919 UT football team?

A. Ghent "Doc" Graves, who was quite a pole vaulter for the Longhorns track team and later earned a medical degree from Harvard University.

Q. This Austin native was an all-SWC end his sophomore year and helped the baseball team win four conference championships. Who was he?

A. Maxey Hart.

CAPT. KING
TEXAS

CAPT. BARTLETT
A.&M.

OFFICIAL PROGRAM

PRICE 50¢

LONGHORNS

"VS"

The 1928 UT–A&M clash drew 45,000 fans, which was then the largest crowd ever to see a game in the Southwest. Clyde Littlefield's Longhorns won, 19–0, and secured the Southwest Conference title. (Photo courtesy of the University of Texas.)

AGGIES

Texas Memorial Stadium Nov. 29, 1928

College football, momentarily put on hold during World War I, came of age in the 1920s as America's greatest sporting spectacle—in a different way from baseball, which remained the national pastime. It was the era of Red Grange, Knute Rockne and the Four Horsemen, crowds in excess of 100,000 witnessing games at Soldier Field in Chicago, and the further weaving of football into the fabric of life in the Southwest. Here as elsewhere, newspapers had begun to see the value of devoting attention to the game. More colleges and high schools were fielding teams than ever before, and the quality of play was better. Members of the SWC still played somewhat provincial schedules, but they were rising to the level of those who purported to be the best. Apart from Grange's Illini and Rockne's Irish, the powers in the 1920s were California, Cornell, Michigan, and Alabama.

The University of Texas, among other institutions of higher learning, was eager to join the big time but fearful of the implications. Lutcher Stark had been increasingly brazen about bringing jocks to UT and helping them out here and there. Other schools had begun to award athletic scholarships, a term those in the ivory tower found amusing if not horrific.

The 1920s have come to be known as the golden age of college stadium building. Consider how many schools erected stadiums then that remain in use: Washington, Kansas, Tennessee, Stanford, Ohio State, Illinois, Nebraska, Michigan State, California, Colorado, Army, Purdue, LSU, Oklahoma, Northwestern, Missouri, Michigan, North Carolina, Alabama, Arizona, Duke, Georgia, and Iowa. One might include UCLA and Southern California because the Rose Bowl and Los Angeles Memorial Coliseum were built in the 1920s as well.

The construction of Texas Memorial Stadium was incalculably significant in UT history—not just by helping the athletic program but also by bringing the alumni and students together, and solidifying the school's identity. Until the stadium was built, there had been growing discussion about moving from the Forty Acres (Guadalupe Street [also known as "the Drag"] on the west, 24th Street on the north, Speedway on the east, and 21st Street on the south) to the 500-acre Brackenridge Tract alongside the Colorado River. The building of Memorial Stadium gave the campus roots that had been lacking before. After the stadium was constructed, there was no more talk of moving out to the Brackenridge Tract. Within a decade, these other substantial buildings dotted the campus: Biological Laboratories

(1925), Garrison Hall (1926), Littlefield Dormitory (1927), Clark Field II (1928), Weaver Power Plant (1928), Gregory Gymnasium (1930), Women's Gym (1931), Welch Hall (1931), Waggener Hall (1931), Brackenridge Hall (1932), Goldsmith Hall (1933), Will Hogg Building (1933), Painter Hall (1933), Texas Union (1933), and Hogg Auditorium (1933). It did not hurt that, by the mid-1920s, royalties from the university's west Texas oil fields had begun to flow.

As to the stadium itself: Stark, L. Theo Bellmont, Bill McGill, Max Fichtenbaum, and many others devoted themselves to the project. Students, alumni, and friends of the university from around the state labored valiantly in a six-month fundraising drive. While the original goal of $500,000 was not met, $275,000 was enough to erect a large but rather bare-bones stadium; any and all money was welcome, including one donation from the Ku Klux Klan. When completed in the fall of 1924, Memorial Stadium was far bigger than anything else within a 1,000-mile radius. Herbert M. Greene was the architect, List & Gifford did the excavation, and Walsh & Burney built a pair of steel-and-concrete stands on the east and west with a total seating capacity of 27,000. It was a dual-purpose facility from the start, with a 440-yard cinder track surrounding the football field. The stadium was built to honor the 198,293 Texans who had served and especially the 5,280 who had died in World War I.

By the Numbers

-47 Yards of offense for Austin College in a 60–0 loss to Texas in 1921.

2 SWC games (Rice and Texas A&M) the Longhorns played in 1921.

8 Touchdowns scored by Howard "Bully" Gilstrap in 1921, leading the team.

10 Straight shutouts by the 1928 and 1929 Texas teams.

18 Offensive snaps for Dana X. Bible's Aggies in the 1920 UT–A&M game.

31 Winning games coached by E. J. "Doc" Stewart in 1923, 8 of them in football and 23 in basketball. There were no losses and 1 tie.

95 Yard punt return by Cy Leland doomed the Longhorns in a 1929 loss to TCU.

600 Fans in attendance at the 1927 Texas–TCU game at Memorial Stadium on a cold and wet day.

33,000 Dollars brought in by the 1922 UT–A&M game at Clark Field.

93,283 Dollars made from the Longhorns–Aggies tilt at Memorial Stadium in 1928.

Archive

Home games in **bold**

1920 Record: 9–0 (Southwest Conference champions)
Coach: Berry Whitaker
Texas 63, Simmons 0
Texas 27, Southwestern 0
Texas 41, Howard Payne 7
Texas 21, Oklahoma A&M 0 (in Dallas)
Texas 54, Austin College 0
Texas 21, Rice 0
Texas 27, Phillips 0
Texas 21, SMU 3
Texas 7, Texas A&M 3

1921 Record: 6–1–1 Coach: Berry Whitaker
Texas 33, St. Edwards 0
Texas 60, Austin College 0
Texas 21, Howard Payne 0
Vanderbilt 20, Texas 0 (in Dallas)
Texas 56, Rice 0
Texas 44, Southwestern 0
Texas 54, Mississippi A&M 7
Texas 0, Texas A&M 0

1922 Record: 7–2 Coach: Berry Whitaker
Texas 19, Austin College 0
Texas 41, Phillips 10
Texas 19, Oklahoma A&M 7
Vanderbilt 20, Texas 10 (in Dallas)
Texas 19, Alabama 10
Texas 29, Rice 0
Texas 26, Southwestern 0
Texas 32, Oklahoma 7
Texas A&M 14, Texas 7

1923 Record: 8–0–1
Coach: E. J. Stewart

Texas 31, Austin College 0
Texas 51, Phillips 0
Texas 33, Tulane 0 (in Beaumont)
Texas 16, Vanderbilt 0 (in Dallas)
Texas 44, Southwestern 0
Texas 27, Rice 0
Texas 7, Baylor 7
Texas 26, Oklahoma 14
Texas 6, Texas A&M 0

1924 Record: 5–3–1
Coach: E. J. Stewart

Texas 27, Southwestern 0
Texas 27, Phillips 0
Texas 6, Howard Payne 0
SMU 10, Texas 6
Texas 7, Florida 7
Rice 19, Texas 6
Baylor 28, Texas 10
Texas 13, TCU 0
Texas 7, Texas A&M 0

George "Hook" McCullough

He arrived on campus by a circuitous route. George McCullough, born in Fayette, Missouri, served in the 36th Infantry during World War I. In between dodging bullets, he played service football and was named to an all-star team while in Europe. Among McCullough's teammates was future Longhorns quarterback Grady "Rats" Watson. Since Watson hailed from Orange, he was well-favored by Lutcher Stark. Both young men were widely thought to have been brought to UT by Stark.

McCullough was, quite simply, one of the finest athletes in the early history of the university—in two sports. He had size (6' 2", 185 pounds) and outstanding reflexes, and was always willing to mix it up with opposing players. On the hardcourts, he was a two-time all-SWC forward and captain of the 1922 team. In football, he was twice all-conference at end and an honorable mention all-American. Nicknamed "Hook" because of his huge hands and a startling ability to catch and handle both kinds of balls, he was remembered by former teammates and coaches in decades to come as one of the school's best ever. He was honored in 1956 when the George "Hook" McCullough Award was instituted; the winner is the football team's MVP, as selected by his teammates.

1925 Record: 6–2–1 Coach: E. J. Stewart

Texas 33, Southwestern 0
Texas 25, Mississippi 0
Vanderbilt 14, Texas 6
Texas 33, Auburn 0 (in Dallas)
Texas 27, Rice 6
Texas 0, SMU 0
Texas 13, Baylor 3
Texas 20, Arizona 0
Texas A&M 28, Texas 0

1926   Record: 5–4   Coach: E. J. Stewart
Texas 31, Southwestern Oklahoma 7
Kansas A&M 13, Texas 3
Texas 27, Phillips 0
Vanderbilt 7, Texas 0 (in Dallas)
Texas 20, Rice 0
SMU 21, Texas 17
Baylor 10, Texas 7
Texas 27, Southwestern 6
Texas 14, Texas A&M 5

1927   Record: 6–2–1   Coach: Clyde Littlefield
Texas 43, Southwestern Oklahoma 0
Texas 0, TCU 0
Texas 20, Trinity 6
Texas 13, Vanderbilt 6 (in Dallas)
Texas 27, Rice 0
SMU 14, Texas 0
Texas 13, Baylor 12
Texas 41, Kansas A&M 7
Texas A&M 28, Texas 7

1928   Record: 7–2 (Southwest Conference champions)
Coach: Clyde Littlefield
Texas 32, St. Edward's 0
Texas 12, Texas Tech 0
Vanderbilt 13, Texas 12 (in Dallas)
Texas 20, Arkansas 7
Texas 13, Rice 6
SMU 6, Texas 2
Texas 6, Baylor 0
Texas 6, TCU 0
Texas 19, Texas A&M 0

1929   Record: 5–2–2   Coach: Clyde Littlefield
Texas 13, St. Edward's 0
Texas 20, Centenary 0

Texas 27, Arkansas 0
Texas 21, Oklahoma 0 (in Dallas)
Texas 39, Rice 0
Texas 0, SMU 0
Texas 0, Baylor 0
TCU 15, Texas 12
Texas A&M 13, Texas 0

20 Big Games

Texas 21, Oklahoma A&M 0 / October 16, 1920 / Fair Park Stadium (Dallas, Texas)

Berry Whitaker's Longhorns have begun the season with three softies—Simmons, Southwestern, and Howard Payne—at home, outscoring them by a 131–7 margin. Next up is a much tougher team in the form of Oklahoma A&M. The game is close until the fourth quarter, when QB Kyle "Icky" Elam scores a pair of touchdowns. Elam's academic standing and eligibility would soon be the subject of heated discussion among SWC brethren.

Texas 7, Texas A&M 3 / November 25, 1920 / Clark Field (Austin, Texas)

Dana X. Bible's Aggies have outscored their opponents, 226–0, in seven games, and Berry Whitaker's Horns have equally impressive numbers: 275–10 in eight games. It is a season-ending confrontation the likes of which the SWC has never seen. A tackle-eligible pass from little-used Bill Barry to Tom Dennis sets up a winning 4-yard TD run by Francis Domingues. Clark Field is bursting at the seams with the weight of nearly 20,000 people—although some watch from telephone poles and the roofs of nearby houses. The need for a real stadium is becoming more and more evident, especially in even-numbered years when A&M comes to town.

Texas 0, Texas A&M 0 / November 24, 1921 / Kyle Field (College Station, Texas)

A crowd of 15,000 gathers in College Station to see the Aggies and Longhorns have at it in the 1921 season finale. The maroon and white put up a series of goal-line stands, and two late field goal tries by Franklin "Punk"

Stacy are tipped at the line. Fans who had called the Horns a "wonder team" at the start of the season are seeking Berry Whitaker's scalp toward the end.

Vanderbilt 20, Texas 10 / October 21, 1922 / Fairgrounds Park (Dallas, Texas)

The Commodores are banged up after playing Michigan the week before, but Gil Reese goes 52 yards for a touchdown and captain Jess Neely limps off the bench to make a key completion late in the game. Jim Marley and Bobby Robertson play well in a losing effort for UT.

Texas A&M 14, Texas 7 / November 30, 1922 / Clark Field (Austin, Texas)

Another overflow crowd at Clark Field sees Whitaker come out with a re-vamped backfield, but it does little good. The Aggies win on a pair of tricky pass plays, both to E. King Gill, who had started the 12th man tradition the year before when A&M beat mighty little Centre College in Dallas. As the Ags board their train in downtown Austin the next day, UT captain Swede Swenson is there to congratulate them although the loss prevents the Longhorns from taking the conference crown.

Texas 16, Vanderbilt 0 / October 20, 1923 / Fairgrounds Park (Dallas, Texas)

Vandy comes to Dallas looking for a third straight win over Texas, but it is not to be. Assistant coach Alex Waite has scouted the Commodores thoroughly, and a 10-point halftime lead is clinched when Oscar Eckhardt makes a great run down the sideline, flattening tacklers like dominoes. Eckhardt and Coach E. J. Stewart are the toast of the state after this defeat of the black and gold.

Texas 7, Baylor 7 / November 10, 1923 / Cotton Palace (Waco, Texas)

Baylor Coach Frank Bridges, always willing to try something different, opens this game with a successful onside kick. BU gets a touchdown from Ralph Pittman, and it seems that may last as the Longhorns have a series of offensive misadventures. But they crank it up in the fourth quarter to drive 50 yards, capped by Joe Ward's short run to tie the defending SWC champs.

Texas 6, Texas A&M 0 / November 29, 1923 / Kyle Field (College Station, Texas)

This game, played on a muddy field, is a defensive battle. The Aggies can only muster two first downs and never get within 48 yards of the Texas goal line. The key play is a punt by Eckhardt, muffed by Clem Pinson of A&M. Buddy Tynes recovers at the 5 and slides all the way into the end zone. Stewart sends no substitutes into this game, which athletic director L. Theo Bellmont uses as a springboard for the idea of building a big new stadium back in Austin.

Texas 7, Florida 7 / October 25, 1924 / Clark Field (Austin, Texas)

It's the final college football game at Clark Field, yet few tears are shed for the charming but outdated edifice. With the construction of Memorial Stadium less than a mile to the southeast moving along, little has been done to maintain Clark Field. Florida is the guest, and the Alligators (as they were then called) and Longhorns are knotted at 7. At the end of the game, Stewart sends in ailing Heinie Pfannkuche. He and his fellow defenders stop big fullback Bill Middlekauff four straight times to preserve the tie.

Baylor 28, Texas 10 / November 8, 1924 / Memorial Stadium (Austin, Texas)

The anticipation to get into the new stadium is just too great, so Bellmont puts the Baylor game there. The surrounding area looks like all construction sites—messy. A crowd of 13,500 sitting in the west stands sees the title-bound Bears roar to an 18-point victory. Bill Coffey, BU's 138-pound quarterback, has scoring runs of 38 and 22 yards.

Texas 7, Texas A&M 0 / November 27, 1924 / Memorial Stadium (Austin, Texas)

Work on the stadium is being rushed to completion. Pomp and ceremony abound this Thanksgiving Day with an address by Governor Pat Neff and solemn reminiscing about those who had given their lives in the war. A crowd of 33,000 sees a game that is dull as dishwater until the very end when substitute halfback Maurice "Rosy" Stallter throws a short pass that Stookie Allen turns into a 52-yard TD. Jim Marley plays a full 60 minutes against the Aggies for the third straight year.

Ike Sewell

He played football at the University of Texas, and he was pretty good—an all-SWC guard in his junior year of 1926. But it is fair to say that Ike Sewell is remembered less for his pigskin prowess than for his many years as a restaurateur. Widely regarded as the inventor of deep-dish pizza, Sewell also opened the first upscale Tex-Mex restaurant in Chicago.

Sewell, born in Wills Point, was a friend to some of the most powerful and wealthy people in Chicago. In 1943, while living in the Windy City, Sewell and a friend began dabbling with the idea of making pizza a full meal rather than just a snack. They opened a restaurant in the basement of an old mansion. After a few hits and misses on ingredients and methods of cooking, Sewell came up with one of Chicago's culinary trademarks. His restaurant was franchised 40 years later, making him rather wealthy, although he continued to work until his death in 1990.

Vanderbilt 14, Texas 6 / October 10, 1925 / Dudley Field (Nashville, Tennessee)

It's homecoming day in Nashville, and the visiting Longhorns accommodate by making enough errors to lose. The most egregious is a fumbled punt by Stuart Wright that is taken back all the way. Vandy gets another score in the fourth quarter when Bill Spears throws a 35-yard touchdown pass to Gil Reese.

Texas A&M 28, Texas 0 / November 26, 1925 / Kyle Field (College Station, Texas)

The SWC title is on the line as the Aggies and Longhorns get together for some old-fashioned brotherly hate. A crowd of 26,000, including Governor Miriam Ferguson, sees A&M turn two of the Horns' offensive miscues into touchdowns. Only the fine play of Mack Saxon prevents it from being worse. UT's honeymoon with coach Doc Stewart is coming to an end.

SMU 21, Texas 17 / October 30, 1926 / Memorial Stadium (Austin, Texas)

The Mustangs, led by Ray Morrison, an early student of the forward pass, are destined to win the conference title, but UT won't make it easy on them. The Longhorns are on the verge of victory with five minutes to go when Gerald Mann (known as the "Little Red Arrow") takes over. He throws a 42-yard TD pass, and with time running out, picks up a fumble by Rufus King and goes in for the winning score as the Mustang Band gleefully plays "Peruna." Brash Chris Cortemaglia had vowed to walk back to Dallas if his Ponies were to lose, but he would be on a north-bound train that night. It remains one of the most dramatic finishes in more than 80 years of stadium history, albeit one not pleasing to the home crowd.

Texas 14, Texas A&M 5 / November 25, 1926 / Memorial Stadium (Austin, Texas)

After another fundraising drive, Memorial Stadium has been expanded for the first time—now with a 13,500-seat horseshoe in the north end. Students, alumni, and others are justifiably proud of a stadium that is now considered "architecturally complete." Some 35,000 patrons witness a 14–5 Texas victory keyed by Saxon, Stallter, King, and Bill Ford. They combine for 11-of-13 passing. Just as important, Aggies star Joel Hunt is held in check. This game allows the Longhorns to end an otherwise ignoble 5–4 season on a high note.

Texas 13, Vanderbilt 6 / October 15, 1927 / Fairgrounds Park (Dallas, Texas)

Texas' first three opponents of the 1927 season offer scant resistance, so new head coach Clyde Littlefield is not sure what kind of team he has until meeting Vandy in Dallas. Quarterback Joe King defies his doctors' suggestions to have immediate knee surgery, wraps it tightly, and plays quite well. He keeps the Commodores off balance, and two early TDs are enough to win. King is a little gamecock; his weight drops from 150 pounds to 132 as the season goes on.

Texas 41, Kansas A&M 7 / November 12, 1927 / Memorial Stadium (Austin, Texas)

Avenging an upset loss to Kansas A&M in Manhattan the season before, the Horns maul the Wildcats in an Armistice Day game played on Friday. Long touchdown runs are the norm as Alfred "Big Un" Rose, Jimmy Boyles, Nona Rees, and even guard Ike Sewell get one apiece. Sewell's comes on a quarterback sack and a 35-yard rumble into the end zone.

SMU 6, Texas 2 / October 30, 1928 / Memorial Stadium (Austin, Texas)

The Longhorns battle the Mustangs in Austin. This long-awaited confrontation features 35 first downs, and a number of great defensive stands and controversial calls, most of which go against UT. One final charge is mounted as Rufus King repeatedly pounds the SMU goal line. Texas partisans insist he got in, but the refs disagree. Heated discussion about this game would go on for a full week.

Texas 19, Texas A&M 0 / November 29, 1928 / Memorial Stadium (Austin, Texas)

The Longhorns' second Southwest Conference title of the decade is there for the taking, and a record crowd of 45,000 sees them do just that. Blocking on off-tackle and end plays is the key to dominance in the line, and Dexter Shelley, UT's versatile and hard-running back, takes full advantage. Ed Beular throws TD passes of 25 and 6 yards to Bill Ford.

Texas 21, Oklahoma 0 / October 19, 1929 / Fairgrounds Park (Dallas, Texas)

For lack of another opponent, Bellmont chooses Oklahoma to replace Vandy in the annual State Fair game. One of college football's greatest rivalries is about to be born, although the schools had played 23 times since 1900. A 10-year contract is signed, and the tradition of revelry on Commerce Street in downtown Dallas begins. The game, before 18,000 fans in creaking old Fairgrounds Park, is a slow-starting affair. Dexter Shelley scores, as does Bull Elkins on a long pass from Nona Rees. Ten days later, the stock market would crash, bringing on the Great Depression.

All-Decade Team

Back	Oscar Eckhardt (1919, 1922, 1923)
Back	Mack Saxon (1925, 1926)
Back	Dexter Shelley (1928–1930)
Lineman	Swede Swenson (1918, 1920–1922)
Lineman	Tom Dennis (1919–1921)
Lineman	Joe Ward (1921–1923)
Lineman	Mortimer "Bud" Sprague (1923, 1924)
Lineman	Clen "Ox" Higgins (1925–1927)
Lineman	Alfred "Big Un" Rose (1927–1929)
End	George "Hook" McCullough (1920, 1921)
End	Bill Ford (1926–1928)
Kicker	Bobby Robertson (1921–1923)

Q & A

Q. What assistant on Bill Juneau's 1919 staff was appointed head coach in 1920, to his utter amazement?

A. Berry Whitaker. He had played football at Indiana University and moved to Austin to start a physical education program in the city's public schools. He soon took the reins of the Austin High School football team, and the Maroons won the unofficial state championship in his first two years. Then Bellmont asked Whitaker to move across town to the university, in order to found a men's intramural program. That he did, but within a year Whitaker was back coaching. He was in charge of the UT basketball team in 1919 and assisted Juneau with the football team. Dissatisfaction was rampant in the ranks, so Juneau was relieved and the mild-mannered Whitaker was the Longhorns' boss at a salary of $3,000. He kept the job for three years and compiled a sparkling 22–3–1 record.

Q. Legend had it that Whitaker was fired by the ever-present Stark almost immediately after the 1922 A&M game, a 14–7 home loss. Was it true?

A. Not according to Whitaker. He had been coming down with ulcers and didn't like the hypercritical nature of fans in general—not just the powerful chairman of the Board of Regents. He quit of his own volition and returned to his beloved intramural program, where he served as director for more than four decades before retiring.

Q. What member of the 1920 and 1921 UT teams had played at Texas A&M in 1918 and 1919?

A. Quarterback Kyle "Icky" Elam.

Q. We know that Louie Smyth, who played for the Canton Bulldogs, was the first ex-Longhorn to make it in pro football. Who was the second?

A. Quarterback Grady "Rats" Watson was a member of the Toledo Maroons in 1920 and 1921. Buddy Tynes would be the next, with the Columbus Tigers in 1924.

Q. This all-SWC tackle captained the 1921 Texas team and later won a couple of state championships at Port Arthur High School. Who was he?

A. Tom Dennis.

Q. Which of Dennis's teammates later served on the Board of Regents?

A. Swede Swenson.

Q. He played fullback for the Longhorns from 1921 to 1923, was an assistant football coach from 1937 to 1956, and coached the UT basketball team to an NCAA Final Four appearance in 1943. Name him.

A. Bully Gilstrap, who also threw the javelin for Littlefield's track team.

Q. What was unique about the 1921 UT–A&M game?

A. Two Aggie cadets transmitted a play-by-play wireless account to three Texas students, using prearranged abbreviations, from station 5XB in College Station to 5XU in Austin. It was the first game account transmitted by wireless in the Southwest.

Q. He was a reserve quarterback on the 1922 team, his son played for UT briefly in the early 1950s, and his grandson would be a four-year starter at that position a generation later. Who was he?

A. George Gardere. The son was George Jr., and the grandson was Peter.

Q. At the 1922 Texas–Vanderbilt game in Dallas, what student group made its first appearance?

A. The 40-member Texas Cowboys, organized by head cheerleader Arno "Shorty" Nowotny and Longhorn Band manager Bill McGill. They wore oilcloth chaps and put on a skit at halftime at Fairgrounds Park. The Commodores won the game, 20–10.

Q. Bobby Robertson was a three-year starter on the Texas basketball team and rotated between quarterback, halfback, and kicker on the football team. What did he do of note in 1922?

A. He booted nine field goals, a school record that would last more than 40 years.

Q. Which of Robertson's teammates helped the 1924 Texas basketball team go 24–0?

A. Abb Curtis, who later became the SWC's supervisor of officials.

Q. What tackle on the 1922 and 1923 teams would later be honored by having a segment of Highway 183 named after him?

A. Ed Bluestein, an engineering graduate who was honored for his 41 years with the Texas Highway Department.

Q. Clark Field's locker rooms were in the adjacent Men's Gym. What did A&M Coach Dana X. Bible do in the visitors' locker room prior to the 1922 Longhorns–Aggies tilt?

A. He conjured Col. William Travis' actions in the Alamo by drawing a line and saying that those who crossed it would be members of the first A&M team to beat Texas in Austin. Each and every one did, and they scored a 14–7 victory.

Q. Texas and Baylor were scheduled to play on December 9, 1922, but the game was cancelled. Why?

A. The Athletics Council stepped in and, by a 6–2 vote, called it off with the explanation that such a late game would interfere with final exams of the players and student body as a whole.

Q. Texas got a new coach in 1923. Who was he?

A. The peripatetic E. J. "Doc" Stewart, who had been the head man at no fewer than seven places—Mount Union, Purdue, Allegheny, Oregon A&M, Nebraska, Camp Gordon (during World War I), and Clemson—before coming to Austin. Stewart, who doubled as coach of the UT basketball team, was a stern taskmaster as well as a man of impeccable speech. His record over four seasons was 24–9–3.

Q. What do we recall about Mortimer "Bud" Sprague?

A. He was a lineman/kicker on the 1923 and 1924 teams who went on to play three years at West Point, becoming an all-American. Eligibility rules were not so strict back then.

Q. Along the same lines, what about K. L. Berry?

A. He was captain of the 1915 Texas team, went off to war, returned and (as a 32-year-old husband and father of three) made all-SWC in 1924. He also fought in World War II, where he was captured by Japanese forces in the Philippines and survived the Bataan death march.

Q. A fine football player, he also had a 6–1 record as a pitcher and batted .440 for Disch's 1924 Longhorns baseball team. Identify him.

A. Oscar Eckhardt, who later played with the Boston Red Sox and Brooklyn Dodgers.

Q. Who was the first Longhorn to score a touchdown in Memorial Stadium history?

A. Jim Marley. He went over on a 1-yard plunge late in the fourth quarter of the 1924 Baylor game.

Q. Memorial Stadium initially lacked any locker rooms. So what did home and visiting players do in their absence?

A. The Longhorns suited up at a shack at the corner of 22nd Street and Speedway. The visitors generally dressed at their hotel and were driven to the stadium in automobiles.

Q. Who was Curtis J. "Shorty" Alderson?

A. A native of Franklin, Kentucky, he came to UT as a student in 1912 and served variously as an assistant coach from 1924 to 1947 in football, basketball, and track. He instituted the swimming program and was the head coach of that sport in the early 1930s. He was also the public address announcer for football, basketball, and baseball games for two decades. Alderson was known as the court of final appeal on rules and regulations pertaining to college sports in Texas.

Q. What was the first SWC football game broadcast via radio?

A. On November 7, 1925, Texas and Baylor met in Memorial Stadium (the Horns won, 13–3). KUT, which had just received its broadcasting license, covered the game. Harold Lissner handled microphone duties.

Q. He had played at several other institutions earlier, but he wasn't the first ringer at UT and he wouldn't be the last. Who was he?

A. Mack Saxon, a do-it-all halfback in 1925 and 1926. He later coached 12 years at Texas College of Mines, the precursor to Texas Western and UT–El Paso.

Q. He played three sports (basketball, football, and track) at Texas in the mid-1920s, became a pilot in the Army Air Corps, and transported bombers during World War II. To whom do we refer?

A. Brigadier General Stuart P. Wright.

Clark Field II

The original Clark Field was not abandoned after the final football game in 1924. Baseball and high school football continued to be played there for two more seasons. Finally in 1927, it was demolished to make way for the Weaver Power Plant and the Mechanical Engineering Building. A new baseball park of the same name was built directly north of Memorial Stadium, across 23rd Street at a cost of $55,000, not including excavation. The flagpole from the old park was transferred to the new one and set in center field, above a unique rock bank soon dubbed "Billy Goat Hill." Clark Field II had a seating capacity of 3,300 and served as home to the Longhorns' baseball program through the 1974 season. (Bass Concert Hall now sits there.) A spot of greenery on the west bank of Waller Creek, long known as Freshman Field, was then renamed Clark Field III in deference to the old-timers.

Q. What sports facility sat just outside the northwest corner of Memorial Stadium from 1927 until the late 1930s?

A. Three tennis courts, named after Dr. Daniel Penick, originator of the varsity tennis program. Here, such players as Wilmer Allison (two-time Wimbledon doubles champ and Penick's successor as coach), Berkeley Bell, Bruce Barnes, Karl Kamrath, and Sammy Giammalva competed. Sometimes, when the stands were full, people observed the action from atop the nearby stadium.

Q. Why was Stewart ousted after the 1926 season?

A. A multitude of reasons. His record as football coach had begun to slip, he was rumored to be overly fond of the ladies, he spent too much time on outside ventures—especially his lucrative boys' and girls' camps in the Hill Country—and he had a personality conflict with Bellmont. The AD himself was also on shaky ground; he had clashed with Disch, and some faculty and regents. So after a great deal of private and public wrangling, Bellmont lost his job although he continued to teach physical education at UT for another three decades. His replacement was H. J. Ettlinger, a math professor whose involvement with Texas sports had begun in 1913 and lasted nearly half a century. Ettlinger, W. E. Metzenthin, and, later, Ed Olle ran the chaotic program until 1937 when Dana X. Bible arrived.

Q. What was Olle's background?

A. He came from nearby Flatonia, played football, basketball, and baseball from 1925 to 1927, coached the basketball team for three years in the early 1930s, and was the business manager of the athletic department for more than 30 years. He then served as AD between Dana X. Bible and Darrell Royal.

Q. What favorite son inherited the football job in 1927?

A. Clyde Littlefield, who was widely admired throughout the athletic department. Memories of his great deeds as a basketball player, football player, and track man from 1911 to 1915 lingered, and he had been doing well as Texas' track coach. He would be paid $6,000 per year to handle both posts. On the gridiron, he would serve for seven years, winning 44 games, losing 18, and tying 6. His 1928 and 1930 teams would win SWC crowns. After giving up the head football coaching job (he assisted through 1948), Littlefield stayed in Austin as track coach, serving for 41 seasons and winning 25 league championships. In 1925, he and Bellmont had originated the Texas Relays, the renowned track festival to which his name was later added. Clyde Littlefield left a huge legacy in University of Texas athletics.

Q. He played football and threw the discus for Littlefield's track team, earned a law degree, and became the voice of the Texas Relays for more than 30 years. Who was he?

A. John "Tiny" Gooch.

Q. A native of Roswell, New Mexico, this man played halfback in football and catcher in baseball from 1925 to 1928. He was later the public address announcer for home football games. Who was he?

A. J. R. "Potsy" Allen.

Q. Who was Mike "Pinky" Higgins?

A. He was on SWC championship baseball and football teams for Texas in the late 1920s. Higgins then had a 14-year career as a third baseman in major league baseball, with the Philadelphia A's, Boston Red Sox, and Detroit Tigers. He managed the Sox from 1955 to 1962.

Q. What did Leo Baldwin of Texas and Merlin Toler of TCU do on October 1, 1927?

A. They combined to punt 63 times in a game played under a downpour and witnessed by a smattering of fans at Memorial Stadium. No one scored.

Q. What was unusual about Baldwin?

A. This Longhorn, who played three years as a lineman, was best in track. He was SWC discus champion twice and shot put champion three times, but he was fast enough to compete on the 440-yard relay team.

Q. Who was captain of the 1927 UT football team?

A. Clen "Ox" Higgins, a native of Dallas. Although he never made all-SWC, he was chosen by Walter Camp as a second-team all-American that year.

Q. Name the third-string player on the 1928 Texas team who died from being electrocuted in a fraternity initiation.

A. Nolte McElroy.

Q. What unfortunate thing happened to the Longhorns' athletic facilities in 1928?

A. The Men's Gym, home of the basketball team since 1917, burned to the ground. The UT hoopsters would play off campus for the next two years before Gregory Gym opened.

Q. There was something new with the UT football uniform in 1928. What was it?

A. From time immemorial, the Longhorns had worn bright orange jerseys, but they tended to fade with repeated washings, which led to the familiar taunts of "yellow bellies" by opponents. Littlefield had a friend in the textile business who came up with a new and darker shade of orange—one that supposedly would not fade. It was used for more than a decade and then dropped due to shortages in World War II. In 1962, Coach Darrell Royal brought back the now-familiar burnt orange—to the great objection of traditionalists.

Q. University administrators were dead-set against postseason play, for which there had been proposals for at least two decades. But they could not prevent what from happening after the '28 season?

A. An SWC all-star team, coached by Littlefield and Bible, met their counterparts from the Texas Interscholastic Athletic Association in Fort Worth on December 29. Three days later, on New Year's Day, they met a team from the Big Six Conference in Dallas. They won the first game and lost the second.

Q. "Big Un" Rose was a three-sport (football, basketball, and track) man at UT. Did he play pro football?

A. Yes—seven seasons with the Providence Steam Roller and Green Bay Packers.

Q. In 1929, Texas was the defending conference champ and had held seven opponents scoreless—albeit two of those games were 0–0 ties. TCU, meanwhile, was also unbeaten and had allowed just one touchdown before playing the Horns. What crazy-legged speedster beat them almost single-handedly?

A. Cy Leland paced the Frogs to a 15–12 victory. It was TCU's first time to win in Austin, dating back to 1897 when the school was known as Add-Ran.

Q. What was different about A&M's football facility?

A. A "new" Kyle Field had been erected on the site of the old one between 1927 and 1929 at a cost of $345,000; some UT fans thought it bore more than a passing resemblance to Memorial Stadium. At any rate, a crowd of 34,000 was there for dedication day—November 28, 1929. The Ags won, 13–0.

Q. Who was the first Longhorn to play in a nationally recognized postseason game?

A. Tackle Gordy Brown, captain of the '29 team, who went out to San Francisco and participated in the East-West Shrine Game.

CHAPTER 5
1930–1939

The 1938 Longhorns lost every game but the
final—and most important—one. A Texas ball
carrier circles right end for yardage against
the Aggies at Memorial Stadium.
(Photo courtesy of the University of Texas.)

Wilson "Bull" Elkins

"Bull" Elkins had led San Antonio's Brackenridge High School to the 1926 state basketball championship. At UT, Elkins was a genuine scholar-athlete, serving as student body president and earning eight letters: three in football, three in basketball, and two in track. He graduated in 1933 with a bachelor's degree and a master's degree. Then it was off to England, where he was a Rhodes scholar and earned a doctorate at Oxford University. Elkins spent 11 years as president of San Angelo Junior College (now Angelo State University) and three at Texas Western. He left his most lasting mark, though, at the University of Maryland, beginning in 1954. Elkins emphasized basic subjects and strict academic standards, which resulted in expulsion of 14% of undergraduate students. Despite a predictable uproar, Elkins prevailed. He also oversaw sweeping changes in the faculty and physical plant before finally retiring in 1978.

Southwest Conference football had not been given its due in the 1920s. The league did not have a consensus all-American, and none of its teams were seriously considered when the various entities named their national champions. Discerning observers, however, knew that changes were taking place. In the 1930s, the SWC proved itself the equal—at least—of any league in the country. There would be no fewer than three national champions in this decade: SMU in 1935 (shared with Minnesota), TCU in 1938, and Texas A&M in 1939. Lineman Barton "Botchy" Koch of Baylor became the first true all-American in 1930, and the Horned Frogs' little quarterback, Davey O'Brien, would be the first player from the SWC to win the Heisman Trophy, in 1938. Grantland Rice attended the 1935 SMU–TCU game in Fort Worth and wrote with ebullience, "This was one of the greatest games ever played in the 60-year history of the nation's finest college sport. [SMU] carved a clear-cut highway right into the middle of the Rose Bowl beyond any argument. This was a swirl of action no other section of the country could approach, the climax game of 1935."

It would be both unfair and untrue to say that the University of Texas did not contribute to the upward movement of the SWC. The Longhorns would have a very bright moment indeed in South Bend, Indiana, in 1934, and there were several athletes whose names (Ernie Koy, Harrison Stafford, Bohn Hilliard, Jack Crain, and others) would be remembered in years to come. Still, no one would say that the 1930s were anything approaching a sweet time for the orange and white. Twelve years would pass (1930 to 1942) between conference championships, and—although it is a very poor way of assessing pigskin prowess—no Longhorns made all-America during this decade either.

Austin got through the Great Depression somewhat easier than other cities due to the steadying influence of state government and the university. But attendance at Longhorns football games sagged, especially in 1933, when five home games drew fewer fans than Memorial Stadium's seating capacity of 40,500. After getting off to such a great start, jut-jawed and charismatic Jack Chevigny let things deteriorate in his three seasons at UT. It was so bad that even a proven winner like Dana X. Bible (whom Texas fans had coveted since the late 1910s) could only win three games in his first two years. As valleys go, this one was rather deep. It took time and effort, but Bible's Horns had begun to win by 1939.

Of course, the game had problems and scandals. The publication in 1929 of the Carnegie Report on intercollegiate athletics revealed a number of corrupt practices in college football, which had previously been associated with mounting prosperity. When the economic dam burst, critics were quick to point out the festering issues—from training tables to massive press coverage to slush funds. Many schools wrung their hands over the implications of creating a physical education department; PE majors add value to a society that needs to keep its youth fit and well-trained, after all. If such an academic component had the unintended by-product of drawing athletes and keeping them eligible, so much the better. The Carnegie Report insisted that "football is not a students' game, as it once was. It is a highly organized commercial enterprise." Some people ignored or scoffed at its conclusions and lofty recommendations, while others agreed and tried to implement them. The University of Chicago gave up the game entirely, and the Ivy League schools had begun to scale back.

On the other hand, consider the words of Bob Zuppke, coach at the University of Illinois from 1913 to 1941: "The game of football is to college life what color is to painting. It makes college life throb and vibrate."

By the Numbers

0 Longhorns on the 1935 all-SWC team, the first time that had happened since 1918. It would not happen again until 1956.

$1 Daily payment to Texas football players in the early 1930s, in exchange for janitorial services.

5 UT coaches under whom Clyde Littlefield served as an assistant: Berry Whitaker (1920–1922), Doc Stewart (1923–1926), Jack Chevigny (1934–1936), Dana X. Bible (1937–1946), and Blair Cherry (1947, 1948).

5 Games Texas won between 1936 and 1938.

15 Longhorns who took part in the 1934 Notre Dame game.
18 Members of the 1932 UT team who had gone through Bully Gilstrap's football finishing school at Schreiner Institute, including star halfback Bohn Hilliard.
23 Touchdowns for Hilliard in his UT career.
40 Straight seasons (1893 to 1932) with a winning percentage of .500 or better. It is the third-longest such streak in college football history.
52 Points scored by Texas in the nine-game 1938 season.
92 Yard interception return by Harrison Stafford in the 1932 SMU game.
94 Yard touchdown run by Hilliard against Texas Tech in 1934, a school record that would last more than 30 years.
120 Members of the 1938 Texas freshman team.
$145 Cost of round-trip train ride between Austin and Boston for the 1931 Texas–Harvard game. Some 300 fans took advantage.
10,117 UT enrollment in 1937.

Archive

Home games in **bold**

1930 Record: 8–1–1 (Southwest Conference champions) Coach: Clyde Littlefield

Texas 36, Southwest Texas 0
Texas 28, Texas College of Mines 0
Texas 0, Centenary 0
Texas 26, Howard Payne 0
Texas 17, Oklahoma 7 (in Dallas)
Rice 6, Texas 0
Texas 25, SMU 7
Texas 14, Baylor 0
Texas 7, TCU 0
Texas 26, Texas A&M 0

1931 Record: 6–4 Coach: Clyde Littlefield

Texas 36, Simmons 0
Texas 31, Missouri 0
Rice 7, Texas 0
Texas 3, Oklahoma 0 (in Dallas)
Harvard 35, Texas 7
SMU 9, Texas 7
Texas 25, Baylor 0

Texas 10, TCU 0
Texas 6, Centenary 0
Texas A&M 7, Texas 6

1932　Record: 8–2　Coach: Clyde Littlefield
Texas 26, Daniel Baker 0
Centenary 13, Texas 6
Texas 65, Missouri 0
Texas 17, Oklahoma 10 (in Dallas)
Texas 18, Rice 6
Texas 14, SMU 6
Texas 19, Baylor 0
TCU 14, Texas 0
Texas 34, Arkansas 0
Texas 21, Texas A&M 0

1933　Record: 4–5–2　Coach: Clyde Littlefield
Texas 46, Southwestern 0
Texas 22, Texas College of Mines 6
Nebraska 26, Texas 0
Oklahoma 9, Texas 0 (in Dallas)
Texas 0, Centenary 0 (in San Antonio)
Texas 18, Rice 0
Texas 10, SMU 0
Baylor 3, Texas 0
TCU 30, Texas 0
Arkansas 20, Texas 6
Texas 10, Texas A&M 10

1934　Record: 7–2–1　Coach: Jack Chevigny
Texas 12, Texas Tech 6
Texas 7, Notre Dame 6
Texas 19, Oklahoma 0 (in Dallas)
Centenary 9, Texas 6
Rice 20, Texas 9
Texas 7, SMU 7
Texas 25, Baylor 6

Texas 20, TCU 19
Texas 19, Arkansas 12
Texas 13, Texas A&M 0

1935 Record: 4–6 Coach: Jack Chevigny
Texas 38, Texas A&I 6
LSU 18, Texas 6
Texas 12, Oklahoma 7 (in Dallas)
Texas 19, Centenary 13
Rice 28, Texas 19
SMU 20, Texas 0
Texas 25, Baylor 6
TCU 28, Texas 0
Arkansas 28, Texas 13
Texas A&M 20, Texas 6

1936 Record: 2–6–1 Coach: Jack Chevigny
Texas 6, LSU 6
Texas 6, Oklahoma 0 (in Dallas)
Baylor 21, Texas 18
Rice 7, Texas 0
SMU 14, Texas 7
TCU 27, Texas 6
Minnesota 47, Texas 19
Texas 7, Texas A&M 0
Arkansas 6, Texas 0 (in Little Rock)

1937 Record: 2–6–1 Coach: Dana X. Bible
Texas 25, Texas Tech 12
LSU 9, Texas 0
Texas 7, Oklahoma 7 (in Dallas)
Arkansas 21, Texas 10
Rice 14, Texas 7
SMU 13, Texas 2
Texas 9, Baylor 6
TCU 14, Texas 0
Texas A&M 7, Texas 0

1938   Record: 1–8   Coach: Dana X. Bible
Kansas 19, Texas 18
LSU 20, Texas 0
Oklahoma 13, Texas 0 (in Dallas)
Arkansas 42, Texas 6 (in Little Rock)
Rice 13, Texas 6
SMU 7, Texas 6
Baylor 14, Texas 3
TCU 28, Texas 6
Texas 7, Texas A&M 6

1939   Record: 5–4   Coach: Dana X. Bible
Texas 12, Florida 0
Texas 17, Wisconsin 7
Oklahoma 24, Texas 12 (in Dallas)
Texas 14, Arkansas 13
Texas 26, Rice 12
SMU 10, Texas 0
Baylor 20, Texas 0
Texas 25, TCU 19
Texas A&M 20, Texas 0

20 Big Games

Rice 6, Texas 0 / October 25, 1930 / Rice Field (Houston, Texas)
After four shutouts and a defeat of OU in Dallas, the Longhorns seem unbeatable. In fact, they are looking ahead to SMU, which just went toe-to-toe with 1929 national champ Notre Dame. But the Owls land a staggering upset on them—just the third time Rice has beaten Texas in 17 tries. The key play is a fumbled fourth-quarter punt that Rice takes in for a score. UT's Pap Perkins and Johnny Craig start a rally that comes a bit too late.

Texas 26, Texas A&M 0 / November 27, 1930 / Memorial Stadium (Austin, Texas)
Somewhat to its own surprise, Texas is alone atop the ranks of the SWC entering the A&M game. A sellout crowd on this Thanksgiving Day sees

the Horns roar 66 yards to a TD on their first possession. Dexter Shelley, the team captain playing in his last game, runs it over once and throws for another score. Littlefield has his second league championship in four years.

Harvard 35, Texas 7 / October 24, 1931 / Harvard Stadium (Cambridge, Massachusetts)

H. J. Ettlinger has arranged this game with his alma mater. The team leaves on its 2,000-mile train trip on Wednesday morning, arrives in Boston on Friday night, and walks into historic Harvard Stadium on Saturday afternoon. Some 35,000 fans—with a smattering of Longhorns here and there—see the Crimson humiliate Texas. Barry Wood and Jack Crickard lead the way as Harvard gains 387 yards on the ground. UT's only score is a 66-yard trick play in which Ronald Fagan passes to Johnny Furrh, who then laterals to Jimmie Burr. A chance to impress football writers in the East is wasted; it is a long train ride back to the Lone Star State.

SMU 9, Texas 7 / October 31, 1931 / Ownby Stadium (Dallas, Texas)

Just a week after the Harvard debacle, Littlefield's Longhorns have a date with SMU in Dallas. There is little snap in their legs against the Ponies, as there had been against the Crimson. Weldon "Speedy" Mason does most of the damage, but Texas is still in the game in the fourth quarter. Then Alfred Delcambre blocks Johnny Craig's punt in the UT end zone for a safety and the margin of victory. Lutcher Stark is there after the game, giving the coaches much-appreciated pointers and suggestions. Meanwhile, the Mustangs head to the 1931 SWC championship.

Texas 17, Oklahoma 10 / October 15, 1932 / Fairgrounds Park (Dallas, Texas)

Ernie Koy throws a lateral to Harrison Stafford, who then tosses the ball to Bohn Hilliard. The brilliant soph is surrounded by OU defenders, but he wiggles his way 27 yards for a score. Later in the game, he disregards Koy's advice to let a punt roll into the end zone. He scoops up the ball and takes it 95 yards. Such dazzling performances show why UT assistant Marty Karow, who had played against Red Grange in the Big 10, compares Hilliard favorably with the Galloping Ghost. In decades to come, Hilliard will be compared with James Saxton and Eric Metcalf, which is also high praise.

TCU 14, Texas 0 / November 11, 1932 / Amon Carter Stadium (Fort Worth, Texas)

In one of the most anticipated match-ups in conference history to date, the Longhorns and Horned Frogs meet in Cowtown. Perceived as a clash of UT's great backfield (Koy, Stafford, and Hilliard) versus TCU's stout line (Johnny Vaught, Lon Evans, Ben Boswell, and others), it tilts in favor of the Frogs. Francis Schmidt's team would finish the season with a record marred only by a tie with LSU. Still, one play from this game has endured in the collective memory for more than seven decades, and a man in purple would get the worst of it. Vaught is pursuing Hilliard on a third-quarter punt return when Stafford hits the future Ole Miss coach at full tilt. He goes down like a proverbial ton of bricks.

Texas 21, Texas A&M 0 / November 24, 1932 / Memorial Stadium (Austin, Texas)

Fifteen thousand short of a sellout, the home crowd sees the final game featuring Koy and Stafford. They, along with Hilliard, all excel. Koy throws TD passes to both, and Hilliard scampers 65 yards with a punt return in the third quarter. Matty Bell's Aggies suffer their fifth shutout of the season.

Nebraska 26, Texas 0 / October 7, 1933 / Memorial Stadium (Lincoln, Nebraska)

The Horns journey to Lincoln to take on long-time nemesis Dana X. Bible, then coaching the Cornhuskers. They are led by fullback George Sauer, who would later coach at Baylor and have a son play for Texas. Hilliard injures an ankle, Sauer crosses the goal line for two TDs (he also tends to dominate on defense as a linebacker), and Nebraska shreds Texas by 26.

Texas 7, Notre Dame 6 / October 6, 1934 / Notre Dame Stadium (South Bend, Indiana)

The Irish had whipped the Longhorns twice back in the 1910s, and most fans expect more of the same—especially because it's not in Austin. But Jack Chevigny, thrilled to be playing his alma mater, gives a fiery speech in the locker room. Charley Coates sends the opening kickoff to Fred Carideo. He fumbles, Jack Gray recovers at the 18, and four plays later Hilliard follows a crisp block by Joe Smartt into the end zone. The Horns make it stand up before a disbelieving crowd of 33,000. This is the day Southwest Conference football comes of age. Not only do the Horns beat the Irish, but Rice beats Purdue on the same day up in West Lafayette, Indiana. It is a proud moment for Chevigny, who nine months earlier had made a ringing declaration at a Longhorns basketball game, pledging his best to make the Texas flag fly high.

Rice 20, Texas 9 / October 27, 1934 / Rice Field (Houston, Texas)
Interest in this game is running high, so the Humble Oil Company sets up a network of three stations, thus beginning its long term as sponsor of SWC football games on the radio with Kern Tips behind the microphone. Although he is a Rice alum, Tips is far too gentlemanly to play favorites—then or for the next 30 years or so. The Owls get a 34-yard TD pass from Bill Wallace in the second quarter and a 67-yarder in the fourth. They are on their way to their first conference crown.

LSU 18, Texas 6 / October 5, 1935 / Tiger Stadium (Baton Rouge, Louisiana)
The Bayou State is still reeling from the assassination of Senator Huey Long three weeks before. Ever adroit, he had seen political value in backing the football program at the state's flagship institution. In a night game at Tiger Stadium, Chevigny's Horns strike the first blow when QB Jimmy Hadlock sprints 60 yards to the LSU 4 before Bill Pitzer runs it over. The Tigers are in charge from there on, getting points from a 50-yard punt return and a 21-yard interception return.

TCU 28, Texas 0 / November 16, 1935 / Memorial Stadium (Austin, Texas)
The last half of the 1935 season is awful for the Longhorns as they lose five of six games. Dutch Meyer's TCU team comes to Austin and has an easy time of it. Star QB Sammy Baugh—lightly recruited but destined to be one of the all-time greats of college and pro ball—passes just three times. All are for scores, however. UT is inconsequential in the conference race as TCU and SMU are gearing up for a big battle that draws national attention; the Ponies go to the Rose Bowl and the Frogs to the Sugar.

Baylor 21, Texas 18 / October 17, 1936 / Memorial Stadium (Austin, Texas)
Fresh off a defeat of OU, the Longhorns compile an 18-point lead over Baylor in the first half, keyed by a 95-yard interception return by Jack Col-

lins. Perhaps assuming the game is won, Chevigny removes most of his starters—and the substitution rules of the day mean they cannot return. To his chagrin, the Bears start scoring. Billy Patterson, Lloyd Russell, and Bubba Gernand combine for three TDs in a victory that shocks all 9,000 fans at Memorial Stadium.

Texas 7, Texas A&M 0 / November 26, 1936 / Memorial Stadium (Austin, Texas)

Two weeks after Chevigny asks UT authorities not to renew his contract as head football coach, the Horns face a seemingly hopeless task against Texas A&M. But halfback Red Sheridan has his best day—running, punting, and catching a 39-yard pass from Jud Atchison. A first-quarter TD stands up because of fine defense against the Ags' studly sophomore runner, Dick Todd. With just two wins, Texas is left to ponder a disastrous season and a shared spot in the SWC's basement.

Jack Gray

A rugged Longhorn who started every game of the 1933 and 1934 football seasons, Jack Gray is best known for his hoops prowess. He came to Texas unheralded and left as its greatest basketball player to that time, without a doubt. He led the SWC in scoring all three years and was a consensus all-American in 1935, but Gray never really got credit for popularizing the one-handed shot—a fairly significant advance in the game. Practically an immortal by the time he played his last game on the Gregory Gym hardcourts, Gray impressed all who saw him. He surely could have been an even better basketball player had he not devoted equal energy to football.

"Throughout the Southwest, they are spinning the saga of this singular basketeer," said one *Austin Statesman* writer. "He was an athlete of surprising merit, and we may not see his like again." But by no means was he through with UT. He was an assistant football coach from 1936 to 1949, minus the war years. More significantly, Gray was named head basketball coach in 1935, at age 25. His Longhorns employed a running, pressing style that the fans loved, with a record of 194–97. The 1947 team, headed by future NBA player Slater Martin, came close to winning the national title. Gray quit after the 1951 season and made much bigger money as an oil pipeline mogul.

Rice 14, Texas 7 / October 23, 1937 / Memorial Stadium (Austin, Texas)

The Bible era does not start well. His first Longhorns team has won 1, lost 2, and tied 1 before meeting Rice in Austin. The game is tied midway through the fourth quarter when it takes an unexpected turn as the Owls' Ernie Lain throws an 11-yard touchdown pass to Frank Steen. Referee Harry Viner indicates the catch is good, although Texas partisans beg to disagree. The howl over poor officiating would go on for the rest of the season. Rice wins its second conference championship in four years.

Texas 9, Baylor 6 / November 6, 1937 / Waco Municipal Stadium (Waco, Texas)

Undefeated in six games and ranked No. 4 in the nation, Baylor hosts Bible's Horns in Waco. Passing whiz Billy Patterson is expected to put on a show, but he is held to 11-of-30 and no fewer than five interceptions. Jud Atchison has an 18-yard touchdown run in the first quarter, and Hugh Wolfe kicks a field goal from the BU 26 to end all that talk about the Bears going to the Rose Bowl. Back in Austin, a tradition is born when the orange "victory lights" are turned on atop the new 27-story Main Building, known even then as the Tower.

Texas 7, Texas A&M 6 / November 24, 1938 / Memorial Stadium (Austin, Texas)

Things have gone from bad in 1937 to even worse in 1938. The Longhorns are 0–8 entering the season finale with A&M. And because they have been manhandled in some of those losses, it doesn't look good against an Aggies team with crack players like Marshall Robnett, Dick Todd, and John Kimbrough. The Austin papers are whistling in the dark by recalling UT upsets of the past, but Bible won't let his boys accept defeat. Early in the fourth quarter, a short run by Nelson Puett Jr., creates Texas' 7–0 lead. With 20 seconds left, basketball star-turned-footballer Bobby Moers fumbles, the ball is recovered for a TD—A&M's first ever at Memorial Stadium—and an apparent tie. But Todd's extra-point kick is blocked when Roy Baines climbs a teammate's back and knocks it down. Bible tells reporters it is the happiest day in his long coaching career.

Texas 17, Wisconsin 7 / October 7, 1939 / Camp Randall Stadium (Madison, Wisconsin)

Jack Crain, UT's 165-pound package of dynamite, has already shown his stuff in a win over Florida, and he does it again in the season's second game, against Wisconsin. He goes 35 yards for a touchdown, R. B. Patrick scores, and two safeties are enough to beat the Badgers. It is the Longhorns' biggest intersectional win since defeating Notre Dame in 1934.

Oklahoma 24, Texas 12 / October 14, 1939 / Cotton Bowl (Dallas, Texas)

The Horns are getting their ears boxed by a powerful Sooners team before 27,000 fans at the Cotton Bowl. They are down by 17 in the fourth quarter when lightning strikes twice. Crain takes a pitchout from his quarterback and high-tails it 71 yards for a score. Texas regains possession three minutes later, and Crain replicates the deed almost exactly—71 yards. But OU settles down and drives the length of the field to score and put it away.

Texas 14, Arkansas 13 / October 21, 1939 / Memorial Stadium (Austin, Texas)

The Razorbacks, who had brutalized Texas, 42–6, the year before, get stiffer competition in 1939 but they are in control in the final minute. With Kay Eakin at the helm, they have limited the Horns to 78 yards total offense and five first downs, and are up by six points. Then, on an improvised play, Patrick lobs a short pass to Crain who scoots 67 yards for a score. The fans, at least those who have not left the stadium, are ecstatic and rush the field. It takes several minutes for officials and players to move them back and allow Crain—who else?—to kick the winning extra point. It is an epic victory, one that helps revitalize the entire UT football program.

All-Decade Team

Back	Harrison Stafford (1930–1932)
Back	Ernie Koy (1930–1932)
Back	Bohn Hilliard (1932–1934)
Lineman	Ox Emerson (1929, 1930)
Lineman	Charley Coates (1932–1934)
Lineman	Clint Small (1934–1936)
Lineman	Howard Terry (1935–1937)
Lineman	Jack Rhodes (1937–1938)
End	Jack Gray (1933, 1934)
End	Philip Sanger (1933, 1934)
Kicker	Hugh Wolfe (1934, 1936, 1937)

Q & A

Q. In 1930, the Horns lost to Rice and were decided underdogs the next week against SMU. What defensive surprise did they spring on Ray Morrison's Ponies?

A. A five-man line, instead of the usual six or seven. They won, 25–7, and moved forward to their second SWC title in four years.

Q. Dexter Shelley had been a two-time all-SWC halfback. What did he do after college?

A. He played in the 1930 East-West Shrine game, had one season each with the Chicago Cardinals and Green Bay Packers, and then coached high school football in Orange.

Q. What Corsicana native played end on the 1930–1932 football teams, guard on the basketball team, and was an infielder and pitcher on the baseball team?

A. Ed Price, who would coach the Longhorns from 1951 to 1956.

Q. Memorial Stadium had a new neighbor beginning in 1931. What was it?

A. Gregory Gymnasium, just up the hill at 21st Street and Speedway. The Longhorns basketball team had played off campus for two seasons after the Men's Gym burned. Ground was broken on May 10, 1929, and, at a cost of $510,000, it was completed in time for the 1931 season. It was named in honor of Thomas W. Gregory, a UT alumnus who had long campaigned to have such a facility built on campus. Far more than just the home of Texas hoops for 47 years, Gregory Gym hosted literally thousands of intercollegiate, intramural, and high school sporting events, as well as speeches, dances, commencement ceremonies, and musical performances. The Texas athletic department set up headquarters there, and its T Room would become a repository for photos and trophies. Given an annex in 1962 and greatly modernized in the 1990s, Gregory Gym is now home to the UT women's volleyball program.

Q. He was an all-conference guard in 1930, but an eligibility issue cost him his senior year. So he headed on to the pros and helped the Detroit Lions win the 1935 NFL championship. Who was he?

A. Gover "Ox" Emerson, later an assistant under Ed Price.

Q. Harrison Stafford, an unknown freshman in 1929, was issued a torn jersey and mismatched shoes, but he soon made his presence known with authority. What did Shorty Alderson, coach of the Yearlings, say about Stafford?

A. He breathlessly told Littlefield, "Clyde, I found you the darndest football player you ever saw. He tore up a couple of dummies and hurt a couple of men. He says his name is Harrison Stafford."

Q. How did Littlefield remember him?

A. "I've never seen a player with the all-around ability that Stafford had. There's never been anyone who could block, run, catch passes and play defense like Harrison Stafford."

Q. What did Stafford do in the off-season?

A. He ran hurdles and sprint relays, and threw the javelin and shot put on the UT track team.

Q. What teammate of Stafford's later had two sons play for the Longhorns?

A. Ernie Koy; his boys were Ernie Jr. (1963–1965) and Ted (1967–1969).

Q. What was Koy's greatest day as a Longhorn?

A. Perhaps when he scored four touchdowns in a 65–0 destruction of Missouri in his senior season. Koy was thrice an all-SWC fullback and was equally adept patrolling the outfield at Clark Field—again three times all-conference. He worked his way through the minor leagues before reaching the bigs, playing with the Brooklyn Dodgers, St. Louis Cardinals, Cincinnati Reds, and Philadelphia Phillies. World War II effectively ended Koy's athletic career.

Q. UT baseball coach Billy Disch also helped out with the football team for a few seasons. What used to irk him no end?

A. Disch considered Clark Field his own, but on football game days it was regularly used as a parking lot. Uncle Billy was not pleased.

Jack Crain

They called him "Jackrabbit," "Cowboy," and "the Nocona Nugget." Jack Crain, from the north Texas town of Nocona (where he scored 71 touchdowns his senior year), was given a one-year scholarship. If he didn't show something, he was out. Crain showed a lot, though, both with the 1938 Yearlings and up on the varsity. He was small but fast, hard to tackle, and possessed of a fierce stiff-arm. There were other great players on those 1939–1941 Texas teams, but Crain was the alpha male among them. Twice all-SWC, he was tenth in Heisman Trophy voting his last year. He was in the Navy during World War II and served three terms in the Texas legislature. Crain retired from politics and went back home, where he worked as a farmer and rancher. Today, the Nocona High School football team plays at Jack Crain Stadium.

Q. When was the term "Hook 'em, Horns" first used?

A. In a *Daily Texan* advertisement, circa 1932.

Q. Duke Washington of Washington State (1955) is often credited with being the first black football player to set foot on the turf of Texas Memorial Stadium, but that is not quite correct. Who was it, then?

A. In 1933, the historically black colleges Paul Quinn and Prairie View played a game at the stadium. Hilliard and other UT players served as referees.

Q. Despite UT's losing record and falling to fifth place in the SWC in 1933, Clyde Littlefield still had a lot of support; the Athletics Council voted unanimously to keep him for another year, but Stark was hounding him to resign and he finally did. Who came next?

A. John Edward "Jack" Chevigny, who had gaudy credentials as part of the great legend of Notre Dame football. Five years earlier, he had scored the winning touchdown against Army after Knute Rockne's famous "win one for the Gipper" halftime speech. A native of Hammond, Indiana, he coached the Chicago Cardinals in 1932 (with a 2–6–2 record) and then, in a move that mystified some, took the job at St. Edward's University in south Austin. While there, he was not shy about promoting himself, impressing local sportswriters and some UT regents. Chevigny got the UT job and 20 lettermen, who helped him go 7–2–1 his first year with that big victory over his alma mater.

Q. What popular idea did Chevigny come up with soon after his arrival on the Forty Acres?

A. He instituted the annual Orange–White game at the end of spring football. The first one was seen by 4,000 fans.

Q. *What did Chevigny receive at the UT football banquet in December 1934?*

A. An $800 raise from the university and a LaSalle touring car from ecstatic boosters.

Q. *Why did he leave Austin so soon?*

A. A variety of reasons. Chevigny did little to maintain relationships with high school coaches in Texas, preferring to recruit in his native Midwest, but that brought little in return. Some people thought he was a phony or a skirt-chaser. A practicing lawyer, he did some legal work on the side and occasionally did not show up for football practice. None of that would have mattered in the least if the Horns had kept winning, but they did not.

Q. *What did he do later on?*

A. Chevigny worked briefly as an attorney for the State Tax Commission, moved to Illinois, struck it rich in the oil business, and lost it all. He joined the Marines in World War II and died fighting at Iwo Jima. The story may be apocryphal, but it is said that a gold pen given to him after the big upset of Notre Dame in 1934 was in use by a Japanese admiral during the signing of the peace treaty in Tokyo Bay 11 years later. It was inscribed, "To Jack Chevigny, an old Notre Damer who beat Notre Dame."

Q. *Charley Coates made all-SWC at two different line positions. What were they?*

A. He was a tackle in 1933 and a center in 1934.

Q. *Did Bohn Hilliard play any other sports at Texas?*

A. Yes. He helped Billy Disch's baseball team win the SWC crown in 1935 and 1936, and made all-conference as an outfielder.

Q. *He played in the UT line from 1935 to 1937 and later was head coach at Texas Tech in the 1960s. Name him.*

A. J. T. King, who served an apprenticeship as an assistant under Ed Price in the 1950s before taking over the Red Raiders program.

Q. The football gods had created something in the Southwest in 1937. What was it?

A. The Cotton Bowl Classic, played each New Year's Day in Dallas. The game, held at the newly erected stadium of that name at the State Fair Grounds, was the brainchild of oil executive J. Curtis Sanford, who financed the first one out of his own pocket. There was not yet a contractual tie-in with the SWC, but Sanford and his successors liked having the conference champ come to Dallas. For 40 years, the Cotton Bowl would be among the big four postseason games, joining the Rose, the Sugar, and the Orange.

Q. An end on the UT football teams of the mid-1930s, he was also a basketball star. Identify this native of Denton.

A. Jack Collins. He was an all-conference center in 1936 (he led the SWC in scoring with 9.8 points per game) and captain of the 1937 team. His son of the same name would play football at UT from 1959 to 1961.

Q. Ever the innovator, what practice did Chevigny implement in the 1936 season?

A. Filming games for study later. This soon became an indispensable tool for coaches and players, not to mention its archival and historical value.

Q. Chevigny was also responsible for a short-lived change to the Longhorns' headgear. What was it?

A. He put a three-pronged design, similar to that for which Michigan was most famous, in orange on otherwise white helmets.

Q. The 1936 Longhorns went 2–6–1 and scored just 69 points. What was the bright side of that dreary season?

A. Probably the play of junior running back Hugh Wolfe. He had a 37-yard touchdown run against LSU and a 95-yard kickoff return against the Minnesota Golden Gophers, who went on to win the first Associated Press national championship. Wolfe was a two-time all-SWC running back (he also handled kicking duties), was a Texas Relays discus champion, and was UT's first NFL draft pick, by the Pittsburgh Steelers. Traded to New York, he spent one season with the Giants.

Q. It has been said that this man saved UT football twice—when he was hired as coach and AD in 1937, and then again 20 years later when he chose Darrell Royal to coach the Horns. To whom do we refer?

A. Dana X. Bible.

Q. What was Bible's background?

A. A native of Jefferson City, Tennessee, he attended Carson-Newman College and studied the game at the knees of such legends as Amos Alonzo Stagg and Glenn "Pop" Warner. Bible had been an assistant coach at Texas A&M, spent one season "on loan" to LSU and returned to College Station as head coach the next year. The work he did there can hardly be overstated. In 11 seasons, his teams had a winning percentage of .768 and deserved more national recognition than they got—especially the 1917 and 1919 teams, which were undefeated and unscored upon. Bible's Aggies had won five SWC titles when he took the Nebraska job in 1929. It was more of the same in Lincoln, as the Cornhuskers won the Big Six crown six times in eight seasons. Any list of the greatest college football coaches of the 1920s and 1930s would have to include Ray Morrison of Vanderbilt, Howard Jones of Southern California, Bob Neyland of Tennessee, Jock Sutherland of Pittsburgh, Wallace Wade of Alabama—and Bible. He coached a total of 33 years and had an impressive record of 198–72–3 (63–31–3 at Texas). He was the third-winningest coach in the history of the game, behind only Stagg and Warner, both of whom worked much longer. Bible was not only an excellent coach but an exemplary sportsman, admired by all.

Q. What was the big controversy when Bible was hired?

A. It was his $15,000 salary, almost double that of university president Harry Benedict. So the Board of Regents decided to give Benedict a raise to $17,500.

Q. How was Bible recalled by one of his former players?

A. "He was as confident as a banker, astute as a schoolmaster, poised as a preacher, and expressive as a salesman."

85

Q. The 1938 freshman squad (known as the Yearlings) achieved what rare thing?

A. They won the annual freshman–varsity game. This game, which had been going on for about 15 years, was usually an informal affair in which the older players beat the younger ones to a fare-the-well. It was a baptism of sorts, or perhaps it could be called an initiation. This time, however, the frosh returned the favor.

Q. Bobby Moers was twice all-conference in both basketball and baseball. But what was he doing out on the field at the end of the 1938 A&M game when he had a crucial fumble?

A. In mid-season, the coaches persuaded him to put on a football uniform. It is indicative of just how short-handed Bible's '38 Longhorns were.

Q. Who were the first female cheerleaders at Texas?

A. Glenn Appling and Louise Billings in 1939.

Q. What co-captain of the 1939 Texas team later was head coach at Virginia?

A. Ned McDonald, who played end.

Q. What was the first on-campus dorm for UT football players?

A. Hill Hall, a $125,000 four-story facility on 21st Street, built in 1939. It was named after Dr. Homer Hill, team physician from 1893 until his death in 1923.

Q. The woman who served as housemother there for many years was hard on the outside but really quite warm and loving. Who was she?

A. Mrs. J. M. Griffith, known to her charges as "Ma Griff" and "Miz Griff."

Q. Identify her predecessor.

A. That would be Mrs. D. B. Emmons. At her boarding house west of campus, she fed the football entourage beginning in the mid-1920s.

86

Dana X. Bible and the 1941 Horns, probably the best team in UT history up to that time. Bible's offensive sparkplug, Jack Crain, is No. 44 on the top row.
(Photo courtesy of the University of Texas.)

Just before the turn of the decade, the NCAA sought to institute the so-called Purity Code (after many a snickering jest, it was redubbed the Sanity Code). A sanctimonious policy that forbade athletic scholarships and off-campus recruiting, it exposed the gulf separating big schools and their smaller brethren. These regulations were widely opposed, and a move to overturn them was successful at the 1951 NCAA convention.

The drumbeat of war was audible well before the bombing of Pearl Harbor in December 1941. As Germany and Japan menaced their neighbors, college football continued its evolution. Most significantly, a rule change allowed much more liberal substitution, although it would be reversed in the early 1950s and reversed again in 1965. Done for two main reasons—to mitigate injuries and to reduce player drain in the event of war—this policy would help keep the game going during the early and mid-1940s. Texas' Dana X. Bible, like most of his coaching colleagues, sometimes had to play physically unfit 4-Fs, freshmen, and whatever military trainees he could find on campus.

College football had become such a big part of the larger culture that the U.S. government wished it to continue on military bases, both here and abroad. There was an implicit agreement that football amounted to good exercise, it kept soldiers' spirits up, and it provided wholesome entertainment. Generals George Marshall, Douglas MacArthur, Dwight Eisenhower, and Omar Bradley all were on record as saying that football produced the best soldiers.

As we will see, World War II affected college football even after the fighting stopped. The University of Texas lost a plethora of athletes to military service, but it gained a few as well through the Navy V-5 and V-12 training programs that were held on the Forty Acres. After the war, the student population at UT grew by leaps and bounds, largely because of the GI Bill. It sent more than 2 million vets to college, and at times all of them appeared to be in Austin. Housing was impossibly tight, and there were scarcely enough classrooms to hold the multitude of students. Admission to basketball games at Gregory Gym was done on a lottery basis.

In the 1940s, the Longhorns won three Southwest Conference titles, reached the top spot in the national rankings twice, and had their first bona fide all-Americans. Bible would turn over the coaching reins to his longtime assistant, Blair Cherry, but keep his AD post for another decade. As much as anything, fans of that time got to witness the brilliance of Bobby Layne, the finest quarterback in UT history until the advent of Vince Young some 60 years later.

There is no doubt that the Texas athletic department had aspirations of reaching the top. National champions from the 1940s included Notre Dame (4 times), Minnesota (2), Army (2), Georgia, and Michigan. So why not Texas? It was a university of 15,000 students with a large alumni base, the flagship institution in a state overflowing with high school athletes. It had coaches with vast experience and the incentive to join the elite of college football. UT also had a newly enlarged facility in which to play.

In April 1947, the Athletics Council approved the plans of architect George Dahl. The east and west stands of Memorial Stadium were to get 26 more rows (for a total of 78), plus a section to the south, boosting seating capacity to 60,130. Dahl had estimated the cost at $600,000, but the low bid came from a Houston company: $1.4 million. The boss—Bible—was not pleased, but the project went forward. With the days of student fundraisers long past, the athletic department was responsible for paying the bill. A double-decked press box and other changes inside and out gave UT a much more substantial and accommodating stadium. The home opener of the 1948 season was on September 18 against LSU, at which time a ceremony was held. Memorial Stadium was rededicated to honor the Texans who had died in the recent war. University president T. S. Painter said, "This stadium will always stand as a lasting memorial to those who so gallantly gave their lives that we might be free."

By the Numbers

0 Losing seasons in the 1940s.

1 Week the Longhorns were No. 1 in the country, twice: in 1941 and in 1946.

1 Round in which Orban "Spec" Sanders was chosen by the Washington Redskins in 1942; he was the first of many Longhorns who would go in the first round of the NFL draft.

4 Touchdowns by Bobby Layne against Oklahoma in 1946, then a school record.

8 Straight years SMU beat or tied Texas (1933–1940) before a 34–0 Longhorns victory in Dallas in 1941.

9 1/2 Months separating Texas' Cotton Bowl win over Missouri on New Year's Day, 1946, and the Horns' 42–0 defeat of the Tigers in the opening game of the 1946 season.

10 Games won in the 1945 season, the most yet for the Horns.

27 Years Jack Crain's school career record of 23 touchdowns lasted until Chris Gilbert broke it in 1968.

34 Points Crain scored in his three games against Oklahoma.

34 Games started by Bobby Layne; it would have been more except he was serving in the Merchant Marine in the first half of the 1945 season.

40 Points for which Layne was responsible in the 1945 Cotton Bowl against Missouri—4 rushing touchdowns, 2 extra-point kicks, and 2 scoring TDs.

48 Fumbles by the Texas offense in 1945, a record that would last 31 years.

76 Points scored against Colorado in 1946, the third most decisive win in UT history.

78–21–3 Texas' record in the 1940s.

99 Jersey number worn by 4' 9" dropkicker/trainer/waterboy Billy "Rooster" Andrews in the mid-1940s.

Archive

Home games in **bold**

1940   Record: 8–2   Coach: Dana X. Bible
Texas 39, Colorado 7

Texas 13, Indiana 6

Texas 19, Oklahoma 16 (in Dallas)

Texas 21, Arkansas 0 (in Little Rock)

Rice 13, Texas 0

SMU 21, Texas 13

Texas 13, Baylor 0

Texas 21, TCU 14

Texas 7, Texas A&M 0

Texas 26, Florida 0

1941   Record: 8–1–1   Coach: Dana X. Bible
Texas 34, Colorado 6

Texas 34, LSU 0

Texas 40, Oklahoma 7 (in Dallas)

Texas 48, Arkansas 14

Texas 40, Rice 0

Texas 34, SMU 0

Texas 7, Baylor 7

TCU 14, Texas 7

Texas 23, Texas A&M 0
Texas 71, Oregon 7

1942 Record: 9–2 (Southwest Conference champions) Coach: Dana X. Bible

Texas 40, Corpus Christi Naval Air Station 0
Texas 64, Kansas State 0
Northwestern 3, Texas 0
Texas 7, Oklahoma 0 (in Dallas)
Texas 47, Arkansas 6 (in Little Rock)
Texas 12, Rice 7
Texas 21, SMU 7
Texas 20, Baylor 0
TCU 13, Texas 7
Texas 12, Texas A&M 6
Texas 14, Georgia Tech 7 (Cotton Bowl in Dallas)

1943 Record: 7–1–1 (Southwest Conference champions) Coach: Dana X. Bible

Texas 65, Blackland Army Air Field 6
Southwestern 14, Texas 7
Texas 13, Oklahoma 7 (in Dallas)
Texas 34, Arkansas 0
Texas 58, Rice 0
Texas 20, SMU 0
Texas 46, TCU 7
Texas 27, Texas A&M 13
Texas 7, Randolph Field 7 (Cotton Bowl in Dallas)

1944 Record: 5–4 Coach: Dana X. Bible

Texas 20, Southwestern 0
Randolph Field 42, Texas 6
Texas 20, Oklahoma 0 (in Dallas)
Texas 19, Arkansas 0 (in Little Rock)
Rice 7, Texas 0
Texas 34, SMU 7
Oklahoma A&M 13, Texas 8

TCU 7, Texas 6
Texas 6, Texas A&M 0

1945   Record: 10–1 (Southwest Conference champions) Coach: Dana X. Bible

Texas 13, Bergstrom Field 7
Texas 46, Southwestern 0
Texas 33, Texas Tech 0
Texas 12, Oklahoma 7 (in Dallas)
Texas 34, Arkansas 7 (in Little Rock)
Rice 7, Texas 6
Texas 12, SMU 7
Texas 21, Baylor 14
Texas 20, TCU 0
Texas 20, Texas A&M 10
Texas 40, Missouri 27 (Cotton Bowl in Dallas)

1946   Record: 8–2   Coach: Dana X. Bible

Texas 42, Missouri 0
Texas 76, Colorado 0
Texas 54, Oklahoma A&M 6
Texas 20, Oklahoma 13 (in Dallas)
Texas 20, Arkansas 0
Rice 18, Texas 13
Texas 19, SMU 3
Texas 22, Baylor 7
TCU 14, Texas 0
Texas 24, Texas A&M 7

1947   Record: 10–1   Coach: Blair Cherry

Texas 33, Texas Tech 0
Texas 38, Oregon 13 (in Portland)
Texas 34, North Carolina 0
Texas 34, Oklahoma 14 (in Dallas)
Texas 21, Arkansas 6 (in Memphis)
Texas 12, Rice 0
SMU 14, Texas 13

Texas 28, Baylor 7
Texas 20, TCU 0
Texas 32, Texas A&M 13
Texas 27, Alabama 7 (Sugar Bowl in New Orleans)

1948   Record: 7–3–1   Coach: Blair Cherry
Texas 33, LSU 0
North Carolina 34, Texas 7
Texas 47, New Mexico 0
Oklahoma 20, Texas 14 (in Dallas)
Texas 14, Arkansas 6
Texas 20, Rice 7
SMU 21, Texas 6
Texas 13, Baylor 10
Texas 14, TCU 7
Texas 14, Texas A&M 14
Texas 41, Georgia 28 (Orange Bowl in Miami)

1949   Record: 6–4   Coach: Blair Cherry
Texas 43, Texas Tech 0
Texas 54, Temple 0
Texas 56, Idaho 7
Oklahoma 20, Texas 14 (in Dallas)
Texas 27, Arkansas 14 (in Little Rock)
Rice 17, Texas 15
SMU 7, Texas 6
Texas 20, Baylor 0
TCU 14, Texas 13
Texas 42, Texas A&M 14

20 Big Games

Texas 19, Oklahoma 16 / October 12, 1940 / Cotton Bowl
(Dallas, Texas)
Jack Crain has done little in the first two games—defeats of Colorado at home and Indiana on the road—but that changes against OU in Dallas. The Longhorns trail by nine points late in the third quarter when Crain sprints

63 yards to the 2, where fullback R. L. Harkins scores. It still appears that Oklahoma will win until a late fumble gives UT hope. Crain circles left end for the winning score with three minutes to play.

Texas 7, Texas A&M 0 / November 28, 1940 / Memorial Stadium (Austin, Texas)

It is a cool, cloudy day in the fall of 1940. Some 45,000 fans are packed into Memorial Stadium, and UT is about to take the field against a team with a 20-game winning streak—the defending national champion Texas A&M Aggies, who are led by ferocious fullback John Kimbrough. In the locker room, the sonorous-voiced Bible reads "It Can Be Done," a 16-line nugget of poetic inspiration. With copious adrenaline flowing through their veins, the Longhorns proceed to do it. In the first 57 seconds, Pete Layden throws a 32-yard strike to Crain, Noble Doss snags an over-the-head ball at the 1, and Layden goes over for the TD. Crain's extra point will prove to be the final score of the day for either team. Doss has three interceptions for the Horns, and Kimbrough is magnificent for the Aggies. The doors to the visitors' locker room are closed as Homer Norton preaches a quiet sermon to his heartbroken players. This is a game Texas fans will talk about for years to come.

Texas 40, Rice 0 / October 25, 1941 / Memorial Stadium (Austin, Texas)

Rice, which had precipitated UT's downfall the year before, is expected to give Bible's 4–0 team a tough test before a sellout crowd in Austin. But the Owls (whose new coach, Jess Neely, will stay 25 years) can't get any traction. They are demoralized when Layden gallops 35 yards for an early score. In the second quarter, Crain fields a punt, gets a block from Henry Harkins and goes 82 yards for another TD. Harkins' brother, R. L., has three of his own in cleanup duty. The Longhorns have been rising in the Associated Press poll, and this shutout of Rice moves them into a tie for the No. 1 spot with Minnesota.

Texas 71, Oregon 7 / December 6, 1941 / Memorial Stadium (Austin, Texas)

The Longhorns have just beaten A&M in College Station, the first time that has happened since 1923. Left out in the cold by machinations of the Rose, Sugar, Orange, and Cotton bowls, they meet Oregon in the season finale.

The unsuspecting Webfoots have no chance against a furious Longhorns team, which scores at least two touchdowns every period and four in the last one. UT finishes with 495 yards of total offense, more than triple that of Oregon. Bible, criticized for pouring it on against a hapless opponent, denies any such thing. The glow of victory lasts less than 24 hours because of news that the Japanese have attacked Pearl Harbor. America's involvement in World War II has begun, and most of the 16 seniors on the 1941 Texas team will be in the service before the year is out.

Northwestern 3, Texas 0 / October 3, 1942 / Dyche Stadium (Evanston, Illinois)

UT's first trip to the Windy City since 1904 is a loss, although not nearly as bad as that 68–0 drubbing by the University of Chicago. It appears that this defensive struggle between Bible's Horns and Pappy Waldorf's Wildcats may go scoreless until Northwestern's Al Pick boots a 36-yard field goal with six minutes to play. Purple-clad quarterback Otto Graham has little success this day, tossing two interceptions, but he will soon be named all-American in both football and basketball, do his part in World War II, and have a Hall of Fame career with the Cleveland Browns.

Bobby Layne

His name was Robert Lawrence Layne, and he had grown up with Doak Walker in Highland Park, adjacent to the SMU campus. It's hard to believe, but he came to UT mostly for baseball reasons. Since Bibb Falk was serving in the Army Air Force, the Longhorns baseball team was in the hands of Blair Cherry. Assistant football coach and soon to replace Bible as head man, Cherry urged the 6' 1", 200-pound Layne to give football a fling as well.

First, though, his baseball exploits. Layne had a 35–3 record as a pitcher, threw two no-hitters, and averaged more than 10 strikeouts per game. There is little reason to think he would not have been quite successful in professional baseball, but he went in a different direction. Four times all-SWC in football, he was a consensus all-American in 1947 and was sixth in Heisman Trophy voting. Layne finished his Texas career with a school record 3,145 yards passing on 210 completions, with 25 touchdown passes. The latter record would not be surpassed until 1992 (by Peter Gardere). Known more for charisma, leadership, and determination than for pure athletic ability, Layne was the third pick in the 1948 NFL draft. He was traded twice in his first three years but found a home in Detroit, where he turned around the Lions' franchise—with some help from his old buddy, Doak Walker. Wearing a blue jersey and blue helmet, minus a facemask, Layne appeared on the cover of the November 29, 1954, issue of *Time* magazine. He retired in 1962 after spending his last years with the Pittsburgh Steelers. A member of the Pro Football Hall of Fame, he was surely one of the best players of his era. Had the mercurial Layne not been an alcoholic his entire adult life, he might have been even better; at the very least, the nonstop drinking and nightlife led to his premature death at age 60.

Texas 14, Georgia Tech 7 / January 1, 1943 / Cotton Bowl /
Cotton Bowl (Dallas, Texas)
Bible had promised a conference champion in five years, but it takes six. The
Longhorns accept the Cotton Bowl bid, are ranked No. 11 and facing No.
5 Georgia Tech. Some scribes think they don't belong on the same field with
Bill Alexander's team. They quiet the naysayers on a warm, sunny New Year's
Day in Big D before a crowd of 36,620. The winning score comes in the
third quarter when Jackie Field takes a punt at his 39, sidesteps a tackler, and
races down the sideline in front of a madly cheering Texas bench for a TD.
The Horns outgain the Rambling Wreck by a margin of 201 to 57 yards, and
Jack Freeman wins the most outstanding lineman award.

Southwestern 14, Texas 7 / October 2, 1943 / Memorial Stadium
(Austin, Texas)
Virtually every member of the 1942 varsity—and most of the frosh, too—
have gone into the service. Seven of them (Jackie Field, Ken Matthews, Spot
Collins, Jack Sachse, Harold Fischer, Les Proctor, and Zuehl Conoly) are
at nearby Southwestern University as Marine trainees, and they enjoy an
impressive homecoming. The Pirates thoroughly dominate play, and Texas
is fortunate to keep it to 14–7. Matthews scores the decisive TD. It will be
the Longhorns' only loss of the season.

Texas 27, Texas A&M 13 / November 25, 1943 / Kyle Field
(College Station, Texas)
It's the last game of the regular season as the No. 12 Longhorns and No.
16 Aggies come into a Thanksgiving Day confrontation for the SWC title.
Homer Norton's team, known as the Kiddie Korps because of its youth, is a
serious underdog and they fall 13 points behind early on. They soon tie it up
with a couple of touchdown runs by Red Burditt and Babe Hallmark. But
shortly before halftime, Ralph Park takes a pitchout and goes 32 yards for
a score, and Texas heads to victory. It is a sweet one for Bible, who still has
many friends and admirers in College Station. The Aggies go on to the Orange Bowl, and the Horns are picking Cotton for the second straight year.

Texas 7, Randolph Field 7 / January 1, 1944 / Cotton Bowl /
Cotton Bowl (Dallas, Texas)
UT had destroyed one service team, Blackland Army Air Field, by a score
of 65–6, but a much tougher one would be the opponent in the '44 Cotton

Bowl. Randolph Field is a pass-happy team, thanks largely to its fine quarterback, Glenn Dobbs. The former Tulsa player and future coach there is the nation's leading passer and kicker, too. On a cold and rainy day, Dobbs completes just 3 of his 16 passes, but one of them is for a first-quarter touchdown. While Texas is limited to 110 yards of total offense, a 35-yard strike from Ralph Ellsworth to George McCall ties the score. The Ramblers drive to the 8-yard line toward the end of the game, but a banged-up Texas defense manages to keep them out of the end zone. Four Horns—Ellsworth, fullback J. R. Callahan, halfback Ralph Park, and center Kiefer Marshall—go the whole 60 minutes.

Texas 6, Texas A&M 0 / November 30, 1944 / Memorial Stadium (Austin, Texas)

Through no fault of his own, this is Bible's worst team since the desultory days of 1937 and 1938; with war raging in Europe and in the Pacific theater, many able-bodied males of college age are otherwise occupied. Texas has dropped games to Randolph Field, Rice, Oklahoma A&M, and TCU. Only the Texas A&M game is left, and from time immemorial it has been the biggest to both schools. Some 43,000 fans fill the stadium to see UT score early, but once is all it takes in a 6–0 game. After an Aggies punt, Bobby Layne completes a 26-yard pass to Jimmie Watson. On the next play, Bible's star freshman evades a heavy rush and picks his way to a TD. The Aggies later have chances to score but can't do it in Texas' 11th straight win over the maroon and white in Austin.

Texas 12, SMU 7 / November 3, 1945 / Ownby Stadium (Dallas, Texas)

The Longhorns are 5–1 and ranked No. 19 coming into this game with Matty Bell's Ponies, and they have done it without their top offensive player, Bobby Layne. He and his Highland Park schoolboy friend, Doak Walker, had joined the Merchant Marine but events are happening swiftly. The two are in New Orleans when they get their discharge papers. Walker plans to enroll at UT but reverses field and stays home at SMU. (Walker's parents emphatically do not want him down in Austin, exposed to Layne's drinking and carousing.) The very next week, the Longhorns and Mustangs face each other in Dallas. Walker thrills the 23,000 fans with a 30-yard scoring run in the first quarter, but Layne tosses TD passes to Dale Schwartzkopf and

Ralph "Peppy" Blount. He also snags an interception to secure a victory in a game with lots of ebb and flow. Layne and Walker will meet once more in college and be teammates as the Detroit Lions rule the NFL in the early and mid-1950s.

Texas 40, Missouri 27 / January 1, 1946 / Cotton Bowl / Cotton Bowl (Dallas, Texas)

Bible has his third SWC championship in four years, and the 10th-ranked Horns face Missouri in the Cotton Bowl. UT is favored by 14 points over Chauncey Simpson's Tigers, who run a Split-T offense. A few personnel adjustments are made in the weeks before the game, and they seem to work. It helps that Layne, playing as a fullback, is at his best. He has 28 points—scoring four touchdowns and kicking two extra points—and throws two TD passes. The Blond Bomber completes 11 of 12, and 8 of them are to Hub Bechtol, in the midst of his three all-America seasons. Mizzou gives the Horns a game though, gaining 408 yards on the ground and getting a 65-yard scoring pass from Bill Dellastatious to Roland Oakes. It is the last bowl game for Bible, who has announced plans to retire from coaching after the 1946 season.

Texas 20, Oklahoma 13 / October 12, 1946 / Cotton Bowl (Dallas, Texas)

It is a team bulging with talent, and some pigskin prognosticators are saying the Longhorns may be among the nation's best. Waltzing over Missouri, Colorado, and Oklahoma A&M by a combined score of 172–6 does nothing to invalidate such notions. Ranked No. 1, Bible's boys travel to Dallas to take on the Sooners in front of 50,000 patrons. It is the biggest crowd ever to see UT play football, and what they see is Layne engineering three long scoring drives. OU's happiest moment of the day comes when Joe Golding swoops in to intercept Layne's pass to Bechtol, returning it 95 yards Several of the Horns express admiration for a young halfback on the Oklahoma team—Darrell Royal.

Texas 24, Texas A&M 7 / November 28, 1946 / Memorial Stadium (Austin, Texas)

Having fallen from their lofty No. 1 perch with surprise losses to Rice and TCU, the Horns are out of the running for the conference title. Nor will there be a bowl game. So the players are determined to finish on a high note for Bible, who is honored again and again in pre-game ceremonies before 48,000 fans. Layne leads methodical touchdown drives of 51, 75, and 47 yards, and Texas A&M is held to a measly 27 yards of total offense. In the days after this game, there will be discussions in the media and among fans about the loss of two games, and some criticism of Bible's use of an archaic offensive system (and perhaps too heavy a reliance on Layne). The college game seems to be shifting to the deceptive and fast-striking T formation. But Bible pays no mind. His 33-year coaching career is at an end, and his record speaks for itself. In 10 seasons, he has written an admirable chapter in Texas football—winning three SWC titles, twice reaching No. 1 in the country, and restoring the entire athletic program to order and prosperity when it had been in disarray before his arrival in Austin.

Texas 34, North Carolina 0 / October 4, 1947 / Memorial Stadium (Austin, Texas)

In the third game of the '47 season, Blair Cherry's Longhorns have roared past Texas Tech and Oregon, and Bobby Layne is in his senior year (at QB now). Somehow, they are underdogs to a visiting North Carolina squad coming off a big win over Georgia. It is the most important intersectional game in college football that week, and 47,000 fans are at the stadium on a hot day to bear witness. Layne throws a 44-yard TD pass to Byron Gillory on the Horns' sixth play from scrimmage, and the "upset" is on. The Longhorns put the leather to the Tar Heels, some of whom limp off the field and do not return. Their all-America runner, Charlie "Choo-Choo" Justice, is held to 18 yards on six carries, leading some wags to comment that "Justice was done" and "Choo-Choo didn't run." The Longhorns need not have been too smug, however; the next year in Chapel Hill, they would absorb a 34–7 spanking.

Texas 34, Oklahoma 14 / October 11, 1947 / Cotton Bowl (Dallas, Texas)

The third-ranked Horns travel to Dallas to cross swords with OU. Cherry and new Sooners Coach Bud Wilkinson have flattered each other's teams shamelessly in the last few days. A crowd of 50,000 is inside the Cotton Bowl, and hundreds more linger at the gates, wishing for a miracle to get them in. Little do they know, the game will be so controversial that some people will later suggest the Texas–Oklahoma series be halted.

With the score tied at 7 in the waning seconds of the first half, the Horns are knocking on the Sooners' goal line. The clock hits zero, but referee Jack Sisco gives UT one last play because a timeout has been called. There is a fumble by Jimmy Canady, a lateral by Layne, a score by Randall Clay, and wild protestations from the men in red. Another Clay TD in the fourth quarter further enrages the OU partisans, who interrupt play with a hail of bottles. When the game is over, an angry crowd threatens Sisco, who is hustled into a police car and out of the Cotton Bowl. The next day, Wilkinson issues an apology from Norman. It is the eighth straight win over OU, but things will be changing "Sooner" rather than later.

Texas 27, Alabama 7 / January 1, 1948 / Sugar Bowl / Tulane Stadium (New Orleans, Louisiana)

Only a one-point mid-season loss to SMU mars the Longhorns' regular season record. So they are off to New Orleans to face Alabama, which has its own backfield whiz, Harry Gilmer. The venerable Grantland Rice has called Gilmer the best passer he has ever seen, although Layne's 1947 stats are better. In bright, chilly weather, 73,000 fans see something less than the offensive fireworks they expect. Layne has 10 completions (including a short TD pass to Peppy Blount) in 24 attempts, plus a fourth-down sneak from one foot out. Gilmer is far from great—leading the Crimson Tide to just seven first downs, throwing an interception, and fumbling once. The Longhorns finish No. 5, and the Bobby Layne era ends with this Sugar Bowl defeat of 'Bama.

SMU 21, Texas 6 / October 30, 1948 / Memorial Stadium (Austin, Texas)

Unlike the year before, neither the Horns nor the Ponies are undefeated coming into this game, but the level of collegiate enthusiasm is even higher. UT students hold three large rallies, a torchlight parade down the heavily decorated Drag, and an auto caravan through campus. Half an hour before kickoff, the newly expanded Memorial Stadium is packed with 66,000 fans, 18,000 more than it had ever held before. They see a game dominated, naturally, by the golden boy, Doak Walker. On the third snap, he blows down the east sideline for a 67-yard touchdown and SMU is ahead for good. Despite having far more first downs and rushing yards, Texas loses at home for the first time since 1945. Walker, who would win the Heisman Trophy that year, passes, runs, kicks, returns kicks, and plays defense marvelously, in a time when the game is not yet so specialized. Most sportswriters of the era concur: Doak Walker is the greatest football player yet to roam the wide-open spaces of Southwest gridirons.

Texas 41, Georgia 28 / January 1, 1949 / Orange Bowl (Orange Bowl in Miami, Florida)

It appears that the season is over, but the bowl invitation scramble has a lovely result for Cherry's unranked 6–3–1 Longhorns. When the announcement comes that Texas has been chosen to meet Southeastern Conference champ Georgia in the Orange Bowl, a howl arises. Wally Butts, coach of the Bulldogs, is accused of seeking a weak opponent, so the Horns have considerable motivation in the weeks leading up to the New Year's Day game in Miami. After the pre-game pageantry, the two teams engage in a lively back-and-forth tussle that is in doubt un-

Tom Landry

In 1943, assistant coach Bully Gilstrap was dispatched to Mission, down in the Rio Grande valley, to seek the services of a promising player. Tom Landry would play freshman ball before his education was interrupted by the war. He was soon in the U.S. Army Air Force, a bomber pilot at the helm of a B-17. Landry crisscrossed the skies of Europe, flying 30 missions and surviving a crash in Belgium. After the war, he returned to UT and was a two-way player for the Longhorns.

By his own admission, Landry was a half-step slow. But he became a heady defensive back for the New York Yankees of the All-America Football Conference in 1949 and soon moved across town to join the Giants. In a seven-year career, Landry snagged 32 interceptions in just 80 games. A player–coach his last two seasons, he became the head coach of the expansion Dallas Cowboys in 1960 and kept that job for 29 years. The Cowboys would win two Super Bowls (following the 1971 and 1977 seasons) during his tenure, and he finished with a record of 270-178-6. He was elected to the Pro Football Hall of Fame in 1990—not bad for a guy who figured he would play a couple of years in the NFL before going into the insurance business. A bronze statue of Landry stands outside soon-to-be-abandoned Texas Stadium in Irving, and a section of Interstate 30 between Dallas and Fort Worth is named in his honor.

til the end. All-SWC running back Ray Borneman suffers a knee injury and is replaced by Tom Landry, who gains 117 yards on 17 carries. There is jubilation in the locker room at the Orange Bowl, and the sportswriters who had labeled Texas a third-rate team are suitably apologetic.

Texas 27, Arkansas 14 / October 15, 1949 / War Memorial Stadium (Little Rock, Arkansas)

Fresh off a hard-fought six-point loss to OU, Cherry's team goes to Little Rock to engage the Razorbacks. Much to their consternation, the Horns fall behind by 14 when a quick-kick is blocked and a handoff is fumbled. But

Ken Jackson and the UT defense prevent any more scores and create some turnovers of their own. Quarterback Paul Campbell (14-for-23 and 237 yards, a school record) has a 45-yard TD pass to Ben Procter, and the Horns go on to win. Arkansas Coach John Barnhill will soon announce his retirement because of the onset of multiple sclerosis but remains as AD until 1971.

All-Decade Team

Quarterback	Bobby Layne (1944–1947)
Back	Jack Crain (1939–1941)
Back	Pete Layden (1939–1941)
Back	Jackie Field (1941–1942)
Lineman	Chal Daniel (1939–1941)
Lineman	Stan Mauldin (1940–1942)
Lineman	Joe Parker (1941–1943)
Lineman	George Petrovich (1944, 1947, 1948)
Lineman	Dick Harris (1945–1948)
End	Malcolm Kutner (1939–1941)
End	Hub Bechtol (1944–1946)
Kicker	Bobby Layne (1944–1947)
Punter	Frank Guess (1946–1948)

Q & A

Q. What did sportswriters call Noble Doss' twisting, 32-yard pass reception in the first minute of the Horns' win over A&M in 1940?

A. "The impossible catch."

Q. Who were "the immortal 13"?

A. These were the men Bible sent on the field that day—the starting 11 and just two subs.

Q. Who was known as the "all-American substitute?"

A. Spec Sanders, a junior college tailback and safety from Oklahoma. Due to the presence of Crain, he didn't get to play as much as he might have. But when he did, he excelled. For example, Sanders finished sixth in SWC rushing in 1941. After military service, he had a nice career with the New York Yankees of the AAFC.

Q. In the fifth year of Bible's five-year plan, the '41 Horns went 8–1–1, outscored their opponents 338–55, and reached No. 1 for the first time in school history. Name the players featured on the cover of the November 17 issue of Life magazine.

A. Wally Scott, Vernon Martin, Spec Sanders, Malcolm Kutner, Julian Garrett, Henry Harkins, Noble Doss, R. L. Harkins, Preston Flanagan, Chal Daniel, Buddy Jungmichel, Pete Layden, Bo Cohenour, and Jack Crain.

Q. After watching his team get beat like a rented mule (34–0), what did SMU Coach Matty Bell call the 1941 Horns?

A. The greatest team the Southwest Conference had yet seen.

Q. UT fans were in a state of bewilderment after their seemingly unbeatable team was tied by Baylor and lost to TCU in successive weeks in November 1941. What did Austin American-Statesman writer Weldon Hart have to say about matters?

A. "When the spry young blades of Texas U., current vintage, are old and gray and come back to the Forty Acres as honor guests, they will still be trying to explain the inexplicable Texas Longhorns of 1941."

Q. So how exactly did the mighty 1941 Horns get shut out of participating in any of the major bowls?

A. Bowl invitations were being given while UT had a final game with Oregon. The Texas A&M Aggies, SWC champs, would meet Alabama in the Cotton Bowl. Bible rejected an invite from the Orange Bowl, looking for a better deal—meaning the Rose or Sugar. Officials at the latter game grew tired of waiting and chose other teams, which meant the Horns had to get the bid to Pasadena—or nothing. The Rose Bowl committee disregarded the urging of Percy Locey, AD of Oregon State, the host team. Duke seemed a safer choice, so the Blue Devils (who ended up hosting the game in Durham, North Carolina) were in and Horns were left to take their frustrations out on Oregon on December 6.

Q. An all-American along with Chal Daniel in 1941, this man won seven letters at Texas—three each in football and basketball, and one in track. Identify him.

A. Malcolm Kutner. His pro football career was short but splendid: rookie of the year with the Chicago Cardinals in 1946, MVP of the National Football League in 1947, and twice all-pro.

Q. Noble Doss set the UT career record for interceptions, with 17. How long did that record stand?

A. Until 2003, when it was tied by Nathan Vasher. It should be pointed out that Doss played for just three years—Vasher played four—and in an era of little passing. His record was a remarkable one.

Q. This Dallas native was central to the success of the Longhorns' resurgence of the late 1930s and early 1940s. All-SWC in football and baseball, he played both sports in the pros. Who was he?

A. Pete Layden. Following the war, he spent three years with the New York Yankees of the AAFC and one as an outfielder with the St. Louis Browns.

Q. What co-captain of the 1942 team later earned a law degree from UT and founded one of the top firms in Austin?

A. Wally Scott. He would help organize the Longhorn Club (a now-defunct booster organization) and serve on the Athletics Council for several years.

Q. This native of Amarillo was an all-SWC tackle in 1942 and flew bombing missions with the 15th Army Air Force in World War II. Who was he?

A. Stan Mauldin, who played with the Chicago Cardinals when they won the 1947 NFL title. His two sons, Dan and Stan Jr., later played for Texas.

Q. What social engagement came in the middle of the '42 season?

A. The players and coaches were treated to a buffet dinner at the Governor's Mansion, courtesy of Governor Coke Stevenson.

Q. What blocking back on the 1942 team transferred to Kansas where he became a star and later the Jayhawks' coach?

A. Don Fambrough.

Q. Another player on that 1942 UT team went on to do big things at another school. Who was he?

A. Jack Mitchell, who helped with the war effort, transferred to Oklahoma, and became quite a T-formation quarterback for Bud Wilkinson. Mitchell, an all-American in 1948, also coached at Arkansas.

Q. Name the UT lettermen who died in the war.

A. Chal Daniel, Mike Sweeney, J. W. "Red" Goodwin, Ralph Greear, Shelby Buck, Glenn Morries, Jack Seale, and Bachman Greer.

Q. How futile was SMU's offense when the Ponies and Horns met in Dallas in 1943?

A. They gained but 19 yards on 26 offensive plays, for a 0.7-yard average. Perhaps the Mustangs should have followed the lead of the Baylor Bears, who sat out the 1943 and 1944 seasons due to the war.

Q. This halfback, a native of Austin, led the SWC in scoring in 1943 with 59 points. Who was he?

A. Ralph Park, a four-year letterman.

Q. What track man came out for football and did quite well for Bible's Horns?

A. Ralph Ellsworth, who led the SWC in rushing in 1943 with 507 yards.

Q. Who was the first player of Japanese descent to play for Texas?

A. Lineman Jim Shiro Kishi in 1943.

Q. He played center for the 1943 Longhorns, took part in the Battle of Iwo Jima, and came back to play two more seasons, although he was no longer a starter. Name him.

A. Kiefer Marshall.

Q. What was the big news at UT during the week before the 1944 SMU game?

A. The Board of Regents, meeting in Houston, fired President Homer Rainey for his liberal political views and failure to curb faculty members of the same inclination. The news was greeted with a mass student protest and a funeral march that purported to mourn the death of academic freedom at the University of Texas.

Q. This man played his freshman year at Texas Tech, came to Austin as a military trainee, and had a fabulous career: thrice an all-American (1944–1946). Name him.

A. Hubert "Hub" Bechtol. At UT, this lanky native of Amarillo set school records in receptions and career TD passes caught. He played three years with the Baltimore Colts, became a success in real estate and insurance, and served on the Austin City Council. Bechtol was said to be on a first-name basis with every Texas governor from Allan Shivers to Rick Perry.

Q. What number did Layne wear on his UT jersey?

A. He had three—41 as a freshman, 33 as a sophomore, 41 again as a junior, and 22 as a senior.

Q. One of Layne's teammates shares a rare honor with him—that of making all-SWC four years running. Who was he?

A. Offensive lineman/linebacker Dick Harris (1945–1948). A first-round pick by the Chicago Bears, he chose not to play pro football.

Q. He was a substitute halfback on the 1945 Longhorns team before transferring to Southwest Texas State, won three state championships as a high school coach, helped Darrell Royal develop the Wishbone offense in the late 1960s, and was the head coach at Texas A&M and Mississippi State. Who was he?

A. Emory Bellard.

Q. Identify Frank Medina.

A. Medina, a full-blooded Cherokee Indian, became the UT trainer in 1945 and held that position for 33 years. Unsentimental and demanding of his athletes, he posted a sign in the dressing room that read, "Hats off to the past, roll up your sleeves for the future." When Medina had them running the steps of Memorial Stadium, if he detected anything less than total effort he'd bellow, "What are you saving it for?"

Q. What substitute running back in the mid-1940s later coached Reagan High School in Austin to three state titles?

A. Travis Raven.

Q. Who, exactly, was Ralph "Peppy" Blount?

A. He was a rare individual—a 6' 5" native of Big Spring who earned a few medals in World War II, played basketball and football at UT, and won election to the Texas Legislature even as an undergraduate. A gregarious raconteur, Blount wrote two books: *We Band of Brothers* (about his wartime experiences) and *Mamas, Don't Let Your Babies Grow Up to Play Football* (about his days as a Longhorn under Bible and Cherry).

Q. What three Texas players from the 1940s gained more than 1,000 yards in their careers?

A. Jack Crain (1,436), Randall Clay (1,076), and Ray Borneman (1,005).

Q. Who was UT's punter from 1946 to 1948?

A. Frank Guess, whose 39.5-yard average in 1947 would stand as a school record for another decade.

Q. Has UT ever worn white at home?

A. Yes. For some reason, the Horns were outfitted in white jerseys for Austin games periodically between 1938 and 1950.

Q. Did Bobby Layne play basketball at UT?

A. He did, rather briefly. Layne was a member of Bully Gilstrap's 1945 team. Far more adept at football and baseball, he scored a couple of points and lent enthusiasm to the proceedings.

Q. How was Blair Cherry chosen to succeed Dana X. Bible?

A. Bible, as AD and the eminently respected person he was, had the only vote that counted. An assistant since Bible first got to UT, Blair Cherry had

107

been practically groomed for the job for 10 years. Cherry had no shortage of experience and was the school's first Texas-born coach. He was a native of Corsicana and played college football at TCU. Beginning in 1930, he was an extraordinarily successful high school coach in Amarillo. His teams there went 84–5 and won three state championships. If Bible had not taken the UT job back in 1937, Blair Cherry was reputedly the next choice.

Q. Was Cherry as polished as Bible had been?

A. Not exactly. He was gruff, intense, and moody, although some people say he mellowed a bit in Austin. A football man through and through, he never learned to handle inquisitive writers, meddlesome alums, or the PR aspects of the job. Another difference: Bible had favored lectures along with practice, whereas Cherry liked long, hard drills with plenty of hitting.

Q. The 1947 Texas–Oregon game in Portland (a 38–13 Longhorns victory) was important in what respect?

A. The Ducks' team was integrated; this appears to have been the first instance of UT taking the field against a team with black players.

Q. What else is unique about that game?

A. It was the first time the Longhorns football team had flown; a DC-4 had been chartered at a cost of $8,000.

Q. Who was Bobby Layne's roommate during his UT years?

A. Rooster Andrews, who was the team manager and occasional drop-kick specialist. The diminutive Andrews, once known as the "all-American water boy," played baseball, served on the officiating crew at the Texas Relays for more than 50 years, and ran a sporting goods store on North Lamar Boulevard (replete with Texas sports memorabilia) from 1971 to 2006.

Q. After just two seasons as coach of the Horns, Cherry got feelers from which two pro teams?

A. The Washington Redskins and Chicago Cardinals. He chose to stay in Austin.

Q. Who kicked an 18-yard field goal with eight seconds to go, enabling Rice to beat Texas in 1949?

A. Jim "Froggie" Williams.

Q. What Longhorn caught 43 passes in 1949 to lead the SWC in that category?

A. Ben Procter.

Q. UT beat Baylor, 20–0, at home in 1949. What makes the game memorable?

A. A minor stampede by Bevo IV.

CHAPTER 7
1950–1959

Oklahoma had beaten the Longhorns six straight
times until this day in Dallas in October 1968.
Darrell Royal gets a ride from two of his players
after overcoming the Sooners.
(Photo courtesy of the University of Texas.)

Two factors were gradually changing the economics of college football in the 1950s: the continued rise of the National Football League and live television broadcasts. Every school, big and small, feared that the popularity of the NFL—which, by all standards, had a better and more polished product—would result in a decline in attendance and media focus on the campus version of the sport. In the case of Southwest Conference schools, a shudder could be felt most of all by SMU and Rice, since Dallas would soon be home to the Cowboys of the NFL and the Texans of the fledgling AFL, and the Oilers were coming to Houston.

Pro football was actually played three times at Memorial Stadium in the late 1950s. An exhibition contest between the Chicago Cardinals and Green Bay Packers in August 1957 drew 19,000 spectators. The Cardinals and Baltimore Colts played in 1958, and the Cardinals and Pittsburgh Steelers (quarterbacked then by Bobby Layne) in 1959. These games came to a halt because the UT athletic department saw no wisdom in aiding and abetting the enemy.

Even athletic administrators at schools in smaller cities knew they would no longer have the stage to themselves, as they had for many decades. Television, too, was something they found threatening. Would their fans stay home on Saturday to watch a regional or national game rather than go to the stadium and buy a ticket? Yet money could be made by appearing on the small screen, and it certainly changed the dynamic of playing games and marketing them.

The 1950s, it must be said, were not the greatest of times for the SWC. Instances of challenging for the national title were very few. The two best teams that decade were probably Blair Cherry's 1950 Longhorns and Bear Bryant's 1956 Aggies, who went 9–0–1. A&M was on NCAA probation; some boosters, unknown to Bryant but surely with his thirst for victory in mind, had been overly persuasive in tempting schoolboys to think well of a future at Aggieland. They had some consolation because after 32 years of trying, the Ags won at Memorial Stadium. Yes, they finally colored it maroon.

No members of the conference had moved even an inch on integrating their teams although "off-Broadway" schools like North Texas State (with Abner Haynes) and Texas Western (Leford Fant) were doing it—and the sky never fell. The University of Oklahoma, too, benefited splendidly from the contributions of Prentice Gautt. UT athletic director Dana X. Bible had canceled a scheduled game with Indiana in 1953 because the Hoosiers insisted on bringing their black players to Austin. Bible may not have liked it, but Duke Washington came with his Washington State teammates the following year and made history. For decades, fine black athletes from Texas had been given two options—play at Prairie View A&M or such obscure schools or go out of state. Photographs from that time show a smattering of fans in the Jim Crow section at the far southeast corner of Memorial Stadium. The thoughts of the people attending those games were not sought out and recorded, but they surely knew that by not opening up, the University of Texas and its SWC brethren were missing out on a richer and more appealing game.

By the Numbers

0 Texas players made all-SWC from 1955 to 1957.

3 Years left on his contract when Blair Cherry quit in 1950.

3 Championship teams Ed Price played on while at UT: football in 1930, baseball in 1932, and basketball in 1933.

3 Longhorns won MVP honors in the College All-Star Game against the NFL champs—Bud McFadin in 1951, Gib Dawson in 1953, and Carlton Massey in 1954.

4 Longhorns in the 1952 all-SWC backfield: T. Jones, Richard Ochoa, Gib Dawson, and Billy Quinn.

4 Hours after Darrell Royal arrived in Austin in December 1956 for his interview by Dana X. Bible, the Athletics Council, and Board of Regents, he was given the job as head football coach.

14 Touchdowns scored by Byron Townsend in 1950, tying a school record set 36 years earlier by Len Barrell.

28 Points OU scored in the first 10 minutes, 50 seconds against Texas in 1952. The final score was 49–20.

228 Carries for Townsend in 1950, which led the nation.

$6,920 Collected by students during the 1956 UT–A&M game, which was sent to support Hungarians fleeing the Soviet invasion of their country.

Archive

Home games in **bold**

1950   Record: 9–2 (Southwest Conference champions)
Coach: Blair Cherry
Texas 28, Texas Tech 14

113

Texas 34, Purdue 26
Oklahoma 14, Texas 13 (in Dallas)
Texas 19, Arkansas 14
Texas 35, Rice 7
Texas 23, SMU 20
Texas 27, Baylor 20
Texas 21, TCU 7
Texas 17, Texas A&M 0
Texas 21, LSU 6
Tennessee 20, Texas 14 (Cotton Bowl in Dallas)

1951   Record: 7–3   Coach: Ed Price
Texas 7, Kentucky 6
Texas 14, Purdue 0
Texas 45, North Carolina 20
Texas 9, Oklahoma 7 (in Dallas)
Arkansas 16, Texas 14
Texas 14, Rice 6
Texas 20, SMU 13
Baylor 18, Texas 6
Texas 32, TCU 21
Texas A&M 22, Texas 21

1952   Record: 9–2 (Southwest Conference champions)
Coach: Ed Price
Texas 35, LSU 14
Texas 28, North Carolina 7
Notre Dame 14, Texas 3
Oklahoma 49, Texas 20 (in Dallas)
Texas 44, Arkansas 7
Texas 20, Rice 7
Texas 31, SMU 14
Texas 35, Baylor 33
Texas 14, TCU 7
Texas 32, Texas A&M 12
Texas 16, Tennessee 0 (Cotton Bowl in Dallas)

1953   Record: 7–3 (Southwest Conference co-champions)
Coach: Ed Price

LSU 20, Texas 7

Texas 41, Villanova 12

Texas 28, Houston 7

Oklahoma 19, Texas 14 (in Dallas)

Texas 16, Arkansas 7

Rice 18, Texas 13

Texas 16, SMU 7

Texas 21, Baylor 20

Texas 13, TCU 3

Texas 21, Texas A&M 12

1954   Record: 4–5–1   Coach: Ed Price

Texas 20, LSU 6

Notre Dame 21, Texas 0

Texas 40, Washington State 14

Oklahoma 14, Texas 7 (in Dallas)

Arkansas 20, Texas 7

Rice 13, Texas 7

Texas 13, SMU 13

Baylor 13, Texas 7

Texas 35, TCU 34

Texas 22, Texas A&M 13

1955   Record: 5–5   Coach: Ed Price

Texas Tech 20, Texas 14

Texas 35, Tulane 21

Southern California 19, Texas 7

Oklahoma 20, Texas 0 (in Dallas)

Arkansas 27, Texas 20 (in Little Rock)

Texas 32, Rice 14

Texas 19, SMU 18

Texas 21, Baylor 20

TCU 47, Texas 20

Texas 21, Texas A&M 6

1956 Record: 1–9 Coach: Ed Price
Southern California 44, Texas 20
Texas 7, Tulane 6
West Virginia 7, Texas 6
Oklahoma 45, Texas 0 (in Dallas)
Arkansas 32, Texas 14
Rice 28, Texas 7
SMU 20, Texas 19
Baylor 10, Texas 7
TCU 46, Texas 0
Texas A&M 34, Texas 21

1957 Record: 6–4–1 Coach: Darrell Royal
Texas 26, Georgia 7 (in Atlanta)
Texas 20, Tulane 6
South Carolina 27, Texas 21
Oklahoma 21, Texas 7 (in Dallas)
Texas 17, Arkansas 0
Texas 19, Rice 14
SMU 19, Texas 12
Texas 7, Baylor 7
Texas 14, TCU 2
Texas 9, Texas A&M 7
Mississippi 39, Texas 7 (Sugar Bowl in New Orleans)

1958 Record: 7–3 Coach: Darrell Royal
Texas 13, Georgia 8
Texas 21, Tulane 20
Texas 12, Texas Tech 7
Texas 15, Oklahoma 14 (in Dallas)
Texas 24, Arkansas 6
Rice 34, Texas 7
SMU 26, Texas 10
Texas 20, Baylor 15
TCU 22, Texas 8
Texas 27, Texas A&M 0

1959 Record: 9–2 (Southwest Conference tri-champions)
Coach: Darrell Royal

Texas 20, Nebraska 0
Texas 26, Maryland 0
Texas 33, California 0
Texas 19, Oklahoma 12 (in Dallas)
Texas 13, Arkansas 12 (in Little Rock)
Texas 28, Rice 6
Texas 21, SMU 0
Texas 13, Baylor 12
TCU 14, Texas 9
Texas 20, Texas A&M 17
Syracuse 23, Texas 14 (Cotton Bowl in Dallas)

20 Big Games

Oklahoma 14, Texas 13 / October 14, 1950 / Cotton Bowl
(Dallas, Texas)

The Cotton Bowl is brimming with 75,504 fans as UT and OU get together for 2½ hours of hand-to-hand combat. The Sooners, sporting a 23-game winning streak, have a dandy sophomore running back, Billy Vessels, who will win the Heisman Trophy two years hence. He scores the decisive TD in the waning minutes after a weird series of events that would take on added significance in the week to come as an Austin sports columnist does a recapitulation that reeks of sour grapes. Meanwhile, Oklahoma goes on to win the 1950 national championship. Texas beats its next seven opponents before falling to Tennessee in the Cotton Bowl.

Texas 23, SMU 20 / November 4, 1950 / Memorial Stadium
(Austin, Texas)

Before a full house in Austin, the No. 7 Longhorns host top-ranked SMU. Athletic director Dana X. Bible gives a pre-game speech in the locker room, and it seems to help. The Ponies' quarterback, Fred Benners, has a nice game but running back Kyle Rote can barely dent the Texas line and finishes with minus-3 yards rushing. When SMU's final drive is snuffed, there is widespread rejoicing among the Horns, who will move up to No. 5 in the polls.

117

But Cherry offers these words of wisdom: "Football neither began nor ended with Saturday's great victory over SMU."

Texas 7, Kentucky 6 / September 22, 1951 / Memorial Stadium (Austin, Texas)

UT's 1951 season opener is against Kentucky, coached by a young Paul "Bear" Bryant. His Wildcats are ranked sixth and have a top pass–catch tandem in Babe Parilli and Steve Meilinger. The visitors from the Bluegrass State get 21 first downs to 8 for Texas, but they score just once and miss the extra point. The Horns have a 13-yard scoring pass from T. Jones to Don Barton, with Gib Dawson making the crucial PAT. Texas' upset of Kentucky merits national headlines and makes the Bear wish he could go into hibernation as UK loses its next two games. For Price, this is an excellent start to his career as coach of the Longhorns.

Texas A&M 22, Texas 21 / November 29, 1951 / Kyle Field (College Station, Texas)

The Aggies are reeling. Their last five games have consisted of three losses and two ties, but with UT coming to town they are ready. And the chance to knock the hated Tea-Sippers out of contention for an Orange Bowl spot is mighty enticing. Ray George's team does it with a 22–21 upset keyed by an injury to Bobby Dillon. The Ags' Glenn Lippman rushes for 174 yards in a bruising battle that features several fights. Price summarizes his 7–3 maiden campaign this way: "We beat the strong ones and lost to some weak ones." The weaklings to which he referred are Arkansas, Baylor, and Texas A&M.

Notre Dame 14, Texas 3 / October 4, 1952 / Memorial Stadium (Austin, Texas)

After dispatching North Carolina in Chapel Hill and LSU in Baton Rouge, the No. 3 Longhorns are at home, facing Notre Dame. The game is dedicated to the memory of ex-coach Jack Chevigny, who had beaten his alma mater in 1934. But that is to no avail as the Irish dominate in the second half to win, 14–3, before a record Memorial Stadium crowd of 67,600. Notre Dame is paced by Ralph Guglielmi and John Lattner (winner of the '53 Heisman Trophy). The Horns play with fury but get no more than a field goal from Gib Dawson. The 400th win in Notre Dame history is achieved under a broiling sun that prompts Coach Frank Leahy—ever the glib psychologist—to move his team to the west sideline, sharing it with Texas.

Texas 16, Tennessee 0 / January 1, 1953 / Cotton Bowl / Cotton Bowl (Dallas, Texas)

The Longhorns have won the SWC with ease and are matched up in the Cotton Bowl against Tennessee—the defending national champion—which has the nation's top defense. Having lost to the Volunteers in this game two years earlier, motivation is not in short supply. Harley Sewell and Carlton Massey lead a defense that smothers its SEC foe, 16–0. Despite pulled muscles in both legs, Richard Ochoa gains 108 yards and scores once in the final game of General Bob Neyland's long career. Sewell and Tom Stolhandske, both all-Americans, celebrate their big New Year's Day win by heading to Honolulu where they are the first Longhorns to participate in the Hula Bowl. Little does anyone suspect that Texas, which finishes the 1952 season 9–2, will not go bowling for five more years.

Darrell Royal

The Hollis, Oklahoma, native had been quite a player (quarterback, defensive back, and punter) for OU in the late 1940s, so he was not exactly unknown. As a head coach, however, his resume was slim. He had spent a year with Edmonton of the Canadian Football League, two at Mississippi State, and one at Washington. The fact that he was leaving Seattle after just one season did not bespeak loyalty or willingness to adhere to a task. Furthermore, Royal's record in college football was a pedestrian 17–13. When the selection process began, his name was nowhere to be found. But Bobby Dodd of Georgia Tech, who initially appeared to have the inside track to the job, turned it down and gave the 32-year-old Royal a glowing recommendation. So did Duffy Daugherty of Michigan State, and so did Bear Bryant over at A&M. Nevertheless, Royal, who got a five-year deal with a salary of $17,500, later admitted that athletic director Dana X. Bible took a gamble in hiring him. Things turned out rather well as DKR quickly changed the losing culture that had gripped Texas football in the mid-1950s. By the time he gave up coaching two decades later, Royal would be widely seen as a towering figure in UT sports history.

Rice 18, Texas 13 / October 24, 1953 / Memorial Stadium (Austin, Texas)

Texas has lost 23 fumbles in its first five games but manages to hang onto the ball against Rice in front of a crowd of 48,000 in Austin. This game features a strange denouement as UT gives up two intentional safeties, then watches as Leroy Fenstemaker throws a 31-yard TD pass to Dan Hart with 55 seconds left on the analog clock in Memorial Stadium's south end, threading the needle between Delano Womack and Charley Brewer. The Owls and Horns will share the SWC crown, but Rice goes to the Cotton Bowl to face Alabama and Texas gets no bowl invite—at least not one it wants—and stays home.

119

Texas 21, Baylor 20 / November 7, 1953 / Memorial Stadium (Austin, Texas)

Collegiate spirit is riding high in the week before this game, although the Longhorns are just 4–3: Pep rallies almost every day, boozy "panty raids" at the co-ed dorms, and an offer by one high-ranking official to jump in the Littlefield Fountain if Baylor could be defeated. That seems unlikely since George Sauer's senior-laden team has not lost and is ranked No. 3. Some pundits say the Bears might go all the way to the 1953 national title. On a cold, misty day at the stadium, L. G. Dupre has three touchdowns for BU, but on one of those scores Carlton Massey blocks the PAT. That turns out to be the difference. The UT locker room is a scene of joy, packed with well-wishers, sports writers, and photographers. Price gets UPI national coach of the week honors, and the aforementioned official takes a well-publicized dip.

Notre Dame 21, Texas 0 / September 25, 1954 / Notre Dame Stadium (South Bend, Indiana)

Ranked No. 4, an overwhelming choice to win the SWC championship, and coming off a convincing defeat of LSU, the Longhorns fly to Indiana to meet No. 2 Notre Dame. It starts well but then things fall apart. QB Charley Brewer is benched in the third quarter in Texas' first shutout in 77 games. There are four pass interceptions, three lost fumbles, and a couple of drive-stopping 15-yard penalties, all of which leads *Houston Post* writer Jack Gallagher to offer this assessment in his column the next day: "Fumbling, bumbling, and utterly inept." At least it is a nice debut for Notre Dame's 26-year-old coach, Terry Brennan.

Texas 22, Texas A&M 13 / November 25, 1954 / Memorial Stadium (Austin, Texas)

It has been a disappointing and tumultuous season, one featuring a shutout loss, harsh comments in the press and from opponents, a temporary dismissal of nine players who have been spending too much time at campus-area watering holes, and rumors that the Longhorn Club would publicly seek Price's dismissal. But against visiting Texas A&M, all of that seems to be forgotten. Brewer throws TD passes of 20 yards to Joe Youngblood and 34 yards to Menan Schriewer as Bear Bryant's Aggies are subdued, 22–13. Nevertheless, there will be changes in offensive strategy and the coaching staff before next season starts.

TCU 47, Texas 20 / November 20, 1955 / Memorial Stadium (Austin, Texas)

Price's Longhorns have a three-game winning streak snapped by eventual SWC champion TCU. Because smooth running back Jim Swink enters the contest averaging 8.3 yards per carry, the defense is primed to stop him. But Swink puts on quite a show—gaining 235 yards with four touchdowns, kicking two extra points, intercepting a pass, and returning punts and kickoffs. The Horned Frogs' all-American is lionized by players, coaches, and media after the game. Virtually the only highlight of the day for Texas is when defensive back Curtis Reeves returns an interception 83 yards for a TD.

Southern California 19, Texas 7 / September 30, 1955 / Los Angeles Memorial Coliseum (Los Angeles, California)

Price, who has been moving personnel around, is convinced he has the right combination with Joe Clements at quarterback, and Walt Fondren, Delano Womack, and Joe Youngblood as his running backs. But in a Friday night game in the City of Angels, that does not last long. Clements suffers a concussion on the fourth play from scrimmage, which necessitates a series of shifts. A crowd of 62,000 sees the No. 9 Trojans assert their superiority with touchdown drives of 76 and 94 yards. The UT offense moves spasmodically against a USC team that will finish in the middle of the pack in the Pacific Coast Conference. Price praises his plucky team after the game, but the Horns will lose their next two—to Oklahoma and Arkansas.

Texas 7, Tulane 6 / September 29, 1956 / Tulane Stadium (New Orleans, Louisiana)

The Longhorns have just suffered a shattering home loss to Southern California. One of the few bright spots is the play of sophomore quarterback Vince Matthews, so Price starts him against the Green Wave in this game at venerable Tulane Stadium. When Matthews falters, in comes Joe Clements. He throws a 6-yard TD pass to Jack Hobbs, who had earlier blocked Tulane's extra point attempt. Walt Fondren's kick is good, and that is all the scoring for the day. Unfortunately, that is also the last game UT will win in the 1956 season as the Mountaineers, Sooners, Razorbacks, Owls, Mustangs, Bears, Horned Frogs, and Aggies take turns whipping the Longhorns.

Texas 26, Georgia 7 / September 21, 1957 / Grant Field (Atlanta, Georgia)

Darrell Royal has been in Austin for a few months now, striving to create a paradigm shift wherein the Longhorns (accused in recent seasons of being soft and easily deflated) will play hard-nosed football—and most important, win games. His first opportunity comes on the road against Georgia before a crowd of 33,000. DKR is pleased to see his team seize the initiative with a couple of first-half touchdowns. Fondren atones for a fumble by leading a late scoring drive to clinch this victory over Wally Butts' Bulldogs. Almost 230 yards on the ground tops anything the 1956 team had been able to do.

Texas 17, Arkansas 0 / October 19, 1957 / Razorback Stadium (Fayetteville, Arkansas)

It's been said that moral victories are for losers. Nonetheless, Texas' 21–7 loss to top-ranked OU seems to have a beneficial effect. Conference play begins in Fayetteville against the Hogs. Jack Mitchell's team has just moved into the top 10, but Texas gets all the breaks in a 17–0 win, the first shutout in more than four years. It includes a 27-yard TD strike from Max Alvis to George Blanch, an interception by Mike Dowdle, and a 29-yard field goal by sidewinder Fred Bednarski.

Texas 19, Rice 14 / October 26, 1957 / Memorial Stadium (Austin, Texas)

A crowd of 50,000 gathers in 40° weather to see the Longhorns and Owls. The star of the night is Rene Ramirez, also known as the "Galloping Gaucho." He has 76 yards rushing and one TD on eight carries, a 22-yard punt return, one pass completion, two catches, an interception, and a brilliant 80-yard kickoff return that wins the game. That has not happened since Hugh Wolfe did it against Minnesota 21 years earlier. In the locker room after the game, a jubilant Ramirez says, "This is my greatest thrill ever. I saw this big hole, and there I go. Oh, San Antone, I did it!" Jess Neely's Rice team will go on to represent the SWC against Navy in the Cotton Bowl.

Mississippi 39, Texas 7 / January 1, 1958 / Sugar Bowl / Tulane Stadium (New Orleans, Louisiana)

The senior-heavy, 11th-ranked Longhorns face Mississippi in the Sugar Bowl. Royal works his guys hard in the week before the game and will later regret it. With nearly 79,000 fans looking on, Rebels quarterback Raymond

Brown engineers one score after another. The cruelest cut is when he fakes a punt, circles left end, and goes 92 yards for a TD. Texas' offensive maneuvers are utterly ineffective at scaring Ole Miss as the final stats include four fumbles lost, four interceptions, and three crucial penalties. The New Orleans misadventure takes the edge off an otherwise remarkable season.

Texas 15, Oklahoma 14 / October 11, 1958 / Cotton Bowl (Dallas, Texas)

The Longhorns have lost six straight to OU, and second-year coach Darrell Royal doesn't like it. He sounds like a man determined to stop "that bloodletting up at Dallas," as he puts it. Bud Wilkinson's Sooners, national champs in 1955 and 1956, are still a formidable opponent. Bobby Lackey, Vince Matthews, and Rene Ramirez combine on 12-of-17 passing as UT scores a big comeback victory. Lackey's 7-yard jump-pass TD to Bobby Bryant with three minutes left sends Texas fans into ecstasy. Lackey also kicks the extra point and makes a one-handed interception on OU's next drive to seal the win. When the game concludes, Royal is lifted onto the shoulders of his players. That night, as the airplane carrying the team gets to Austin, it must circle for 15 minutes while police move back a crowd that has gathered to welcome the conquering heroes back home.

Texas 21, SMU 0 / October 31, 1959 / Cotton Bowl (Dallas, Texas)

Pre-season favorites to take the conference crown, the SMU Mustangs enter this game expecting to win. After all, they have beaten Texas three times in a row and have a fine quarterback in Don Meredith. The Longhorns' first play from scrimmage begins with Lackey fumbling the snap. But he then shovels the ball to Jack Collins, who throws to Monte Lee for a 51-yard bomb. The Ponies threaten to score just once, and that ends with Lee's sack of Meredith late in the first half. Meredith will call the Cotton Bowl home for the next seven years, with the expansion Dallas Cowboys.

Syracuse 23, Texas 14 / January 1, 1960 / Cotton Bowl / Cotton Bowl (Dallas, Texas)

Tri-champs of the SWC (along with TCU and Arkansas), the Horns are paired up with Syracuse, which has already been awarded the 1959 national title. Ben Schwartzwalder's muscular team, which outgained its opponents by a margin of 355 yards per game, is the subject of rapturous articles in the national press. And with players like Roger Davis, Bob Yates, Fred

Mautino, and Ernie Davis (1961 Heisman Trophy winner), the Orangemen are indeed tough. The game, played in humid 43° weather, is much closer than most anyone anticipates, although Syracuse gets the trophy. This Cotton Bowl will be best remembered for a mini-brawl late in the first half that supposedly has racial overtones. Some of the Orangemen also whine about being penalized for the repeated application of forearm shivers; Schwartzwalder claims that the umpire who threw the flag on those penalties "can't expect to go to heaven."

All-Decade Team, Offense

Quarterback	T. Jones (1950–1952)
Back	Byron Townsend (1949–1951)
Back	Gib Dawson (1950–1952)
Lineman	Bud McFadin (1948–1950)
Lineman	Harley Sewell (1950–1952)
Lineman	Phil Branch (1951–1953)
Lineman	Buck Lansford (1952–1954)
Lineman	Ken Jackson (1948–1950)
Lineman	Maurice Doke (1957–1959)
End	Tom Stolhandske (1950–1952)
End	Menan Schriewer (1953–1955)
Kicker	Gib Dawson (1950–1952)
Punter	Walt Fondren (1955–1957)

All-Decade Team, Defense

Lineman	Bud McFadin (1948–1950)
Lineman	Harley Sewell (1950–1952)
Lineman	Bill Georges (1950–1952)
Lineman	Carlton Massey (1952,1953)
Linebacker	Don Menasco (1949–1951)
Linebacker	June Davis (1949–1951)
Linebacker	Jack Barton (1950–1952)
Defensive back	Bobby Dillon (1949–1951)
Defensive back	Bobby Raley (1950–1952)
Defensive back	Joe Youngblood (1953–1955)
Defensive back	Bobby Lackey (1957–1959)

Q & A

Q. From 1948 to 1950, he erased many of Hub Bechtol's receiving records. Who was he?

A. Ben Procter. He was a Phi Beta Kappa at UT, earned a doctorate at Harvard, and went on to write several books on early Texas history.

Q. He was twice an all-SWC tackle, all-American in 1950, served in the Air Force during the Korean War, and then spent five years with the Los Angeles Rams. He retired prematurely due to a freak shooting accident. After three years of healing, he was ready to play some more, and the Denver Broncos had the good fortune to get him. Name this mountain of a man.

A. Lewis "Bud" McFadin, who was all-AFL his first three years in Denver. McFadin finished his career by playing two seasons with the Houston Oilers.

Q. What second-string offensive lineman on the 1949–1951 teams later made a fortune in the home construction industry?

A. Bill Milburn.

Q. He was Texas' quarterback in 1950 and played shortstop on two straight national champion baseball teams for Bibb Falk. Who was he?

A. Ben Tompkins.

Q. The Longhorns first played in Rice Stadium in 1950. The state-of-the-art facility with two curved upper decks was jam-packed with 70,000 fans. Did the Owls send them home happy?

A. No—except for the UT students and alumni who attended. Texas won, 35–7. Baylor, too, opened a new stadium in 1950. Two weeks later in Waco, the Horns were again unkind visitors, securing a seven-point victory.

Q. LSU was in Austin for the 1950 regular season finale. What was poignant about halftime ceremonies of that game?

A. They were dedicated to Cherry. Since his team was up by 21 points, he stayed out on the field and watched. As the Longhorn Band serenaded him with "The Eyes of Texas" and students in the west stands made a caricature of his face with cards, Cherry wept.

Fred Bednarski

Without a doubt the most intriguing player on the '57 team was Fred Bednarski. A native of Poland, he and his family had survived three years in a Nazi labor camp before finding their way to the United States, Texas, and Austin. At Fulmore Junior High School, at Travis High School, and then at UT, Bednarski displayed a skill that simply amazed anyone who saw it. Instead of the traditional straight-ahead kicking style, he would boot the ball with the instep of his right foot; almost invariably, it traveled high and far. There were references in the *Austin American-Statesman* about his "peculiar sideways kick." He used it with the Yearlings in 1955 and on some kickoffs in 1956 as a sophomore. Not until 1957 was Bednarski called upon to try long-distance field goals—unsuccessfully against Georgia and Oklahoma, but he made a 29-yarder against the wind in a 17–0 defeat of Arkansas. (Future UT Coach Fred Akers, one of the Hogs' defensive backs on the field for that play, suspected trickery but could only watch as the ball sailed between the goalposts.) The Associated Press and *Sports Illustrated* both took note. So let the record show that the first soccer-style kicker was not Pete Gogolak, his brother Charlie, nor Jan Stenerud. These other men, all foreign-born too, did their part to revolutionize kicking in American football, but it started with Zdzislaw "Fred" Bednarski of the University of Texas.

Q. What native of Douglas, Arizona, was a two-time all-SWC running back and finished his career at Texas with 1,724 yards and 14 touchdowns?

A. Gib Dawson.

Q. This defensive back was a co-captain, all-SWC, and all-American in 1951, and finished his UT career with 13 interceptions. Who was he?

A. Bobby Dillon, whose achievements are truly impressive given that he was blind in one eye. He went on to play eight years with the Green Bay Packers.

Q. Bob Neyland, Tennessee's long-time coach, insisted that his team be allowed to wear orange jerseys in the 1951 Cotton Bowl. Did he prevail?

A. He did, because Blair Cherry was a gracious host and agreed to have the Horns wear white. Two years later, in the same game Neyland made the same request. This time, however, the general got a different answer. His Vols wore white.

Q. During the 1950 season, Cherry announced he would be quitting as Texas' coach. In a magazine article published soon thereafter, what was his pithy explanation?

A. Too much pressure and an overemphasis on winning, and he failed to mention his ulcers and insomnia. But in the winter of his discontent, Cherry's Horns, led by Bud McFadin, Ben Procter, Don "Tiger" Menasco, Byron Townsend, and Bobby Dillon, finished 9–2, losing to Tennessee in the Cotton Bowl.

Q. Bear Bryant, then at Kentucky, was mentioned as a possibility to re-place Cherry in 1951. Who got the job?

A. Athletic history turns on moments like these. Bryant, chafing under the presence of basketball coach Adolph Rupp, was available—showing up at Texas A&M in 1954 and then going to Alabama for 25 years and six national championships. Instead, UT chose soft-spoken Ed Price, whose six-year reign began well before the wheels came off at the end.

Q. What was Price's background?

A. He had won eight letters in three sports at UT in the early 1930s, wrote for the *Daily Texan,* put in two years as a flight deck officer in the Pacific theater during the war, and been an assistant since 1936 (except for the war years) under Chevigny and Bible. During his summers, Price earned a master's degree in education.

Q. What quarterback for Texas (1950–1952) later served as AD at Texas Tech?

A. T. Jones.

Q. The Longhorns were adorned with what kind of sartorial splendor from 1951 to 1956?

A. Orange helmets with a white stripe down the middle.

Q. Name the reserve back who went on to become a Hollywood stunt man.

A. Dean Smith. He was better known for his track exploits, such as winning a gold medal with the 400-meter relay team in the 1952 Helsinki Olympics and being the leadoff man on UT's world-record-setting 440-yard relay team in 1955. Besides three decades in the movie business—he made 10 films with John Wayne—Smith was quite a cowboy, specializing in bareback bronco riding and calf roping.

Q. The 1952 season opener, a 35–14 defeat of LSU at Tiger Stadium in Baton Rouge, was played at night. What was Texas' previous game under the lights?

A. It was in 1937, against the Bayou Bengals in the same venue. A few weeks after that 1952 game, Notre Dame and UT played in Austin with the temperature around 90° at kickoff. University officials had discussed lighting Memorial Stadium before, and now the idea picked up steam.

Q. How was Harley Sewell brought to UT?

A. Sewell, who hailed from a hamlet on the banks of the Red River, was working as a telephone lineman when Buddy Jungmichel showed up. His recruiting spiel was given while Sewell remained atop a telephone pole. A 6' 1", 220-pound two-way player with an unusually high threshold for pain, Sewell would go on to spend 10 years with the Detroit Lions and 1 with Los Angeles Rams.

Q. How about Sewell's teammate, Carlton Massey?

A. This native of Rockwall was playing at Southwestern University, but the Pirates dropped football after his sophomore season. Thus, his transfer to Texas. He helped lead the Horns to the 1952 conference championship, was all-SWC and all-American, and had a five-year NFL career.

Q. He was a rugged and dependable guard for Texas from 1953 to 1955 who went on to play 10 seasons with the Winnipeg Blue Bombers of the CFL. Name him.

A. Herb Gray.

Q. When did UT first play the University of Houston?

A. It was the third game of the 1953 season. The Cougars lost, 28–7.

Q. What quarterback came off the bench and threw a 49-yard TD pass to Menan Schriewer to clinch the Longhorns' victory over TCU in 1953?

A. John "Bunny" Andrews, the younger brother of the inimitable Rooster.

Q. As is well known, interracial competition at Memorial Stadium began when Duke Washington of Washington State stepped on the field in 1954. How did he do in that game and how did he remember it?

A. Washington, whose team lost, 40–14, had a 73-yard touchdown run. He had no complaints about his UT counterparts, saying it had been a good, hard-hitting football game. The Longhorns had flattering words for him, as well. Perhaps it is indicative that when Washington crossed the goal line on that long run, most of the Texas student section stood and cheered loudly.

Q. The scene was Cowtown in 1954. TCU was up, 27–7, toward the end of the first half. What then transpired?

A. Price's boys girded up their loins and came back to win, 35–34. The final score was a 4-yard run by Delano Womack. Buck Lansford's extra point hit the right post and bounced through.

Q. Who helped coach the UT quarterbacks during spring training in 1955?

A. Bobby Layne, then the toast of the NFL.

Q. Price brought in an assistant from Auburn in 1955 who later became head coach of the San Diego Chargers. Identify him.

A. Charley Waller.

Q. What took place outside the hallowed walls of Memorial Stadium on May 17, 1955?

A. A huge brawl among baseball fans. For the first time in 14 years, Texas did not win the SWC baseball title. To make matters worse, the new champs were none other than the Texas A&M Aggies, and more than 3,000 of their supporters came over from College Station to cheer them and rag the Longhorns. Clark Field had a seating capacity of 2,400, but some 6,000 rambunctious young people got in. The trouble began early. There was jousting and fighting in the stands, which the UT authorities were unable to stop. When the game (won by the Ags, 7–4) ended, the fisticuffs spilled outside of the park and escalated into a wild free-for-all with several hundred combatants. The main event involved a pair of football stars, Buck Lansford of UT and Jack Pardee of A&M, whaling at each other. The Austin city police finally arrived in sufficient numbers to quell the proceedings. No arrests were made.

Q. In the summer of 1955, UT invested $200,000 to install four sets of lights on the east and west sides of Memorial Stadium. When were they first put to use?

A. In the season opener, a 20–14 loss to Texas Tech. Coincidentally or not, the Red Raiders' 30-year campaign to get into the Southwest Conference soon bore fruit.

Q. What else was new on the UT sports scene in 1955?

A. D. Harold Byrd and Moton Crockett refurbished and donated "Big Bertha"—a 500-pound, eight-foot-high drum—to the Longhorn Band, and head cheerleader Harley Clark unveiled the "Hook 'em, Horns" hand signal in a Gregory Gym pep rally the night before the TCU game. The men in the purple silks won, anyway.

Q. Identify the first female sportswriter to get inside the press box at Memorial Stadium.

A. Norma Mills of the *Daily Texan,* who stormed that male bastion in the 1955 season.

Q. Who was known as "a rich man's Jack Armstrong"?

A. Walter Fondren, heir to an oil fortune estimated at $10 million. Fondren led the team in rushing and scoring in 1955 and 1956, passing in 1957, and punting all three years.

Q. The 1956 Horns were considered a passing team, such as it was for that time. How did they do in the air?

A. The numbers say it all: QBs Joe Clements, Vince Matthews, and Walter Fondren combined to throw 9 touchdowns and 22 interceptions.

Q. The 1956 season (1–9) was certainly a nadir in Texas football history. How did the home opener against Southern Cal go?

A. Not well at all. Running back Cornelius "Chocolate Rocket" Roberts had TD runs of 73, 50, and 74 yards in a 44–20 USC victory.

Q. Roberts' performance made it evident that, like it or not, athletic integration was coming. Identify the UT student who paid a surprise visit to Ed Price's office the following week.

A. Marion Ford Jr. He had been a standout at Houston's Wheatley High School in the segregation days and was among a smattering of black undergrads on the Forty Acres in 1956. Brash and fearless, he told the coach, "Ed, you need me. I can help you." One may only speculate about the repercussions sure to follow had Price chosen to defy the traditions of the culture in which he was raised and put Ford in a Longhorns uniform. He lacked the vision and nerve to do it, however. The two shook hands as the meeting ended. Price would soon quit as football coach, whereas Ford got his chemical engineering degree from UT and then a DDS, was a Fulbright Scholar in Germany, established dental clinics in Africa as a Peace Corps volunteer, made enough money to have a collection of Bentleys and, if that were not enough, was a world-class dancer. When he died in February 2001, the Texas House of Representatives passed a resolution honoring the extraordinary life of Dr. Marion Ford.

Q. What rather hateful behavior may have caused Price to pen a letter of resignation late in the 1956 season?

A. He was being hanged in effigy on the Drag and around campus. After his retirement from coaching, Price worked in the university's physical education department and later became the assistant dean of students.

Q. What trusted lieutenant left Seattle for Austin along with Royal in 1957?

A. Mike Campbell, who would be the primary defensive coach at UT for 20 years. As we will see, Royal wanted Campbell to succeed him in 1976, but that did not happen.

Q. After he was hired as the Longhorns' range boss, what did Royal do?

A. He took a look at the facilities and was a bit dismayed. He was offended by grass growing high up the seven-foot fence surrounding the stadium. In fact, Royal did not like the fence at all and urged its removal. Nor did he like the peeling paint in the locker rooms or the ragged furniture in the coaches' office over at Gregory Gym. Although his primary task was to rebuild UT football, Royal soon had these and other cosmetic changes done to the stadium and its grounds.

Q. Who kicked a field goal to beat Texas A&M and its Heisman Trophy winner John David Crow, in 1957?

A. Bobby Lackey, who also led the team in interceptions that year.

Q. As a sophomore in 1957, Max Alvis was one of Royal's top halfbacks. But he never played football again. What happened?

A. Alvis signed a $50,000 contract to play baseball. A third baseman, he had a 10-year major league career, primarily with the Cleveland Indians.

Q. Royal was downright obsessive about field position early in his career. What ploy did he sometimes use to gain it?

A. The third-down quick kick, which has gone from rare to virtually unheard of.

Q. What was Royal's big innovation prior to the 1958 season?

A. The hiring of Lan Hewlett as the nation's first full-time academic counselor for a football team. Known widely as the "brain coach," Hewlett was a liaison between the athletic department and faculty, set up a compulsory study hall for freshmen, and kept close tabs on all eligibility matters. What Hewlett began almost 50 years ago has grown into a far-flung operation, involving scholarship athletes of both genders and all sports.

Q. Who was UT's new public address man beginning in the 1958 season?

A. Wally Pryor, who took over from Dr. Curtis Alderson. A swimming letterman at Texas in 1950, Pryor would handle microphone duties for both football and basketball for the next three decades.

Q. What was done at the stadium after the 1958 season?

A. The sod and grass first planted in 1924 were wearing out, so the field was dug up and replanted. This was done under the direction of agricultural experts from Texas A&M and gave the stadium a plush new playing field. The second-generation grass field only lasted 10 years, however, before giving way to artificial turf.

Q. Maurice Doke had started every game his first two seasons as an end, but he moved to guard in 1959. How did he do?

A. He again started all 11 games (including a Cotton Bowl loss to Syracuse) and made all-America.

Q. Name the TCU speed merchant who scampered 56 yards on a snowy day at Memorial Stadium to beat the Longhorns in 1959.

A. Harry Moreland.

Q. He led the 1959 Longhorns in rushing, receiving, and all-purpose yards. Who was he?

A. Jack Collins, an all-SWC pick that year. Unfortunately, his junior and senior seasons were not quite so impressive.

Q. Royal, who coined the phrase "three things can happen when you pass, and two of them are bad," was not enamored of the forward pass. How did his Horns do through the air in 1959 and 1960?

A. His top two pass-catchers were Collins (8) and James Saxton (9).

Q. The press loved Royal's colloquial sayings. What was his quip about Saxton?

A. He said that his halfback from east Texas "ran faster than small-town gossip."

There was drama aplenty in the Big Shootout, which took place on a gray day in the Ozarks in 1969. Jim Bertelsen crosses the Arkansas goal line as teammates Forrest Wiegand and Randy Peschel celebrate.
(Photo courtesy of the University of Texas.)

The Southwest Conference in the 1960s was dominated by two teams, Texas and Arkansas. The Longhorns and Razorbacks represented the SWC in the Cotton Bowl eight of those years, and only once—SMU in 1966—did another team crack the Associated Press' final top 10 poll. Between them, UT and Arkansas won three national championships during this decade. Darrell Royal and Frank Broyles saw their programs flourish as never before.

Royal, national coach of the year twice, was in great demand. He deflected feelers from teams in the National Football League until they finally stopped asking. After the Horns won the 1963 national title, his alma mater, the University of Oklahoma, came calling. DKR was tempted, but he declined. Two years later, the Sooners were still floundering and again in need of a coach. They begged him to return to Norman, offering a relatively big contract. In the end, Royal decided that Austin was home.

The University of Texas' football fortunes in the 1960s can be described as two high peaks surrounding something of a valley. As valleys go, this one was not very deep. It hardly compared with 1936 to 1938, when only five games were won, or Ed Price's final, excruciating season, when the Longhorns lost all but one. Nevertheless, the three-year drop-off, when the Horns lost a total of 12 games, is impossible to ignore. Royal himself came to agree that he had spent too much time with interviews, banquets, and coaching clinics. There were key injuries, and some recruits didn't pan out. Complacent or not, Texas threw fear into few opponents from 1965 to 1967. "Longhorn fans are finding out what I've known all along: I ain't no genius," he said after consecutive losses to Arkansas, Rice, and SMU in mid-1965. But he also reaffirmed confidence in himself and his methods. Time would prove Royal right, because the best was yet to come.

It was no coincidence that the UT Ex-Students' Association chose to build its new $410,000 home on San Jacinto Boulevard, directly across from Memorial Stadium. Such was the importance of the stadium and the football program to the university as a whole. So the alumni were aghast when W. W. Heath, chairman of the UT Board of Regents, announced in March 1965 that the land on which Memorial Stadium sat might be better utilized. Heath recited a litany of problems on UT's congested campus—especially the shortage of parking, classroom, office, and dormitory space. Shocking though the idea seemed, it had been discussed in the 1940s and 1950s, and the Athletics Council was behooved to consider alternatives. Two in particular, the Brackenridge Tract (500 acres belonging to UT, along the Colorado River) and the Balcones Research Center in north Austin, were the most likely possibilities if it came to that. But many people were determined that it never would. The Ex-Students rather passionately lobbied the administration, regents, and legislators (65% of whom were Texas grads). Royal, football coach and AD, was curiously neutral about the matter. One person who spoke up was L. Theo Bellmont, largely responsible for the stadium's construction 41 years earlier. Naturally, he was opposed to any plan to demolish it.

A tentative decision was reached in November 1965 that the stadium would remain. The UT athletic department went forward with a $200,000 facelift prior to the 1967 season. A study was commissioned to see about expanding and modernizing the stadium. In the end, the cost of moving off campus convinced the regents to give a reprieve to Memorial Stadium. Royal, J. Neils Thompson (chairman of the Athletics Council), and Frank Erwin (Heath's successor as chairman of the Board of Regents) led the way in implementing many changes at the stadium. They would not be completed until early in the 1971 season.

Even the most cursory description of that process must include a reference to the "battle of Waller Creek." In the late 1960s, the University of Texas, like virtually every other school across the country, was in upheaval. Protests against the Vietnam War, countercultural lifestyles, and rebellion were the order of the day. Austin may not have been on the level of Madison, Ann Arbor, or Berkeley, but it was easily the most freewheeling college town in the South. Expansion of the stadium entailed moving San Jacinto Boulevard 56 feet to the west, toward Waller Creek. That, in turn, entailed the loss of 15 cypress and oak trees, all of which long predated the university. Students and a few professors who bore signs and proclaimed a calling higher than mere football protested, to the extent of climbing into the upper reaches of the trees. It came to a head when Erwin drove up in his orange Cadillac and gave orders that the bulldozers and chainsaws be cranked up and put to use. It was a nasty scene, with the chairman of the Board of Regents applauding, cheering, and trading insults with anyone he considered to be in opposition. Almost 30 people were arrested; others were so incensed that they dragged tree limbs to the steps of the Tower as the cameras rolled.

By the Numbers

0 College running backs who had gained 1,000 yards in their first three varsity seasons until Texas' Chris Gilbert (1966–1968) did it.

3 Games lost between 1961 and 1964.

4 Members of the UT team that beat Alabama in the 1965 Orange Bowl who would be teammates of Joe Namath when the New York Jets won the Super Bowl five years later: Jim Hudson, Pete Lammons, George Sauer, and John Elliott.

5 Straight years (1961–1965) the Horns reached No. 1 in the nation.

5 Points scored in the 1960 Texas–TCU game in Fort Worth, 3 by the Longhorns.

7.9 Yards per carry for James Saxton in 1961.

8 Players who quit in 1968 spring training, which prompted speculation about dissension and other problems in the UT football program.

12 Years between UT's visits to Lubbock to play Texas Tech (1950–1962).

20 Years between Texas' first No. 1 ranking (November 8, 1941) and its second (November 11, 1961).

25 Tackles by linebacker Tommy Nobis against Rice in 1964.

40 Point-per-game average in the last seven games of the 1968 season.

67 Prospects signed to scholarships in the 1964 recruiting season.

245 Yards gained by Gilbert against Baylor in 1967, then a school record.

$4,000 Raise given to Coach Darrell Royal after winning the 1963 national championship, bumping his salary to $24,000.

28,000 People in attendance at a Memorial Stadium pep rally the Wednesday night before the 1969 Texas–Arkansas game in Fayetteville.

Archive

Home games in **bold**

1960 Record: 7–3–1 Coach: Darrell Royal

Nebraska 14, Texas 13

Texas 34, Maryland 0

Texas 17, Texas Tech 0

Texas 24, Oklahoma 0 (in Dallas)

Arkansas 24, Texas 23

Rice 7, Texas 0

Texas 17, SMU 7

Texas 12, Baylor 7

Texas 3, TCU 2

Texas 21, Texas A&M 14

Texas 3, Alabama 3 (Bluebonnet Bowl in Houston)

1961 Record: 10–1 (Southwest Conference co-champions) Coach: Darrell Royal

Texas 28, California 3
Texas 42, Texas Tech 14
Texas 41, Washington State 8
Texas 28, Oklahoma 7 (in Dallas)
Texas 33, Arkansas 7
Texas 34, Rice 7
Texas 27, SMU 0
Texas 33, Baylor 7
TCU 6, Texas 0
Texas 25, Texas A&M 0
Texas 12, Mississippi 7 (Cotton Bowl in Dallas)

1962 Record: 9–1–1 (Southwest Conference champions) Coach: Darrell Royal

Texas 25, Oregon 13
Texas 34, Texas Tech 0
Texas 35, Tulane 8
Texas 9, Oklahoma 6 (in Dallas)
Texas 7, Arkansas 3
Texas 14, Rice 14
Texas 6, SMU 0
Texas 27, Baylor 12
Texas 14, TCU 0
Texas 13, Texas A&M 3
LSU 13, Texas 0 (Cotton Bowl in Dallas)

1963 Record: 11–0 (Southwest Conference champions, national champions) Coach: Darrell Royal

Texas 21, Tulane 0
Texas 49, Texas Tech 7
Texas 34, Oklahoma State 7
Texas 28, Oklahoma 7 (in Dallas)
Texas 17, Arkansas 13 (in Little Rock)
Texas 10, Rice 6
Texas 17, SMU 12

Texas 7, Baylor 0
Texas 17, TCU 0
Texas 15, Texas A&M 13
Texas 28, Navy 6 (Cotton Bowl in Dallas)

1964   Record: 10–1   Coach: Darrell Royal
Texas 31, Tulane 0
Texas 23, Texas Tech 0
Texas 17, Army 6
Texas 28, Oklahoma 7 (in Dallas)
Arkansas 14, Texas 13
Texas 6, Rice 3
Texas 7, SMU 0
Texas 20, Baylor 14
Texas 28, TCU 13
Texas 26, Texas A&M 7
Texas 21, Alabama 17 (Orange Bowl in Miami)

1965   Record: 6–4   Coach: Darrell Royal
Texas 31, Tulane 0
Texas 33, Texas Tech 7
Texas 27, Indiana 12
Texas 19, Oklahoma 0 (in Dallas)
Arkansas 27, Texas 24
Rice 20, Texas 17
SMU 31, Texas 14
Texas 35, Baylor 14
TCU 25, Texas 10
Texas 21, Texas A&M 17

1966   Record: 7–4   Coach: Darrell Royal
Southern California 10, Texas 6
Texas 31, Texas Tech 21
Texas 35, Indiana 0
Oklahoma 18, Texas 9 (in Dallas)
Arkansas 12, Texas 7
Texas 14, Rice 6

SMU 13, Texas 12
Texas 26, Baylor 14
Texas 13, TCU 3
Texas 22, Texas A&M 14
Texas 19, Mississippi 0 (Bluebonnet Bowl in Houston)

1967   Record: 6–4   Coach: Darrell Royal
Southern California 17, Texas 13
Texas Tech 19, Texas 13
Texas 19, Oklahoma State 0
Texas 9, Oklahoma 7 (in Dallas)
Texas 21, Arkansas 12
Texas 28, Rice 6
Texas 35, SMU 28
Texas 24, Baylor 0
TCU 24, Texas 17
Texas A&M 10, Texas 7

1968   Record: 9–1–1 (Southwest Conference co-champions)   Coach: Darrell Royal
Texas 20, Houston 20
Texas Tech 31, Texas 22
Texas 31, Oklahoma State 3
Texas 26, Oklahoma 20 (in Dallas)
Texas 39, Arkansas 29
Texas 38, Rice 14
Texas 38, SMU 7
Texas 47, Baylor 26
Texas 47, TCU 21
Texas 35, Texas A&M 14
Texas 36, Tennessee 13 (Cotton Bowl in Dallas)

1969   Record: 11–0 (Southwest Conference champions, national champions)   Coach: Darrell Royal
Texas 17, California 0
Texas 49, Texas Tech 7
Texas 56, Navy 17

Tommy Nobis

The primary newcomer on the 1963 Texas team was a 230-pound package of football ferocity named Tommy Nobis. Twice a consensus all-American, he played linebacker and in the offensive line, and was equally effective in both spots. Royal called Nobis the best two-way player he had ever seen. Winner of the Maxwell Award and the Outland Trophy, he would be the top overall pick in the 1966 NFL draft, by the Atlanta Falcons. He played there for 11 years (strictly as a linebacker), was rookie of the year, and made the Pro Bowl five times. Unfortunately, the Falcons were an expansion franchise, which meant a lot of losing, regardless of Nobis' fine play. This man, who once said, "Football is like a jealous woman—it needs constant attention," was among the best linebackers ever, both in college and in the pros. His jersey number (60) was retired by the Falcons, but not by UT. Still, the few who have been given it know about the legacy of Tommy Nobis. When Derrick Johnson had No. 60 from 2001 to 2004, he often spoke about the honor of wearing the jersey made famous by the big redhead.

Texas 27, Oklahoma 17 (in Dallas)
Texas 31, Rice 0
Texas 45, SMU 14
Texas 56, Baylor 14
Texas 69, TCU 7
Texas 49, Texas A&M 12
Texas 15, Arkansas 14
Texas 21, Notre Dame 17 (Cotton Bowl in Dallas)

20 Big Games

Arkansas 24, Texas 23 / October 15, 1960 / Memorial Stadium (Austin, Texas)

After a one-point loss to Nebraska in the season opener, the Longhorns put together three shutouts. No. 11 in the nation, they host Arkansas before a surprisingly small gathering of 35,000. Texas goes up by two touchdowns in the first half, and it looks like a decisive victory is in the making. But the Razorbacks regain the momentum due to the passing of quarterback George McKinney and the running of halfback Lance Alworth. With 30 seconds left, Mickey Cissell checks in and boots a 20-yard field goal. This narrow loss to Frank Broyles' team turns the SWC race around; the Hogs advance to the Cotton Bowl and not the Horns.

Texas 3, Alabama 3 / December 17, 1960 / Bluebonnet Bowl (Rice Stadium in Houston, Texas)

The second annual Bluebonnet Bowl features an attractive coaching match-up of Darrell Royal and Bear Bryant, still a drawing card in the Lone Star State because of his years at A&M. The Crimson Tide, with just one starter weighing more than 200 pounds, is favored by one point and the final score is even closer than that. Tommy Brooker of 'Bama kicks a field goal, as does Dan Petty of UT. The game ends with Petty trying one from 36 yards out, but it is wide and short. Jimmy Saxton (86 yards running and receiving) is named the offensive MVP, and Alabama's Lee Roy Jordan gets the honor on defense.

Texas 28, California 3 / September 23, 1961 / Memorial Stadium (Berkeley, California)

Royal has re-tooled his offense during the summer to better utilize the talents of the 5' 11", 160-pound Saxton. He shows why in the season opener against Cal out in Berkeley. On the third snap, Saxton breaks a 49-yard run that sets the tone for the No. 4 Longhorns. They compile 419 yards of total offense and keep the Golden Bears from making a single first down in the second half. It's early, but Royal knows his 1961 team can go far.

TCU 6, Texas 0 / November 18, 1961 / Memorial Stadium (Austin, Texas)

The Longhorns are motoring at high speed. They have won all eight games, none by fewer than 21 points. Ranked No. 3, they jump to the top when Michigan State and Mississippi lose on the same Saturday. UT's first national championship seems not just possible but likely. There is simply no way Texas will fall to the TCU Horned Frogs, who are coming off two decisive defeats and are 24-point underdogs for a game to be played in Austin. No wonder Coach Abe Martin uses the analogy of climbing into the ring with the heavyweight champion. On the Horns' first drive, Saxton runs for 16 yards on a sweep and grabs a pass from Mike Cotten, taking it 45 yards before a violent collision with two Frogs knocks him unconscious. TCU's gangly quarterback, Sonny Gibbs, connects with Buddy Iles on a 50-yard TD pass. Saxton returns, gets kayoed again, and returns yet again—but to no avail. It is a stunning, staggering loss, and the Texas locker room is as quiet as a funeral parlor. To their credit, the Longhorns shut out Texas A&M five days later, beat a hefty Mississippi team in the Cotton Bowl, and finish No. 3 in the nation.

Texas 7, Arkansas 3 / October 20, 1962 / Memorial Stadium (Austin, Texas)

"The strong get stronger, and the weak get weaker." These are the words Johnny Treadwell and his UT teammates had used to motivate each other during head-knocking practice sessions before the 1962 season. They will be put to the test when the No. 1 Longhorns and the No. 7 Razorbacks meet at Memorial Stadium in front of 64,350 patrons. Broyles' players want little more than to avenge last year's 33–7 whacking in Fayetteville. Tom McKnelly's 41-yard field goal gives Arkansas a 3–0 halftime lead. With eight minutes left, there is a goal-line stand that the old-timers love to recall. Treadwell and his fellow linebacker Pat Culpepper hit big Danny Brabham and make him cough it up. As the Horns start to move downfield, the fans are pogoing on the stadium's old wooden bleachers, the Texas Cowboys are firing their wheeled cannon "Smokey" on almost every play, and the weary Hogs are giving ground on a hot, sweaty night. Just 36 seconds remain on the clock when Johnny Genung pitches to Tommy "T-Bird" Ford, who gets the ball into the end zone. In the 70th season of Texas football, this is a dramatic and unforgettable victory.

LSU 13, Texas 0 / January 1, 1963 / Cotton Bowl (Cotton Bowl in Dallas, Texas)

Only a mid-season tie with Rice stands between the Horns and an undefeated regular season record. In the Cotton Bowl, they will meet LSU. Oddly enough, Charley McClendon's team has also been tied by the Owls. The Longhorns, criticized by some fans and sportswriters as an offensive dud, are determined to prove otherwise on this 55° day in Dallas. Jimmy Field scoots around UT's right flank for a 22-yard TD, Lynn Amedee kicks a pair of field goals, and the Tigers pitch a shutout. Johnny Treadwell and Scott Appleton have excellent games on defense for the No. 4 Horns.

Texas 7, Baylor 0 / November 9, 1963 / Memorial Stadium (Austin, Texas)

Texas has come close to the brass ring in the past three years, and this time it will happen. The Horns start the season ranked fifth and move up one spot per week, per victory. After beating OU in Dallas, they stand at the top—as they had in 1961 and 1962, and both of those stints had lasted just two weeks. Pass-happy Baylor intends to be the spoiler, what with Don Trull throwing and all-American Lawrence Elkins catching. Trailing by 7, the Bears take over at their own 13-yard line with 2 minutes left. Three completions, two runs, and a 27-yard pass-interference penalty put them at the UT 19 with 29 seconds to play. Aiming to tie the game (or win with a two-point conversion), Trull zings it toward the sure hands of Elkins, but safety Duke Carlisle drifts across, leaps, and intercepts the ball. Pandemonium reigns in the stands.

Texas 28, Navy 6 / January 1, 1964 / Cotton Bowl (Cotton Bowl in Dallas, Texas)

Royal's Longhorns have been No. 1 since the fifth week of the season and have won every game—albeit some of those are near-defeats. The Associated Press and United Press International have already awarded the 1963 national championship to Texas before the Cotton Bowl against No. 2 Navy and its superlative quarterback, Roger Staubach, winner of the Heisman Trophy. Before three minutes have elapsed, Duke Carlisle lobs a 58-yard touchdown pass to Phil Harris, and the same pair combines on a 63-yarder in the second quarter, sweeping away all doubt about the outcome. Staubach is 21-of-31 through the air, but the star of the day is Carlisle, who sets a Cotton Bowl total offense record of 267 yards. Royal is coach of the year for the second time, and the Texas Longhorns have finally climbed the mountain of college football.

Arkansas 14, Texas 13 / October 17, 1964 / Memorial Stadium (Austin, Texas)

The Horns, defending national champs, have beaten four teams smartly and are ranked first. But they have a serious challenger from within the Southwest Conference: Frank Broyles' Razorbacks pay a visit on this Saturday night. In the first quarter, Ken Hatfield has an 81-yard touchdown on a punt return to dampen the spirits of UT fans. Just 87 seconds are left in the game when Ernie Koy Jr. culminates a 70-yard drive with a short scoring run that leaves Texas down by one. Royal consults with his coaches and decides to roll the dice, but Marvin Kristynik's pass to Hix Green falls short, effectively ending the game. Delirious Arkansas fans come down from the stands and grab handfuls of grass to take back to the Ozarks. Royal makes his way to the Arkansas locker room and offers congratulations and encouragement to go all the way. Indeed, the Hogs would win the rest of their regular season games, beat Nebraska in the Cotton Bowl, and win one version of the 1964 national championship.

Texas 21, Alabama 17 / January 1, 1965 / Orange Bowl (Orange Bowl in Miami, Florida)

After dispatching the Aggies for the eighth straight time, Texas has a 9–1 record and a date with Alabama in southern Florida. The AP and UPI polls have already given the '64 national crown to the Crimson Tide, whose star quarterback, Joe Namath, is doubtful with a bad knee. Namath does not start, but he plays. Ernie Koy has a 79-yard TD run, and Jim Hudson hits George Sauer on a 69-yard scoring strike. But this game will always be remembered for the goal-line stand in which Tommy Nobis and his pals keep Namath from scoring with 6:30 left.

Arkansas 27, Texas 24 / October 16, 1965 / Razorback Stadium (Fayetteville, Arkansas)

Tommy Nobis, Ken Ehrig, Phil Harris, and others are dealing with injuries, but they won't miss this game. The state of Arkansas is in a football frenzy, what with the defending national champions taking on Texas. Tommy Trantham returns a fumbled punt 77 yards for a score, and Jon Brittenum connects repeatedly with Bobby Crockett as the Hogs take a 20-point lead. The small UT delegation among the 42,000 at Razorback Stadium finds hope as Marvin Kristynik leads a comeback that puts the Horns up by four. But Brittenum has more magic, taking his team 80 yards for the winning score. Frank Broyles calls it "the greatest game in the history of football," but he can be forgiven the overstatement. Few suspect that, with this loss to the Razorbacks, Texas football is entering a three-year decline.

Texas 21, Texas A&M 17 / November 25, 1965 / Kyle Field (College Station, Texas)

The Aggies' Gene Stallings concocts the "Texas Special," in which QB Harry Ledbetter intentionally underthrows an almost-forward pass to end Dude McLean. He picks up the ball on one bounce and, continuing the charade, kicks the ground in disgust. The A&M linemen do their part by turning back to the huddle. Only then does McLean streak by the relaxed UT defenders, all the way to a 91-yard touchdown that has no equal in SWC history. His team down by 17 at the half, Royal dispenses with the X's and O's, gives a very short speech, and then proceeds to write "21–17" on the blackboard. The torch is lit and, of course, Texas scores the final 21 points. Amid a joyous locker room, DKR is regarded as a modern-day Nostradamus.

Southern California 10, Texas 6 / September 17, 1966 / Memorial Stadium (Austin, Texas)

Not even given an obligatory pre-season top-10 ranking, the Longhorns host a husky Southern Cal team in the opener. It is also the debut of a pair of sophomores who will largely define UT football over the next three seasons: quarterback Bill Bradley and running back Chris Gilbert. Most of the USC defensive effort focuses on Bradley, which helps Gilbert get 103 yards on the night. At midfield after the game, Royal shakes hands with his counterpart, John McKay and concedes the Trojans were better. They are building toward a national title in 1967.

SMU 13, Texas 12 / October 29, 1966 / Memorial Stadium (Austin, Texas)

On the third play from scrimmage, Gilbert takes a pitchout from Bradley and goes 74 yards for a score against the visiting Mustangs. They come back, however, on a 10-yard TD pass from Mike Livingston to Jerry LeVias. Although the Horns regain the lead, a fumble allows Dennis Partee to kick a 32-yard field goal with 18 seconds left. SMU wins and moves on to its first conference title since Doak Walker roamed the gridiron. Along with John Westbrook of Baylor, LeVias integrates SWC football. This speedy and elusive receiver is the league's 1966 player of the year, but he does it under harrowing conditions as many opposing players target him for rough treatment. Some of the worst wear orange, a fact that causes Gilbert and Bradley—with whom LeVias had played in a high school all-star game—to issue a quiet apology.

Texas 9, Oklahoma 7 / October 14, 1967 / Cotton Bowl (Dallas, Texas)

"'67, Year of the Horns." So read the bumper stickers that started popping up on cars around Austin after UT's shutout of Mississippi in the 1966 Bluebonnet Bowl. But Bill Bradley has major knee surgery and the Horns lose their first two games, so all that talk is forgotten. They look dead and listless against OU, trailing by 7 at the half. Royal tells his players to get in on the fight, and they do. Rob Layne kicks a 35-yard field goal into the wind, and an 84-yard drive culminates with Bradley going around left end to score. On the Sooners' final thrust, Corby Robertson replaces the injured Joel Brame at linebacker and makes a key tackle on Steve Owens. This loss will prove to be the only one for Chuck Fairbanks' team in 1967.

Texas 20, Houston 20 / September 21, 1968 / Memorial Stadium (Austin, Texas)

What a difference 15 years makes. The University of Houston, Dana X. Bible's choice to replace an integrated Indiana team in 1953, is back in Austin. The Cougars have a number of black players, most notably running back Paul Gipson. The media fancies it a duel between Gipson and Gilbert, who is poised to break the SWC career rushing mark. Both are outstanding: 159 yards and two TDs for Gipson, 173 and three for Gilbert. The Longhorns can't make a single first down in the second half and are on the ropes. The game ends with Texas sitting on the ball, content with a tie. For that perceived lack of gumption, Royal hears boos from the fans of both schools. This game is one of the most important in UH history, bolstering its claim for inclusion in the Southwest Conference. The invitation comes to Bill Yeoman's program soon thereafter.

Texas 36, Tennessee 13 / January 1, 1969 / Cotton Bowl (Cotton Bowl in Dallas, Texas)

The Wishbone offense has wiped out a number of team records for the SWC co-champs. They are back in the Cotton Bowl for the first time in six years, ranked fifth, and facing Tennessee. In 33° weather, the Longhorns assert themselves with vim and vigor. Steve Worster goes 14 yards on a triple-option play. Better yet, Cotton Speyrer gets behind the Vols' all-America defensive back, Jimmy Weatherford, and collects James Street's pass for a 78-yard TD. The same pair victimizes Weatherford again in the third quarter, this time for 79 yards. Tennessee tight end Ken DeLong is frustrated and unusually belligerent in his dealings with the refs all day long.

Texas 27, Oklahoma 17 / October 11, 1969 / Cotton Bowl (Dallas, Texas)

Royal's No. 2 Longhorns have not even broken a sweat in beating California, Texas Tech, and Navy. No. 8 Oklahoma, however, is another matter. On a hot day in Dallas, the Sooners go up by 14 points. Then Speyrer has a nice over-the-head catch of Street's pass for a 24-yard TD, and Jim Bertelsen goes 55 yards to set up another score just before the break. It's a hard-nosed battle in the second half, finally won by UT. Steve Owens, OU's thundering fullback, has 123 yards and is on his way to winning the Heisman Trophy.

Texas 15, Arkansas 14 / December 6, 1969 / Razorback Stadium (Fayetteville, Arkansas)

J. T. King of Texas Tech, Hayden Fry of SMU, Fred Taylor of TCU, and Gene Stallings of Texas A&M are some of the coaches who sing the highest praises of the 1969 Longhorns. Top-ranked and dead serious about winning the national title, they travel to the hills to encounter Arkansas, a team that is just as undefeated and ranked No. 2. It's the game of the century, at least to people in the Southwest, the "Big Shootout," as DKR calls it. On a raw and misty day, President Richard Nixon helicopters in, with anti-war protesters chanting from outside the stadium. The Hogs' quarterback, Bill Montgomery, puts them ahead by 14 at the end of the third quarter. Street has a diagonal 42-yard touchdown run (with a two-point conversion), Danny Lester makes a key interception in the end zone, and then comes the most dramatic moment in a game full of drama. Fourth down and three to go at the UT 43-yard line. Royal makes the biggest gamble of his career with 53 Veer Pass, which works to perfection as Street completes a 44-yard strike to Randy Peschel. Within a minute, Jim Bertelsen runs it over, Happy Feller kicks the extra point, and the red-clad fans at Razorback Stadium look on in stony disbelief. Back in Austin, students flood the Drag for 13 blocks, honking horns and making merry. The Tower, lighted orange with a white No. 1, has never looked lovelier.

Texas 21, Notre Dame 17 / January 1, 1970 / Cotton Bowl (Cotton Bowl in Dallas, Texas)

The Irish have not been in a bowl game since 1925, but they are lured back by the opportunity to play Texas—not to mention a $345,000 check. The Horns are not small, but they are outweighed at least 20 pounds a man by the strapping Notre Dame team. QB Joe Theismann puts the Irish up by 10, Texas regains the lead, but briefly as Theismann makes something out of a broken play with a TD pass to Jim Yoder. With just under seven minutes left, Street begins operations 76 yards from pay dirt. A 17-play drive (which includes a couple of fourth-and-twos) is executed flawlessly as Billy Dale follows a block by Bobby Wuensch to score. Notre Dame's final possession ends when Tom Campbell intercepts Theismann's 27th pass of the afternoon. He takes the ball straight to Royal, who in turn presents it to Fred Steinmark, standing on crutches near the Texas bench.

All-Decade Team, Offense

Quarterback	James Street (1967–1969)
Back	James Saxton (1959–1961)
Back	Chris Gilbert (1966–1968)
Lineman	Olen Underwood (1962–1964)
Lineman	Jack Howe (1963–1965)
Lineman	Tommy Nobis (1963–1965)

Lineman	Howard Goad (1964–1966)
Lineman	Danny Abbott (1966–1968)
Lineman	Bob McKay (1967–1969)
End	George Sauer (1963, 1964)
End	Pete Lammons (1963–1965)
Kicker	David Conway (1964–1966)
Punter	Bill Bradley (1966–1968)

All-Decade Team, Defense

Lineman	Don Talbert (1959–1961)
Lineman	Scott Appleton (1961–1963)
Lineman	Loyd Wainscott (1966–1968)
Lineman	Leo Brooks (1967–1969)
Linebacker	Johnny Treadwell (1960–1962)
Linebacker	Tommy Nobis (1963–1965)
Linebacker	Glen Halsell (1967–1969)
Defensive back	Duke Carlisle (1961–1963)
Defensive back	Jim Hudson (1962–1964)
Defensive back	Joe Dixon (1962–1964)
Defensive back	Ronnie Ehrig (1965, 1967, 1968)

Q & A

Q. What obscure Longhorns tackle in 1959 and 1960 later did big things in the business world?

A. Jim Bob Moffett. Born in Houma, Louisiana, of a blue-collar background, he grew up in Houston. Moffett might have done more as a football player, but he took his geology studies very seriously. He soon had a master's degree and formed the company that became New Orleans-based Freeport-McMoRan, one of the world's leaders in the extraction of natural resources. In the Irian Jaya region of Indonesia, it found the mother lode—the largest deposit of gold and copper on earth. Between 1973 and 1997, Freeport-McMoRan excavated 1,650 tons of gold but in the process deposited more than 100,000 of tons of toxic mining waste into local rivers on a daily basis. Forests have been denuded, and many villagers have been displaced and killed by members of the Indonesian military, who are in cahoots with the company. Moffett, who earns about $40 million a year, has been generous to the Texas athletic department and the university as a whole. (Longtime UT President and Chancellor William Cunningham serves on the company's board.) He and his wife were honored in 1997 with the naming of the Louise and James Robert Moffett Molecular Biology Building on Speedway, for which he gave $3 million.

Q. When did Jones Ramsey become sports information director at UT?

A. In 1960, after spending nine seasons at Texas A&M. Ramsey, who stayed on as the Horns' SID until 1982, was a real quipster. His most famous line was that "in Texas, there are only two sports: football and spring football."

Q. What was the history of Room 2001 of the now-razed Villa Capri Hotel, just east of the stadium?

A. That's where Ramsey and Royal played host to the media (Jack Gallagher, Dave Campbell, Blackie Sherrod, Dan Jenkins, Lou Maysel, and Mickey Herskowitz and others), friends, and various hangers-on after home games in the 1960s and early 1970s.

Q. Everyone knows about the Wishbone, which assistant coach Emory Bellard brought to UT in 1968. But what was its precursor?

A. The Flip-Flop, the sole purpose of which was to get the ball to Jimmy Saxton more often in the 1961 season. It worked.

Q. A golden era was certainly dawning in 1961. What happened in Austin after the 10–1 Horns beat Ole Miss in the Cotton Bowl?

A. There was a Darrell Royal Day, and the coach was called on to address the Texas Legislature.

Q. What sophomore on the 1961 team later coached the Longhorns?

A. David McWilliams, a 180-pound lineman from Cleburne.

Q. At least one of a set of brothers from Texas City was on the UT roster every year from 1959 to 1966. Who were they?

A. The Talberts—Don, Charley, and Diron. All three, by the way, were known as "Goose."

Q. What was new on the Longhorns football scene in 1962?

A. Two things. The new, "burnt" orange jerseys Royal had chosen, saying that they were faithful to the color Clyde Littlefield had used three decades earlier. And a giant cotton Texas flag, measuring 111' × 63', had been presented by Mississippi Governor Ross Barnett at the Cotton Bowl nine months earlier. It was originally the responsibility of the Texas Cowboys and later service fraternity Alpha Phi Omega. The flag, which has been replaced three times and is now a bit larger and made of nylon, is unfurled on the field before every home game.

Q. What tragic event happened prior to the 1962 season?

A. Offensive lineman Reggie Grob died. He was a walk-on who made the freshman team, then the varsity, and finally got the validation of a scholarship. Grob collapsed from heat exhaustion, hanging on for 17 days before dying. Royal, who had long adhered to the macho idea that athletes should not be given much water regardless of the heat, changed his ways after Grob's death.

Q. Name the shoeless kicker on the 1962 and 1963 teams.

A. Tony Crosby.

Q. What publications branded the Horns as the top team in the nation entering the 1963 season?

A. *Sports Illustrated* and *Street & Smith Football Yearbook*.

Q. What New Orleans artist was employed to draw covers for UT game programs from the early 1950s until the mid-1960s?

A. John Churchill Chase, whose work typically featured Bevo as a sly trickster, thwarting his opponent in a variety of ways—sometimes by the use of Rube Goldberg-type inventions.

Q. He has been called the greatest player who never was. During his freshman year at UT, this muscular running back with sprinter's speed made four F's and a D, and was soon off to TCU. From there he went to Oklahoma. He played well with the Sooners in 1962 and the first three games of the 1963 season. The week after their game with Texas, he fought an

assistant coach, popped off to the media once too often, and was told to hit the road. Who was he?

A. Joe Don Looney. Despite his considerable baggage, he was a first-round pick of the New York Giants, and they traded him after less than a month. He played with four other NFL teams and did virtually nothing. After his football days, Looney became a convert to Hinduism and lived in many distant lands. He died in a motorcycle accident in 1988.

Q. What was Royal's pungent description of the real nature of football?

A. He said, "It's meat on meat, flesh on flesh, stink on stink."

Q. Besides Tommy Nobis, who was UT's other key defender in '63?

A. Outland Award winner Scott Appleton.

Fred Steinmark

A native of Denver, Fred Steinmark proved himself capable of making it in big-time college football although he was just 5' 10" and weighed 168 pounds. He was a starter by early in his sophomore year and led the team in punt returns. Steinmark had been feeling some pain in his leg for a while, and it seemed to be getting worse toward the end of the 1969 season. Team doctors thought he might have suffered a deep thigh bruise, but he managed to practice and play. Still, Steinmark's performance was not up to par and other defensive backs were being used in his stead. Just six days after the titanic Texas–Arkansas game, joy turned to shock with the announcement that Steinmark had been diagnosed with a tumor in his left leg, which was soon amputated. He attended the Cotton Bowl, walked with a prosthesis to receive his football award at the team banquet on January 12 and re-enrolled at UT. Sadly, the story did not end as all wished—he died in 1971. A large swept-wing scoreboard was already under construction at the south end of the stadium, and it was named in his honor on September 23, 1972.

Q. There was a controversy over a certain play in the 1963 UT–A&M game at Kyle Field. What was it?

A. The Aggies were up, 13–9, with less than 3 minutes to play and the Longhorns threatening at their end of the field. Quarterback Tommy Wade went for a TD pass to George Sauer, but the ball was intercepted by Jim Willenborg. The officials, however, indicated that he was out of bounds before securing the ball and thus Texas retained possession, to the vocal consternation of the Aggies. The drive went forward, with Duke Carlisle scoring the winning touchdown. Willenborg and his coach, Hank Foldberg, said a major injustice had been done, and photographic evidence did seem to validate their views.

Q. What did the UT administration do before the 1964 season to show its appreciation to Royal?

A. He was given a full professorship, which entailed tenure. The *Daily Texan* howled in protest at the very idea that a football coach would wear the same academic cloak as historians and scientists.

Q. What was the unique ending of the 1964 A&M game at Memorial Stadium?

A. A senior end named Garry Brown had toiled in oblivion for three years. In fact, he never even got to wear a uniform on game day until then. Royal put him in with less than 30 seconds on the clock. Quarterback Jim Hudson immediately hit Brown with a 19-yard pass and again with a 10-yard TD pass as time ran out.

Q. Bill Bradley and Chris Gilbert were two schoolboy stars who reached the UT varsity in 1966. Their paths would diverge in varied ways. How so?

A. Bradley started nearly every game for two years but never lived up to his press clippings, suffered a knee injury, and eventually moved to wide receiver and defensive back. He was a fine and consistent punter, however. Gilbert, on the other hand, blossomed almost immediately; he broke Jack Crain's school record of 23 touchdowns and gained more than 1,000 yards all three seasons. Still, Bradley had a nine-year career with the Philadelphia Eagles and Minnesota Vikings, intercepting 34 passes, whereas Gilbert never played a down of pro football.

Q. He was Texas' leading receiver in 1966 and 1967, collecting 19 passes each year. Who was he?

A. Ragan Gennusa, who majored in art at UT. He went on to become a prominent artist, specializing in paintings with Western and natural motifs.

Q. Almost unnoticed, something significant was going on in 1967. What was it?

A. Integration of the football program, at least on the freshman level. E. A. Curry and Robinson Parsons, both walk-on running backs, had made the team, which was full of white stars like Steve Worster, Scott Henderson, Eddie Phillips, Cotton Speyrer, Fred Steinmark, and Bill Atessis. Curry did have one moment of glory, scoring a touchdown against the Rice frosh. Leon O'Neal was signed to a scholarship in February 1968, but grades way-laid him. The 1969 freshmen included scholarship recipient Julius Whittier and walk-on Talmadge Blewitt; not until 1970 did UT have a black varsity player—Whittier.

Q. Along the same line, what was happening outside the stadium before the 1967 season opener against Texas Tech?

A. The Negro Association for Progress (soon re-named the Afro-Americans for Black Liberation) led a protest against UT's hesitance to recruit black football players.

Q. What was the lowest point of the Longhorns' three-year interregnum?

A. They lost their final two games of the 1967 season, and had a tie and a loss to begin 1968. However, the very next week UT beat Oklahoma State by a score of 31–3, and that was the beginning of a 30-game winning streak.

Q. What personnel shift precipitated that change of fortunes?

A. Royal moved Bradley to receiver (and then defensive back) and made James Street his quarterback.

Q. Name the four members of the Longhorns' Wishbone backfield in 1968.

A. Street and runners Worster, Gilbert, and Ted Koy (son of Ernie Sr. and brother of Ernie Jr., both UT greats themselves).

Q. The triple-option offense would prove devastating in time. Who suggested the Wishbone nickname?

A. *Houston Post* writer Mickey Herskowitz.

Q. Gilbert gained 213 yards against Rice in 1968, which moved him past what TCU Horned Frog as the SWC's all-time rusher?

A. Jim Swink.

Q. Who scored the winning touchdown in a 26–20 thriller against OU in 1968?

A. Worster, with 39 seconds to play.

Q. It was 1969, the 100th year of college football. As Royal got his team ready for the season opener, what was happening at Memorial Stadium?

A. A lot. Artificial turf was installed, and the track was converted from cinders to rubber. Aluminum seats replaced the ancient wooden ones throughout the stadium, and construction began on a 15,000-seat upper deck on the west side. It was not complete until halfway through the 1971 season. The cost for these improvements was $17 million, which seems low now but was a scandalously high figure at the time, so university officials did all they could to obscure if not hide it.

Q. As great as Gilbert was, UT coaches found a replacement who might have been even better. Who was this person?

A. Jim Bertelsen. A Wisconsin native, he would end up with 2,510 yards rushing and 33 touchdowns, was twice all-conference, and played five years for the LA Rams. Bertelsen was a key figure with the Horns from 1969 to 1971.

Q. What was the **Daily Texan** *headline when Ohio State lost and UT ascended to the top of the polls in 1969?*

A. "Goodbye Columbus, Hello No. 1."

Q. What was James Street's record as the Longhorns quarterback in games he started?

A. 20–0. There had been some great ones before and there would be more in the future, but his record has never been surpassed—at least not yet.

Q. Street got most of his renown at UT as a football player, but how did he do on the baseball diamond for the Horns?

A. As a pitcher for Cliff Gustafson's team, he went 29–8.

Earl Campbell, the 1977 Heisman Trophy winner, in action against Notre Dame in the Cotton Bowl. A national championship slipped away from Fred Akers' team that day as the Irish took a convincing victory.
(Photo courtesy of the University of Texas.)

Before a single bowl game was played, United Press International (UPI) awarded the 1970 national championship to Texas. Once a common practice, this was the last year in which any of the selecting organizations made their choices prior to bowl games. Some football historians have come to regard this national championship as less than authentic, given that Notre Dame would thrash the Longhorns in Dallas a month later. But it is far more so than what is claimed by many other schools that purported to have won national titles. To wit: Texas was the champ in 1969, the defeats of UCLA and Arkansas loomed large, the Horns averaged 41 points per game in 1970, and that 30-game winning streak speaks for itself—rather loudly.

The culture was changing on the Forty Acres and on the football team. Some players had not been the least bit self-conscious about wearing cowboy hats in the early 1960s, but no more. The percentage of players who smoked marijuana was probably no different than among their fellow students, and their hair was considerably longer than before. Darrell Royal, as befitted his name, was viewed as a king of sorts. He and his wife Edith sometimes vacationed with former President Lyndon B. Johnson, and country and western singer Willie Nelson welcomed him backstage at some shows.

Most of all, integration was a reality by the 1970s. This shift, long awaited and long delayed, was not always easy. If institutional racism lingered in the UT football program—and some black players like Julius Whittier, Lonnie Bennett, Donald Ealey, and Roosevelt Leaks quietly insisted that it did—most parties were eager to work together and move forward. One could scarcely miss the irony that the very people who had for so long been excluded from participation in Texas football were now the engine driving it.

The process by which Royal's replacement was chosen after the 1976 season has never been fully revealed. It's fair to say that after 20 years in Austin, DKR felt he had earned the right to determine who would be the next head coach. And—more important—he was still Texas' athletic director; at virtually any school, the AD hires and fires coaches. Royal wanted his defensive assistant, Mike Campbell (who had come with him from Washington in 1957), to get the job.

But it was not so simple. In a maneuver that would have put Machiavelli to shame, Frank Erwin (whose 13-year tenure on the Board of Regents concluded in 1975), ex-Governor Allan Shivers (then chairman of the board), and President Lorene Rogers took control of a matter in which they really had no standing. Campbell, Maryland Coach Jerry Claiborne, and Jim Wacker (future TCU and Minnesota coach) were given courtesy interviews, but attention was directed to the young, handsome, and energetic Fred Akers. Fairly or not, Campbell, 54, was perceived as "too old" to be the head coach at the University of Texas. Akers was chosen and, furthermore, told that he need not report to Royal, who stayed on as AD for another five years. To say that relations were strained would be putting it very lightly.

Akers, a native of Blytheville, Arkansas, was one of nine children in a family that teetered on the edge of poverty. He played for the Razorbacks from 1957 to 1959 and paid his dues as a coach, starting with the UA freshmen. Then it was on to high school jobs in Port Arthur, Edinburg, and Lubbock before joining the UT staff in 1966. Akers had offensive and defensive duties during his 9 years under Royal before getting the Wyoming job. His first team went 2–9, but his second one had an 8–4 record and played in the Fiesta Bowl. Akers was actually considered more likely to return to his alma mater than to UT in 1977, but Lou Holtz was Frank Broyles' pick. (Like his counterpart, DKR, Broyles was athletic director; unlike Royal, he was allowed to name his successor.) Akers kept just two men from Royal's staff, one of whom, David McWilliams, would replace him 10 years later.

Meat on the Hoof

He was an undersized offensive lineman on the 1964 and 1965 UT teams, but he never played enough to earn a letter at a time when such things mattered. After quitting the sport, Gary Shaw started to compile notes for a book that would be an exposé alleging brutality and corruption in the UT football program. *Meat on the Hoof: The Hidden World of Texas Football,* published in 1972, got national attention and sold more than 350,000 copies.

Shaw wrote about coaches who ran drills that could only be called sadistic, fudging of grades to keep stars eligible, and other dubious practices. His harshest words were reserved for Royal, the man at the top of the pyramid that was Texas football. The book was roundly criticized by many who were there at the time, but it also had its defenders. Accurate or not, *Meat on the Hoof* tarnished the legend of DKR and remains—all these years later—a sore topic. Shaw quickly spent the money he made on the book, spent 10 years as a homeless person, was diagnosed as a paranoid schizophrenic, and died in 1999 at the age of 53.

By the Numbers

4   SMU Mustangs flattened by offensive lineman Jerry Sisemore on one play in 1972.

7   Touchdown passes thrown by Marty Akins in his three years as UT's quarterback.

24   Yards gained rushing in a 30–0 loss to Houston in 1976.

27   Victories by Akins-led teams.

43   Years separating UT's visits to New England (Harvard in 1931 and Boston College in 1974).

49   Years between Texas–Auburn games (1925 and the 1974 Gator Bowl).

54   Seconds it took for Texas to score 14 points against Texas A&M in 1974.

55   Yard field goal kicked by Happy Feller against UCLA in 1970, tying an SWC record. It was topped by Mike Dean's 56-yarder against TCU in 1974, which was topped by Russell Erxleben's 67-yarder against Rice in 1977.

81   Points scored against TCU in 1974, two more than the Horned Frogs scored the entire season.

88   Yard touchdown pass from Jon Aune to Alfred Jackson against Boston College in the 1977 season opener, setting a new school record.

100   Games between shutouts (a 13–0 loss to LSU in the 1963 Cotton Bowl and 27–0 to Oklahoma in 1972).

2,923   Yards gained by Roosevelt Leaks in his three-year career with the Horns.

37,000   Attendance at a Memorial Stadium pep rally before the Big Shootout II against Arkansas in 1970.

$435,205   UT's take in the 1972 Cotton Bowl against Penn State, of which it kept $100,000, sharing the rest with its conference brethren.

Archive

Home games in **bold**

1970 Record: 10–1 (Southwest Conference champions, national champions) Coach: Darrell Royal

Texas 56, California 15

Texas 35, Texas Tech 13

Texas 20, UCLA 17

Texas 41, Oklahoma 9 (in Dallas)

Texas 45, Rice 21

Texas 42, SMU 15

Texas 21, Baylor 14

Texas 58, TCU 0

Texas 52, Texas A&M 14
Texas 42, Arkansas 7
Notre Dame 24, Texas 11 (Cotton Bowl in Dallas)

1971 Record: 8–3 (Southwest Conference champions)
Coach: Darrell Royal
Texas 28, UCLA 10
Texas 28, Texas Tech 0
Texas 35, Oregon 7
Oklahoma 48, Texas 27 (in Dallas)
Arkansas 31, Texas 7 (in Little Rock)
Texas 39, Rice 10
Texas 22, SMU 18
Texas 24, Baylor 0
Texas 31, TCU 0
Texas 34, Texas A&M 14
Penn State 30, Texas 6 (Cotton Bowl in Dallas)

1972 Record: 10–1 (Southwest Conference champions)
Coach: Darrell Royal
Texas 23, Miami 10
Texas 25, Texas Tech 20
Texas 27, Utah State 12
Oklahoma 27, Texas 0 (in Dallas)
Texas 35, Arkansas 15
Texas 45, Rice 9
Texas 17, SMU 9
Texas 17, Baylor 3
Texas 27, TCU 0
Texas 38, Texas A&M 3
Texas 17, Alabama 13 (Cotton Bowl in Dallas)

1973 Record: 8–3 (Southwest Conference champions)
Coach: Darrell Royal
Miami 20, Texas 15
Texas 28, Texas Tech 12
Texas 41, Wake Forest 0

Oklahoma 52, Texas 13 (in Dallas)
Texas 34, Arkansas 6
Texas 55, Rice 13
Texas 42, SMU 14
Texas 42, Baylor 6
Texas 52, TCU 7
Texas 42, Texas A&M 13
Nebraska 19, Texas 3 (Cotton Bowl in Dallas)

1974 Record: 8–4 Coach: Darrell Royal
Texas 42, Boston College 19
Texas 34, Wyoming 7
Texas Tech 26, Texas 3
Texas 35, Washington 21
Oklahoma 16, Texas 13 (in Dallas)
Texas 38, Arkansas 7
Texas 27, Rice 6
Texas 35, SMU 15
Baylor 34, Texas 24
Texas 81, TCU 16
Texas 32, Texas A&M 3
Auburn 27, Texas 3 (Gator Bowl in Jacksonville, Florida)

1975 Record: 10–2 (Southwest Conference tri-champions) Coach: Darrell Royal
Texas 46, Colorado State 0
Texas 28, Washington 10
Texas 42, Texas Tech 18
Texas 61, Utah State 7
Oklahoma 24, Texas 17 (in Dallas)
Texas 24, Arkansas 18
Texas 41, Rice 9
Texas 30, SMU 22
Texas 37, Baylor 21
Texas 27, TCU 11
Texas A&M 20, Texas 10
Texas 38, Colorado 21 (Bluebonnet Bowl in Houston)

1976 Record: 5–5–1 Coach: Darrell Royal

Boston College 14, Texas 13
Texas 17, North Texas 14
Texas 42, Rice 15
Texas 6, Oklahoma 6 (in Dallas)
Texas 13, SMU 12
Texas Tech 31, Texas 28
Houston 30, Texas 0
Texas 34, TCU 7
Baylor 20, Texas 10
Texas A&M 27, Texas 3
Texas 29, Arkansas 12

1977 Record: 11–1 (Southwest Conference champions) Coach: Fred Akers

Texas 44, Boston College 0
Texas 68, Virginia 0
Texas 72, Rice 15
Texas 13, Oklahoma 6 (in Dallas)
Texas 13, Arkansas 9
Texas 30, SMU 14
Texas 26, Texas Tech 0
Texas 35, Houston 21
Texas 44, TCU 14
Texas 29, Baylor 7
Texas 57, Texas A&M 28
Notre Dame 38, Texas 10 (Cotton Bowl in Dallas)

1978 Record: 9–3 Coach: Fred Akers

Texas 34, Rice 0
Texas 17, Wyoming 3

Earl Campbell

In January 1974, Royal paid a visit to an unpainted frame house in a little community south of Tyler. He and assistant coach Ken Dabbs were there to seek the services of a football player named Earl Campbell, who had just led John Tyler High School to the state championship. The meeting did not begin well. The young man was very direct. "Coach Royal, I heard you don't like black people," were almost his first words. Perhaps Royal was prepared for Campbell's challenge, because he talked about his own childhood in Oklahoma during the Dust Bowl. He, too, had lived in a shack. Campbell listened to offers from other white coaches who seemed equally sincere, but as everyone knows he ended up casting his lot with the Longhorns.

What he did over the next four years at UT was the stuff of legend. Campbell gained 4,443 yards rushing, scored 41 touchdowns, won the Heisman Trophy, and almost brought the national championship back to Austin. Unquestionably one of the greatest backs in college football history, his status was further enhanced by what he accomplished in the NFL. The Tyler Rose was the No. 1 overall pick by the Houston Oilers and led the NFL in rushing his first three seasons. Due to the heavy pounding he took, Campbell only lasted nine years in pro football. Upon his retirement in 1986, one sportswriter characterized him this way: "At his best, he was the best."

Perhaps as a thank-you of sorts, shortly after he retired Campbell was given a job at the university—as special assistant to the vice president for student affairs. He remains in that position today. Earl Campbell experienced a lot of football glory, but he has also paid a steep price for it. He now has severe arthritis, has trouble walking, and is sometimes confined to a wheelchair. At halftime of the Ohio State game in 2006, he was honored by the unveiling of a nine-foot statue at the southwest corner of the stadium.

Texas 24, Texas Tech 7
Oklahoma 31, Texas 10 (in Dallas)
Texas 26, North Texas 16
Texas 28, Arkansas 21
Texas 22, SMU 3
Houston 10, Texas 7
Texas 41, TCU 0
Baylor 38, Texas 14
Texas 22, Texas A&M 7
Texas 42, Maryland 0 (Sun Bowl in El Paso)

1979 Record: 9–3 Coach: Fred Akers
Texas 17, Iowa State 9
Texas 21, Missouri 0
Texas 26, Rice 9
Texas 16, Oklahoma 7 (in Dallas)
Arkansas 17, Texas 14
Texas 30, SMU 6
Texas 14, Texas Tech 6
Texas 21, Houston 13
Texas 35, TCU 10
Texas 13, Baylor 0
Texas A&M 13, Texas 7
Washington 14, Texas 7 (Sun Bowl in El Paso)

20 Big Games

**Texas 20, UCLA 17 / October 3, 1970 / Memorial Stadium
(Austin, Texas)**
The defending national champs are 22-point favorites against UCLA. The Bruins, adorned in baby-blue jerseys, are serious about ending UT's 22-game winning streak and they appear to have figured out the Wishbone. Dennis Dummit leads a pair of long third-quarter drives and has UCLA up by four. The Longhorns, with the ball at their 45-yard line and 20 seconds to play, are desperate. Quarterback Eddie Phillips escapes a heavy rush and fires the ball to an angling Cotton Speyrer. Two Bruins miss intercepting it, and a third fails to impede Speyrer who sprints to

the goal line as a huge roar erupts from the 65,500 fans in attendance. The winning streak remains intact, as does UT's run for another national crown.

Texas 42, Arkansas 7 / December 5, 1970 / Memorial Stadium (Austin, Texas)
Fresh off administering a ninth consecutive beating to the Aggies, UT is a solid No. 1 in the polls. Royal closes practice to "everyone, including blood brothers," in the week leading up to the Arkansas game, which is being billed as the Big Shootout II. Needless to say, the No. 4 Hogs wish to atone for last year's loss in Fayetteville. It is not to be, however, as Texas wins in convincing fashion. Scott Henderson leads a key goal-line stand, Jim Bertelsen gains 189 yards, and his backfield mate, Steve Worster, scores the 36th touchdown of his career. Frank Broyles gives a mournful postgame assessment.

Notre Dame 24, Texas 11 / January 1, 1971 / Cotton Bowl (Cotton Bowl in Dallas, Texas)
Texas has already won the UPI's version of the national title before this rematch with the Irish at the Cotton Bowl, now bearing a rock-hard first-generation artificial turf. The game starts with Phillips bolting 63 yards, but the Horns settle for a field goal. Joe Theismann's running and passing has Notre Dame ahead by 13 at the half. The Horns' effort to come from behind, as they have done nine times in their 30-game winning streak, is a study in futility. Worster, with lingering hip, shoulder, and knee injuries, has a miserable day—42 yards on 16 carries, and four fumbles. Royal is gracious afterward, saying the loss was long overdue. His counterpart, Ara Parseghian, calls it one of the biggest moments in Notre Dame history, and he is right.

Oklahoma 48, Texas 27 / October 9, 1971 / Cotton Bowl (Dallas, Texas)
It's almost like that spanking by Notre Dame never happened. Royal's 1971 Horns are off to a fine start with wins over UCLA, Texas Tech, and Oregon. But the Wishbone offense has been adopted—some say perfected—by Oklahoma, as is seen in this game in Big D. Jack Mildren is ever so nimble at quarterback, and Greg Pruitt provides breakaway speed around the corners. The Sooners have won the first of five straight over Texas. The next week is even worse as UT suffers a blowout loss to the Razorbacks on a dark, rainy day in Little Rock.

Texas 34, Texas A&M 14 / November 25, 1971 / Kyle Field (College Station, Texas)

Some 52,000 fans are on hand at Kyle Field to see whether the Aggies can (1) beat UT, (2) earn a spot in the Liberty Bowl, and (3) save Coach Gene Stallings' job. They fail on all three counts as the Longhorns secure a 34–14 win. The Texas defense creates five turnovers, Donnie Wigginton scores twice, and Stallings gets canned that very night. The Horns will return to the Cotton Bowl, losing to Penn State, 30–6.

Texas 35, Arkansas 15 / October 21, 1972 / Memorial Stadium (Austin, Texas)

The Longhorns, coming off a shutout loss to OU, are facing an Arkansas team that started the season with national title aspirations. On a rainy night in Austin, UT loses five fumbles but still comes away with a victory by scoring 20 points in the final quarter. Roosevelt Leaks and QB Alan Lowry score two TDs each, while Donald Ealey scoots 26 yards for the final one. The Razorbacks' Joe Ferguson is held to 14-of-38 passing. More than 80,000 tickets are sold for this game, although the weather suppresses attendance somewhat.

Texas 17, Alabama 13 / January 1, 1973 / Cotton Bowl (Cotton Bowl in Dallas, Texas)

Alabama, too, has switched to the Wishbone and is favored by seven points in a game witnessed by a sellout crowd in Dallas. The Longhorns struggle early on, but the Tide is turned on a key play with 4:22 left. Alan Lowry, struggling with tonsillitis and 100° fever, consults with Royal and suggests a bootleg around the left end. On third down and 2, he fakes to Leaks, hides the ball on his hip, and turns the corner. He eludes one 'Bama defensive back and scores. Somehow, the officials fail to see that Lowry's left foot was clearly out of bounds at the 10. At any rate, UT wins. The Horns and their fans savor it after losing rather badly in this game the past two years.

Miami 20, Texas 15 / September 21, 1973 / Orange Bowl (Miami, Florida)

Texas is ranked third in pre-season polls, but that does not last long against Miami. Joey Aboussie breaks into the open, apparently en route to a 54-yard TD, but he inexplicably fumbles. It is just one of eight fumbles (five recovered by the Hurricanes) this night, although many of them are caused by hard-hitting defenders like Rubin Carter and Tony Cristiani. Sophomore quarterback Marty Akins gets a rough baptism; the main bright spot is Leaks, who gains 153 yards on 30 carries.

Texas 42, SMU 14 / November 3, 1973 / Cotton Bowl (Dallas, Texas)

The Ponies have jumped on the Wishbone bandwagon, as well. With quarterback Ricky Wesson, and halfbacks Wayne Morris and Alvin Maxson, they have the personnel to make it go. SMU is averaging 419 yards on the ground entering this game, which is seen on national TV. The Mustangs are up by 14 early on, but Jimmy Moore has a 94-yard punt return and Leaks gets one big gainer after another. He carries 37 times for 342 yards, breaking a Southwest Conference record that had stood for 23 years. Credit also goes to center Bill Wyman. Royal says that Wyman and Leaks go together like ham and eggs.

Texas 38, Arkansas 7 / October 19, 1974 / Memorial Stadium (Austin, Texas)

Earl Campbell, a "can't-miss" prospect if ever there was one, has gotten off to a fine start in his freshman year—despite sharing the fullback spot with Roosevelt Leaks. He plays a big role in this rollicking defeat of the Razorbacks. In the second quarter, he takes a handoff from Marty Akins, stiff-arms an Arkansas defender, and motors 68 yards for a score. Just before the half, Campbell blocks a punt. The ball is scooped up by Doug English, who strolls into the end zone and thus fulfills every lineman's dream. Frank Broyles says his team has at least 10 injuries, not to mention the worst injury of all: that to the pride of the Hogs, pre-season SWC favorites.

Baylor 34, Texas 24 / November 9, 1974 / Baylor Stadium (Waco, Texas)

In the week leading up to this game, Royal is all nicey-nicey about Baylor and how the Bears will be sky-high when UT comes to town. It sounds like so much coach-speak early in the second quarter, when the Horns are up by a score of 24–7. Who among the 43,100 fans at Baylor Stadium knows that a major turnaround is about to ensue? QB Neal Jeffrey leads the Bears to scores in four of their next five possessions for a stirring 34–24 upset of the six-time conference champions. Royal goes to the BU locker room and congratulates the victors, who will win their first SWC title since 1924. Coach and AD Grant Teaff wants the scoreboard lights to remain on all night long, and some fans sleep on the field. Such is the significance of this win to Baylor football, which is still known as the "Miracle on the Brazos."

Texas 28, Washington 10 / September 20, 1975 / Husky Stadium (Seattle, Washington)

Perhaps some people in Seattle still hold it against Royal that he had left them so suddenly back in 1956. If so, they don't let on as the No. 8 Longhorns pay a visit UW's stadium, perched on the shore of Lake Washington. The Horns win, but it doesn't come easy. The passing of Washington's Warren Moon and the running of 250-pound fullback Robin Earl dominate the first quarter. For UT, Campbell gains 198 yards, and Akins adds 140 of his own. Huskies Coach Don James is impressed with both of UT's offensive stars.

Texas 38, Colorado 21 / December 27, 1975 / Bluebonnet Bowl (Astrodome in Houston, Texas)

The regular season ends with a 10-point loss to Texas A&M, but UT still shares the conference crown with the Aggies and Arkansas. The reward is a Bluebonnet Bowl match-up with Colorado. Royal feels he may not have worked his team hard enough in last year's 27–3 loss to Auburn in the Gator Bowl, so he makes appropriate changes. Akins returns from a knee injury, although he is still not at full speed. Bill Mallory's Golden Buffaloes take a 21–7 halftime lead, which would have been bigger if not for a goal-line interception. It is all Texas in the second half, as the Horns score 24 unanswered points—including a 55-yard field goal by Russell Erxleben. Tim Campbell, who has a blocked punt and resultant TD, is named the game's top defensive player. His more famous brother gets the offensive honors.

Texas 6, Oklahoma 6 / October 9, 1976 / Cotton Bowl (Dallas, Texas)

Even more media attention than usual is devoted to this game in the week before it is played. Barry Switzer (whose team has won the last two national championships) makes sly digs at Royal, whose star is fading. Royal, in turn, is convinced that OU is spying on his practices. The two coaches ignore each other in pre-game warm-ups. The game itself is a ferocious defensive struggle. Erxleben kicks two field goals, and it looks like the Horns might win with just those six points. But with 5:23 left, Ivey Suber fumbles and the Sooners move 37 yards to score. The extra point fails, and the two teams must settle for a tie. As he walks toward the Cotton Bowl locker room, Royal is roundly booed by some students and fans from his alma mater. Worn out by this three-hour football war, the haggard coach stops, puts his hands on his knees, and retches.

Texas 29, Arkansas 12 / December 4, 1976 / Memorial Stadium (Austin, Texas)

UT football fortunes have not been this bad in nearly a decade. The last five games have consisted of losses to Texas Tech, Houston (a disastrous 30–0), Baylor, and Texas A&M, with a defeat of TCU in the middle; Earl Campbell's absence due to injury does not help matters. The nosedive prompts speculation about Royal's resolve to stay in the game. As it happens, Frank Broyles announces his intention to retire after 19 years at the Razorbacks' helm. The game, featuring two SWC also-rans, is a 29–12 Texas triumph in which Campbell gains 131 yards and quarterback Mark McBath gets 118. Raymond Clayborn has two 46-yard punt returns, and Erxleben hits three field goals. Royal and Broyles, both of whom have had their share of highs and lows, meet at midfield after the game for a hug and a warm shake. Both have coached their last game. It is the end of an era.

Texas 13, Arkansas 9 / October 15, 1977 / Razorback Stadium (Fayetteville, Arkansas)

A big win over OU moves the Longhorns up to No. 2, their highest ranking since the heady days of 1970. There is also a revitalization going on in the Ozarks, with Lou Holtz now in charge of the Hogs' program. An overflow crowd witnesses two of the finest kickers in college football history—Russell Erxleben and Steve Little. The former boots field goals of 58 and 52 yards, and the latter has three, of 33, 67, and 25 yards. He also misses from 60 yards out at the end of the first half. UT's winning fourth-quarter touchdown drive begins at its 20 in the face of a stiff wind. It concludes with Johnny "Ham" Jones taking a pitch from Randy McEachern and going the final yard untouched. Campbell has 188 yards, supplanting the Razorbacks' Dickey Morton as the SWC's all-time leading rusher.

Notre Dame 38, Texas 10 / January 1, 1978 / Cotton Bowl (Cotton Bowl in Dallas, Texas)

Firmly established as No. 1 and with the Heisman Trophy winner in its backfield, Texas is all smiles. And yet there are worries aplenty coming into this Cotton Bowl contest with Notre Dame. Linebacker Lance Taylor is out, Erxleben has a thigh bruise, and McEachern's knee is hurting. Although the

Irish are ahead by 21 at the half, Coach Fred Akers tell his team it can still pull out a victory. Hopes for a fourth national title dim and then go out as Notre Dame takes advantage of six turnovers and dominates from start to finish. Vagas Ferguson and Jerome Heavens combine for 201 yards, most of it up the middle. With that kind of success on the ground, quarterback Joe Montana doesn't need to throw much. Akers tries not to dwell on the loss and hits the recruiting road. But he knows such opportunities don't come along often.

Houston 10, Texas 7 / November 11, 1978 / Memorial Stadium (Austin, Texas)

Bill Yeoman's Cougars have shown no fear whatsoever upon entering Memorial Stadium—a tie game back in 1968 and a 30-point clobbering in 1976 prove it. A crowd of 83,053 is there to see the SWC game of the year. UH is up by 10 as the fourth quarter commences. Donnie Little drives the Horns 82 yards on 11 plays—with passes of 27 and 29 yards to tight end Lawrence Sampleton—but they can't get back in the end zone. This victory sends Houston to the Cotton Bowl and Texas out to the west Texas town of El Paso, where a 42–0 mauling of Maryland will take place.

Texas 16, Oklahoma 7 / October 13, 1979 / Cotton Bowl (Dallas, Texas)

The season has begun quite well—three victories and only 18 points surrendered, but it is likely to be a different story against No. 3 OU in Dallas. Johnnie Johnson fumbles a punt and sets up a Sooners TD. But Derrick Hatchett has a 36-yard interception return, after which Donnie Little tosses a short scoring pass to Steve Hall. John Goodson's three field goals make the difference, and A. J. "Jam" Jones records his fourth straight 100-yard game. Beating Oklahoma elevates the Horns to No. 2, but they will drop a close one to Arkansas a week hence.

Texas A&M 13, Texas 7 / December 1, 1979 / Kyle Field (College Station, Texas)

A five-game winning streak is expected to become six after this contest, but the 5–5 Aggies refuse to cooperate. David Hardy kicks two field goals, and speedster Curtis Dickey races 22 yards for a score. Texas' miscues include two bobbled punts and kickoffs, and a missed short field goal. A&M Coach Tom Wilson beats his chest in the locker room after the game, and why not?

A shocking upset has prevented UT from getting an invite to the Sugar Bowl to face 'Bama and Bear Bryant. Instead, the morose Horns go back to the Sun Bowl, where they will fall to Washington.

All-Decade Team, Offense

Quarterback	Marty Akins (1972–1975)
Back	Steve Worster (1968–1970)
Back	Roosevelt Leaks (1972–1974)
Back	Earl Campbell (1974–1977)
Lineman	Bobby Wuensch (1968–1970)
Lineman	Jerry Sisemore (1970–1972)
Lineman	Bill Wyman (1971–1973)
Lineman	Don Crosslin (1971–1973)
Lineman	Bob Simmons (1973–1975)
End	Cotton Speyrer (1968–1970)
End	Johnny "Lam" Jones (1976–1979)
Punt/kick returner	Johnnie Johnson (1976–1979)
Kicker	Russell Erxleben (1975–1978)
Punter	Russell Erxleben (1975–1978)

All-Decade Team, Defense

Lineman	Bill Atessis (1968–1970)
Lineman	Doug English (1972–1974)
Lineman	Brad Shearer (1974–1977)
Lineman	Steve McMichael (1976–1979)
Linebacker	Scott Henderson (1968–1970)
Linebacker	Randy Braband (1970–1972)
Linebacker	Glen Gaspard (1971–1973)
Defensive back	Raymond Clayborn (1973–1976)
Defensive back	Ricky Churchman (1976–1979)
Defensive back	Johnnie Johnson (1976–1979)
Defensive back	Derrick Hatchett (1977–1979)

171

Q & A

Q. There were no night games at Memorial Stadium in 1970. Why?

A. As part of the expansion project, the lights on the west side had been taken down.

Q. After Cotton Speyrer broke his arm in the OU game in 1970, who came over from the defense to take his place?

A. Danny Lester, who led the team with 17 catches that season.

Q. What was TCU Coach Fred Taylor's lament after seeing his team get pounded, 58–0, by the Longhorns in Fort Worth in 1970?

A. "I feel like we were beat when we went on the field."

Q. This rampaging fullback from Bridge City was the centerpiece of the 1967 recruiting class, and his jersey number (30) matched the Longhorns' winning streak over three seasons. Who was he?

A. Steve Worster. Twice an all-American, he finished his career with 2,353 yards. Worster was fourth in 1970 Heisman Trophy voting.

Q. One of Worster's teammates came from Houston, was twice all-SWC as a defensive end, and an all-American in his senior season. To whom do we refer?

A. Bill Atessis.

Q. The expanded Memorial Stadium now held 75,504 seats. The massive west-side upper deck sat atop an eight-story building that would house athletics, classrooms, gyms, racquetball courts, and more. For whom was it named?

A. L. Theo Bellmont, UT's first athletic director a half-century earlier.

Q. Defensive tackle Greg Ploetz was back with the team in 1971 after taking a year off. Where had he been?

A. Focusing on his art studies.

Q. This 5' 8", 167-pound fifth-year senior shared the quarterback spot in 1971 because Eddie Phillips had leg and foot injuries. Identify him.

A. Donnie Wigginton, who had a nose for the end zone, leading the SWC in scoring with 84 points.

Q. This balding, 150-pound junior college transfer broke a 56-yard punt return against Arkansas in 1971. Who was he?

A. Dean Campbell.

Q. What else happened that day in Little Rock?

A. Arkansas fans made the Longhorn Band a target of verbal abuse throughout the game and tossed a few whiskey bottles, too. Band director Vince DiNino swore he would never return.

Q. Identify the first black player in Texas history to score a touchdown.

A. Halfback Lonnie Bennett, who ran it over from 7 yards out in a 39–10 defeat of Rice in '71.

Q. Who did Royal name to coach the defensive backs in 1972?

A. Alvin Matthews, the first black assistant coach in SWC history. He was a part-time coach, working only in the spring because he was still playing for the Green Bay Packers. Texas' first full-time black coach was Prenis Williams, who handled receivers from 1974 to 1976.

Q. Name the lightly recruited player from Dallas who earned a starting job on the defensive line early in the 1972 season.

A. Doug English, who was on his way to two-time all-SWC honors and was an all-American in 1974. He would have a solid, decade-long career with the Detroit Lions.

Q. He was supposed to take Steve Worster's place as fullback in the Wishbone, but he was too valuable to leave his linebacker spot. Who was this native of East Chambers?

A. Glen Gaspard, twice all-SWC. He also kicked a few field goals.

Q. Identify the offensive lineman who starred for the Horns from 1970 to 1972.

A. Jerry Sisemore, who was twice an all-American and spent 13 years with the Philadelphia Eagles.

Q. Another excellent offensive lineman came close on Sisemore's heels. Who was he?

A. Bob Simmons. Three times all-conference and an all-American in 1975, he played seven years with the Kansas City Chiefs.

Q. Who is Emory Bellard in UT football history?

A. Royal's offensive backfield coach from 1967 to 1971, he was most responsible for bringing the Wishbone offense to reality. Bellard took over at A&M in 1972.

Q. Penn State beat the Horns in the 1972 Cotton Bowl. Who was in Joe Paterno's backfield that damp and dreary day?

A. Lydell Mitchell and Franco Harris, both of whom went on to great success in the NFL.

Q. What were linebacker Randy Braband's words to sportswriters as he entered the locker room after that loss to the Nittany Lions?

A. "You grubby buzzards, get out of my way."

Q. He had been a two-year starter in the defensive backfield. But Royal needed a quarterback to replace Eddie Phillips, and he readily made the switch. Who was he?

A. Alan Lowry, who led UT to 10 wins and made all-SWC despite throwing just one touchdown pass the entire season.

Q. Neither Royal nor 'Bama's Bear Bryant had been in a hurry to integrate. But, as seen in the 1973 Cotton Bowl, the segregation days were over. Name some of the black athletes who played in that game.

A. Running back Wilbur Jackson and defensive end John Mitchell for the Crimson Tide, and offensive lineman Julius Whittier, defensive end Howard

Shaw, and running backs Roosevelt Leaks, Donald Ealey, and Lonnie Bennett for the Longhorns.

Q. *After apprenticing under Lowry in 1972, he became UT's starting quarterback for the next three seasons. Who was he?*

A. Marty Akins, who finished with nearly 2,000 yards rushing, 1,188 yards passing, and 25 TDs. Akins was a fine player who went on to do quite well in the legal field. He also made a feeble run for governor in 2002.

Q. *How did Leaks do in 1973 Heisman Trophy voting?*

A. He came in third. In spite of a serious knee injury in '74 spring training, he went on to a productive nine-year career with the Baltimore Colts and Buffalo Bills.

Q. *When Leaks was a sophomore and had turned into UT's first black star, he met some resistance from teammates. What happened to cool the situation?*

A. Two offensive linemen, Jerry Sisemore and Travis Roach, stood up in a players-only meeting and stated rather forcefully that Rosey was a Longhorn like the rest of them and that he should be treated with the respect he deserved. Problem resolved.

Q. *What did the Sooners do to UT in Dallas in 1973?*

A. The Selmon brothers (Lucious, Dewey, and LeRoy), Joe Washington, and quarterback Steve Davis were merciless in a 52–13 defeat. "We lost to a vastly superior football team," said a glum Royal about Oklahoma. Even so, the Horns won their sixth straight SWC title and a trip to the Cotton Bowl (a 19–3 loss to Nebraska). No one knew it at the time, but that would be Royal's last visit to Dallas on New Year's Day.

Q. *This defensive back had an interception and recovered teammate Mike Dean's kickoff in the end zone for a touchdown against Texas Tech in 1973. Who was he?*

A. Jay Arnold.

Q. *Who led Texas in tackles in 1973?*

A. Linebacker Wade Johnston, who had 87 and another 17 in the Cotton Bowl loss to Nebraska.

Q. *When did UT disband its freshman football program?*

A. In 1974. Although frosh had been eligible for varsity competition since 1972, Royal had kept the Yearlings around. He realized, however, that there was no longer any use in making that attempt and integrated them with the varsity. The first-year men who started at least one game in 1974 included Earl Campbell, running back Gralyn Wyatt, defensive end Travis Couch, receiver Alfred Jackson, defensive tackle Brad Shearer, and offensive lineman George James.

Q. *A sophomore on the '74 team was equally effective on offense and defense (and a heck of a kick returner), and went on to a fine 13-year career with the New England Patriots and Cleveland Browns. Name him.*

A. Raymond Clayborn, who also ran the 100 meters in 9.5 seconds, and the 400 meters in 46.9, and competed in the sprint relays on the UT track team.

Q. *What quarterback briefly took Akins' job in early 1974 only to suffer a concussion against Wyoming and lose it right back?*

A. Mike Presley.

Q. *The 1974 Texas–Oklahoma game was not televised. Why?*

A. The Sooners were on NCAA probation, and this was part of their punishment.

Q. *Who was Texas' leading scorer in the 1974 season?*

A. Kicker Billy "Sure" Schott, who had 7 field goals and 44 PATs for a total of 65 points.

Q. *When was the last time fewer than 40,000 fans attended a home game?*

A. The 1975 game against TCU drew a crowd of just 34,500 to Memorial Stadium.

Q. *How did Marty Akins do as a runner in 1975?*

A. He set a school record for quarterbacks by gaining 777 yards. His record would stand for three decades before Vince Young shattered it.

Q. *Who was Texas' kicker from 1975 to 1978?*

A. Russell Erxleben, the last of the great straight-ahead kickers. Blessed with a cannon for a leg, Erxleben's field goals (the longest of which was 67 yards), punts, and kickoffs were something to behold. He was drafted in the first round by the New Orleans Saints but had a mediocre pro career. As a self-taught financial investor, Erxleben was no better. In 1999, he was convicted of securities fraud and spent five years in the slammer.

Q. *When Erxleben had an injury in 1977, who kicked in his place?*

A. Defensive tackle Steve McMichael. He came from the south Texas town of Freer, and made all-SWC twice and all-America once (1979). A fairly ferocious player, McMichael went on to have a 16-year career, mostly with the Chicago Bears. "Bam-Bam" took on a new nickname, "Mongo," after moving into another career of sorts, as a professional wrestler. He brawled and carried on phony feuds with such esteemed gentlemen as Ric Flair, Bobby Heenan, Jeff Jarrett, Stevie Ray Huffman, and Davey Boy Smith.

Q. *In 1976, his 20th season in Austin, what was Royal's salary?*

A. $50,000.

Q. *The Horns had won 42 straight games at home, but that came to an abrupt end in 1976 when Houston visited. What did Bill Yeoman's team do?*

A. With Danny Davis running the offense and Wilson Whitley the defense, the Cougars crushed Texas, 30–0.

Q. *How did Earl Campbell do that season?*

A. A series of injuries caused him to miss four games and parts of others. He gained just 653 yards, did not make all-SWC, and briefly considered giving up football.

Q. *Who put on a stirring performance at the Texas Relays as a high school senior in 1976, went to Montreal to win an Olympic gold medal in the 4 × 100-meter relay, and then wowed them again in the 1977 Relays?*

A. Johnny "Lam" Jones, who then gave up track for football glory. He was drafted in the first round by the New York Jets, but his pro football career was marked by injury and disappointment.

Q. What was the final tally on DKR's two decades as head coach of the Longhorns?

A. Three national championships, twice national coach of the year, a 167–47–5 record (109–27–2 in the SWC), a share of 11 conference titles, 16 bowl games, 9 top-five finishes, 30 weeks ranked No. 1 in the nation, a 30-game winning streak, 77 all-SWC players, and 26 all-Americans.

Q. Fred Akers, who immediately junked the Wishbone, anticipated that 1977 would be a "rebuilding" year. Was it?

A. Given that UT was coming off a 5–5–1 record, how could it be otherwise? The Horns were picked to finish fourth in the SWC, but when the first three games (Boston College, Virginia, and Rice) were won by a 184–15 margin, they were off to the races. They moved into the top 20, the top 10, and higher with every victory—especially a defeat of Oklahoma, UT's first since 1970. With defensive tackle Brad Shearer, Erxleben, and the incomparable Campbell leading the way, they got up to No. 1 by late October and went undefeated in the regular season.

Q. Three quarterbacks started at least one game that season. Who were they?

A. Mark McBath, Randy McEachern, and Sam Ansley.

Q. McEachern was the surprise hero against OU in '77. What had his role been in that game the previous season?

A. He sat in the press box of the Cotton Bowl and worked as a spotter for a radio announcer.

Q. Alfred Jackson caught five balls against Baylor in 1977, setting a UT record for career receiving yardage. Who held the record before that?

A. Ben Procter, in the late 1940s.

Q. What ceremony took place at the stadium on November 12, 1977?

A. At halftime of the TCU game (a 44–4 Texas victory), Memorial Stadium was dedicated for the third time. Just as it was built to honor Texas' World War I soldiers in 1924, and as a 1948 ceremony encompassed those who had served in World War II, the university chose to include Korean and Vietnam war veterans.

Q. What was Earl Campbell's greatest day—statistically speaking—as a Longhorn?

A. It came at Kyle Field in 1977, when he carried 27 times for 222 yards and three TDs.

Q. Campbell finished as the fifth-leading runner in college football history. Who remained in front of him?

A. Tony Dorsett of Pittsburgh, Archie Griffin of Ohio State, Ed Marinaro of Cornell, and Terry Miller of Oklahoma State.

Q. When Campbell first came to UT in 1974, he made clear that he would not be bought or sold. What kind of car did he drive during his Heisman Trophy season?

A. A 1967 Oldsmobile, for which he had paid $300.

Q. Why did Akers' 1978 team lose three times?

A. Campbell was gone, and a dozen starters missed games with injuries.

Q. UT's 38–14 loss to Baylor that year is remembered for what locker room stunt?

A. Grant Teaff told his Bears a story about two Eskimo fishermen, the elder of whom advised about the need to "keep your worms warm." The BU coach then took a worm he had bought at a nearby bait store and dropped it into his mouth, pretending to chew and swallow it. His players, whether amazed or disgusted, went out and beat the Longhorns.

Q. What native of LaGrange was an all-America defensive back in 1978 and 1979?

A. Johnnie Johnson, thrice all-SWC. Nimble and fleet of foot, he was also a fine kick and punt returner. A first-round pick by the LA Rams, Johnson was NFL rookie of the year and had a solid 11-year career.

Q. He was a worthy successor to Russell Erxleben as UT's kicker, booting a school-record 17 field goals in 1979. Who was he?

A. John Goodson.

Q. *This young man stood 5' 8", weighed 160 pounds, and split time between football and track during his years (1979–1982) at Texas. Identify him.*

A. Herkie Walls, who saw action at five different positions during his freshman year.

COTTON
BOWL

The top-ranked UT Longhorns, on the cusp of
the 1983 national crown. They pose outside the
stadium where, the next day, they will suffer a
10–9 upset at the hands of Georgia.
(Photo courtesy of the University of Texas.)

In the summer of 1981, DeLoss Dodds was hired as athletic director at the University of Texas. He came better equipped for the job than anyone since L. Theo Bellmont nearly seven decades earlier. Dodds had run track at Kansas State—winning the quarter-mile in the 1958 Big Eight meet—and earned a couple of degrees while coaching the Wildcats. Soon, he was the AD and happy to be taking care of business at his alma mater. Other schools had sought Dodds' services, but he decided he would leave Manhattan only if Oklahoma or Texas came calling. The Longhorns made their pitch before the Sooners did.

Many UT boosters viewed the 44-year-old Dodds with some suspicion at first, especially when he began to modernize the athletic department and embark on a variety of broad-based fundraising ventures. Before Dodds got to Austin, the annual budget was just over $4 million. With him at the helm, it is now approaching the $100 million mark. Critics say he runs the athletic department like a Fortune 500 company, but at least it's solvent—and many of Texas' NCAA Division I-A counterparts are not.

The 1980s were not an especially good time for Southwest Conference football. In four seasons (1980, 1986, 1988, and 1989), no member cracked the final top-10 rankings. The best the conference had to offer were the 1981 Texas and 1982 SMU teams, both of which finished No. 2, and the 1983 Horns, who came within a fumbled punt of winning the national title. It was a time of recruiting scandals and slush funds, when SWC members turned on each other in almost cannibalistic fashion. Only Rice, Baylor, and Arkansas managed to stay off some form of NCAA probation. SMU, of course, suffered the "death penalty" and sat out two seasons of competition. The conference's market share in television coverage began to dwindle, caus-ing the bigger schools to think pragmatically. Many a sportswriter speculated about the future of the Southwest Conference, which was, indeed, nearing the end of its days.

Virtually nothing had been done to the stadium since erection of the west-side upper deck in 1971. Eleven years later, the Centennial Room opened. Sitting just below the upper deck and extending the length of the field, it was a nice and comfy place to watch a game, drink, and social-ize—for those with the money to spend. The Centennial Room may have been the first, but it certainly would not be the last, instance of catering to wealthy donors; revenue-producing luxury boxes at Memorial Stadium were right around the corner. At least one member of the Athletics Council, John Stuart, expressed concern about creeping commercialism and straying too far from the ideals of an academic institution. Others may have agreed, but few were willing to speak up.

Toward the end of the decade, a group of men from the Dana X. Bible era formed a plan to rename the stadium in honor of the revered coach, who had died in 1980. Rooster Andrews, Malcolm Kutner, Noble Doss, and Wally Scott lined up behind former sports information director Bill Sansing's proposal. Sansing met with UT President William Cunningham and stated his case but was turned down because, Cunningham asserted, the very name "Memorial Stadium" had come to mean so much to generations of students and alumni of the university.

By the Numbers

1	All-SWC player in 1989 (wide receiver Johnny Walker), the fewest since 1960.
1–8–1	Bear Bryant's record against UT, which concluded with the 1982 Cotton Bowl.
2 mins., 53 secs.	Length of athletic director DeLoss Dodds' statement, on November 29, 1986, that Fred Akers was being terminated. He then walked out of the meeting, pursued by reporters.
3	Times the Longhorns played in the Bluebonnet Bowl in this decade (1980, 1985, and 1987).
6	Yards rushing in the second half of the 1986 Arkansas game.
6	Years straight seasons finishing out of the top 20 (1984–1989).
30	Years between losing seasons (1956–1986).
38	Years between home losses to Baylor (1951–1989).
51	Years since UT had back-to-back losing seasons (1937/1938–1988/1989).
173	Points scored by Houston against UT from 1987 to 1989.
282	Points scored by kicker Jeff Ward during his career.
54,768	Average attendance at home games in 1989.

Archive

Home games in **bold**

1980 Record: 7–5 Coach: Fred Akers
Texas 23, Arkansas 17
Texas 35, Utah State 17
Texas 35, Oregon State 0

183

Texas 41, Rice 28
Texas 20, Oklahoma 13 (in Dallas)
SMU 20, Texas 6
Texas Tech 24, Texas 20
Texas 15, Houston 13
Texas 51, TCU 26
Baylor 16, Texas 0
Texas A&M 24, Texas 14
North Carolina 16, Texas 7 (Bluebonnet Bowl in Houston)

1981   Record: 10–1–1   Coach: Fred Akers
Texas 31, Rice 3
Texas 23, North Texas 10
Texas 14, Miami 7
Texas 34, Oklahoma 14 (in Dallas)
Arkansas 42, Texas 11
Texas 9, SMU 7
Texas 26, Texas Tech 9
Texas 14, Houston 14
Texas 31, TCU 15
Texas 34, Baylor 12
Texas 21, Texas A&M 13
Texas 14, Alabama 12 (Cotton Bowl in Dallas)

1982   Record: 9–3   Coach: Fred Akers
Texas 21, Utah 12
Texas 21, Missouri 0
Texas 34, Rice 7
Oklahoma 28, Texas 22 (in Dallas)
SMU 30, Texas 17
Texas 27, Texas Tech 0
Texas 50, Houston 0
Texas 38, TCU 21
Texas 31, Baylor 23
Texas 53, Texas A&M 16
Texas 33, Arkansas 7
North Carolina 26, Texas 10 (Sun Bowl in El Paso)

1983 Record: 11–1 (Southwest Conference champions) Coach: Fred Akers

Texas 20, Auburn 7
Texas 26, North Texas 6
Texas 42, Rice 6
Texas 28, Oklahoma 16 (in Dallas)
Texas 31, Arkansas 3
Texas 15, SMU 12 (in Irving)
Texas 20, Texas Tech 3
Texas 9, Houston 3
Texas 20, TCU 14
Texas 24, Baylor 21
Texas 45, Texas A&M 13
Georgia 10, Texas 9 (Cotton Bowl in Dallas)

1984 Record: 7–4–1 Coach: Fred Akers

Texas 35, Auburn 27
Texas 28, Penn State 3 (in East Rutherford, New Jersey)
Texas 38, Rice 13
Texas 15, Oklahoma 15 (in Dallas)
Texas 24, Arkansas 18
Texas 13, SMU 7
Texas 13, Texas Tech 10
Houston 29, Texas 15
Texas 44, TCU 23
Baylor 24, Texas 10
Texas A&M 37, Texas 12
Iowa 55, Texas 17 (Freedom Bowl in Anaheim, California)

1985 Record: 8–4 Coach: Fred Akers

Texas 21, Missouri 17
Texas 38, Stanford 34
Texas 44, Rice 16
Oklahoma 14, Texas 7 (in Dallas)
Texas 15, Arkansas 13
SMU 44, Texas 14
Texas 34, Texas Tech 21

185

Texas 34, Houston 24
Texas 20, TCU 0
Texas 17, Baylor 10
Texas A&M 42, Texas 10
Air Force 24, Texas 16 (Bluebonnet Bowl in Houston)

1986   Record: 5–6   Coach: Fred Akers
Stanford 31, Texas 20
Texas 27, Missouri 25
Texas 17, Rice 14
Oklahoma 47, Texas 12 (in Dallas)
Arkansas 21, Texas 14
Texas 27, SMU 24
Texas Tech 23, Texas 21
Texas 30, Houston 10
Texas 45, TCU 16
Baylor 18, Texas 13
Texas A&M 16, Texas 3

1987   Record: 7–5   Coach: David McWilliams
Auburn 31, Texas 3
Brigham Young 22, Texas 17
Texas 61, Oregon State 16
Texas 45, Rice 26
Oklahoma 44, Texas 9 (in Dallas)
Texas 16, Arkansas 14 (in Little Rock)
Texas 41, Texas Tech 27
Houston 60, Texas 40
Texas 24, TCU 21
Texas 34, Baylor 16
Texas A&M 20, Texas 13
Texas 32, Pittsburgh 27 (Bluebonnet Bowl in Houston)

1988   Record: 4–7   Coach: David McWilliams
Brigham Young 47, Texas 6
Texas 47, New Mexico 0
Texas 27, North Texas 24
Texas 20, Rice 13

186

Oklahoma 28, Texas 13 (in Dallas)
Arkansas 27, Texas 24
Texas Tech 33, Texas 32
Houston 66, Texas 15
Texas 30, TCU 21
Baylor 17, Texas 14
Texas A&M 28, Texas 24

1989 Record: 5–6 Coach: David McWilliams

Colorado 27, Texas 6
Texas 45, SMU 13
Penn State 16, Texas 12
Texas 31, Rice 30
Texas 28, Oklahoma 24 (in Dallas)
Texas 24, Arkansas 20
Texas Tech 24, Texas 17
Houston 47, Texas 9
Texas 31, TCU 17
Baylor 50, Texas 7
Texas A&M 21, Texas 10

Kenneth Sims

Defensive tackle Kenneth Sims came to UT in 1978 from the little town of Kosse. He was a raw recruit with poor technique, incapable of bench-pressing 170 pounds. Furthermore, Sims didn't play much his first two years because he was learning from guys like Bill Acker and Steve McMichael. By 1981, it was a different story. Sims was a dominant player who manhandled offensive linemen. He was a consensus all-American (despite missing the last few games with torn ligaments in his right ankle), won the Lombardi Award, and was chosen by New England as the first overall pick in the draft. But his pro career could only be called disappointing. Sims played 74 games in eight years with the Patriots, registering just 17 sacks. In April 1990, he showed up at the team's mini-camp out of shape, irking coaches and the front office. A few months later, Austin police arrested Sims and charged him with possession of cocaine. Although he had two years left on his contract, the Pats released him and he soon retired from the game.

20 Big Games

Texas 20, Oklahoma 13 / October 11, 1980 / Cotton Bowl (Dallas, Texas)
With four straight wins, the season shows considerable promise. The Horns are No. 3 as they head to Dallas to meet OU. J. C. Watts has the Sooners up by three with 10 minutes to play, but Donnie Little gets hot at the right time. He repeatedly follows center Mike Baab's blocks for effective quarterback draws. Two drives result in a TD, a field goal, and a UT victory. Akers is effusive in his praise of Little. Nevertheless, this game takes a toll on Texas as seven players are injured.

SMU 20, Texas 6 / October 25, 1980 / Memorial Stadium (Austin, Texas)
Now within one spot of No. 1, the Horns host SMU. Most of the players hurt against Oklahoma still can't go, but this game seems like a lock none-

theless. The Ponies are not used to playing in front of crowds of 73,535, and they have a freshman quarterback—Lance McElhenny—getting his first start. The fuzzy-cheeked McElhenny completes just one pass, but a fine pair of running backs is taking his handoffs: Craig James and Eric Dickerson. James has 146 yards, the Texas receivers manage to drop 11 passes, and the biggest upset of the 1980 season has happened. The Longhorns' season begins to unravel as they lose five of their last seven.

Arkansas 42, Texas 11 / October 17, 1981 / Razorback Stadium (Fayetteville, Arkansas)

Akers' Horns rise in the polls every week, culminating in the coveted No. 1 ranking after a thorough whipping of Oklahoma. Eric Holle and his mates are seen gang-tackling a poor Sooner on the cover of *Sports Illustrated*. On this rainy day in Fayetteville, it is a different story. The Longhorns must start seven drives from behind their own 10-yard line, and Rick McIvor tosses four interceptions in an embarrassing loss. Akers' alma mater shows him no pity.

Texas 14, Alabama 12 / January 1, 1982 / Cotton Bowl (Cotton Bowl in Dallas)

The Longhorns, representatives—but not champions—of the SWC, meet third-ranked Alabama in the Cotton Bowl. Bear Bryant has recently become the all-time winningest coach in college football history, and it appears that he is about to win again. The Crimson Tide is up by 10 early in the fourth quarter. Texas is facing third-and-10 at the 'Bama 30 when quarterback Robert Brewer, a former walk-on, scampers up the middle for a score. (His teammates will later mock his slowness afoot, but he got a very big TD.) Terry Orr wins the game with an 8-yard run in the last two minutes. When all the bowl games are played, the Longhorns trail only national champion Clemson.

SMU 30, Texas 17 / October 23, 1982 / Memorial Stadium (Austin, Texas)

The only reason the Horns played in the '82 Cotton Bowl is that SMU, with its 10–1 record, was on NCAA probation. Bobby Collins' team comes to Austin determined to extract a measure of revenge. This game, featuring more than the usual amount of woofing by muscular young men, is played out before 80,157 fans on a gorgeous Indian-summer day. Lance McElhenny's wobbly pass is deflected by Texas defensive back Jitter Fields into the hands of Bobby Leach, who takes off on a 79-yard TD jaunt. Eric Dickerson rushes for 118 yards, Craig James has a 46-yard touchdown reception, and the Pony Express rides. The Dallas media is out en masse, treating this win as one of SMU's biggest in decades.

Texas 33, Arkansas 7 / December 4, 1982 / Memorial Stadium (Austin, Texas)

After falling to SMU, Akers' team reels off victories over Texas Tech, Houston, TCU, Baylor, and Texas A&M. Still, sixth-ranked Arkansas is favored to win in Austin in the regular season finale. The Razorbacks are routed as Darryl Clark runs for 97 yards, and Robert Brewer and Herkie Walls connect on a 37-yard TD pass. Kiki DeAyala leads a strong defensive effort for the Longhorns. Three weeks later, they will lose to North Carolina in the Sun Bowl.

Texas 15, SMU 12 / October 22, 1983 / Texas Stadium (Irving, Texas)

The second-ranked Horns have flattened every opponent, only one of whom—Oklahoma—scores in double figures. This may be the best Texas team since Earl Campbell's senior year or the national title teams of 1969 and 1970, but the test comes against an equally talented bunch of SMU Mustangs, who are now playing home games at Texas Stadium. The Ponies have not lost in 21 games, and the competition gains extra heat with reports that UT has warned the NCAA about even more recruiting shenanigans by SMU's coaches and boosters. In a game Akers will describe as "an absolute street fight," Jeff Ward kicks field goals of 54 and 47 yards, and Todd Dodge comes off the bench to throw a fourth-quarter TD pass to Bill Boy Bryant. A valiant SMU comeback at the end falls a bit short as the 1983 Longhorns keep winning.

Texas 45, Texas A&M 13 / November 26, 1983 / Kyle Field (College Station, Texas)

For the 10th straight week, Texas is sitting up close to the top of the mountain at No. 2, behind Nebraska but definitely in the running for the national title. On a windy day in College Station, things start badly. The Aggies go up by 13, and their fans are calling on Reveille, the ghost of E. King Gill, and all things maroon. Widespread grumbling about the relatively weak UT offense comes to a halt after Rick McIvor replaces Rob Moerschell at quarterback and starts throwing touchdown passes right and left. All in all, it is a fine way to spend a Thanksgiving Day. The Horns are unbeaten and untied in the regular season for the second time in seven years.

Georgia 10, Texas 9 / January 1, 1984 / Cotton Bowl (Cotton Bowl in Dallas, Texas)

It's a game Texas players will be what-iffing for years to come. At least on paper, they appear to be a much better team than No. 7 Georgia. They drop five passes (one in the end zone), Jeff Ward misses two field goals, and Rick McIvor throws a pair of interceptions. Still, they lead by six points with less than five minutes to play. The Bulldogs punt from their own 34 and it goes to Craig Curry, who is in the game instead of the sure-handed Michael Feldt. Curry fumbles, and within three plays QB John Lastinger has high-tailed it into the end zone. Kevin Butler's extra point gives Georgia the winning margin. What makes it far more excruciating is that Nebraska will soon lose in the Orange Bowl, and just like that a national championship is missed.

Texas 35, Auburn 27 / September 15, 1984 / Memorial Stadium (Austin, Texas)

Despite losing a big and talented senior class, Akers' Horns open the season at No. 4. The first opponent is Auburn, with its dazzling running back, Bo Jackson. Todd Dodge makes his second career start, completes 15-of-24 with one TD through the air and one on the ground. Easily the most memorable play of the night comes when Jackson breaks through the UT line and sprints toward the end zone. But safety Jerry Gray has the angle and refuses to quit, running Jackson down after 53 yards on the southwest corner of the field. The Tigers' star has a separated shoulder and will miss the rest of the season—but he will be back in '85 to win the Heisman Trophy.

Texas 15, Oklahoma 15 / October 13, 1984 / Cotton Bowl (Dallas, Texas)

Impressive wins over Auburn and Penn State have catapulted Texas to No. 1 in the nation. That sets the table for a big game with the No. 3 Sooners. Their freshman linebacker, Brian Bosworth, has issued a variety of putdowns in the week before the game. On a dark, rainy day in Dallas, the Horns can only muster eight first downs and 170 yards of total offense, 58 of which is on a single run by Kevin Nelson. OU leads by three late when the most controversial call of the game happens. Texas is driving when safety Keith Stanberry intercepts a pass in the end zone but the refs say he is out of bounds. He, the Boz, and all persons wearing red howl with indignation—to no avail. Jeff Ward enters and hits a game-tying field goal. The Horns lose their top spot in the polls and will not be there again for two decades and counting.

Texas 15, Arkansas 13 / October 19, 1985 / Razorback Stadium (Fayetteville, Arkansas)

Because of a traffic jam, the bus carrying the team to Razorback Stadium arrives just 20 minutes before kickoff. The fans are ever so hospitable to their visitors from the Lone Star State. James Shibest has a 30-yard TD catch for the fourth-ranked Hogs, but the day belongs to Ward, UT's three-time all-SWC kicker. He boots five field goals, ranging from 33 to 55 yards. Linebacker Ty Allert has 13 unassisted tackles, and defensive back John Hagy recovers a fumble and intercepts a pass. The Horns are on the road again the next week, but they get whacked by SMU, 44–14.

Texas A&M 42, Texas 10 / November 28, 1985 / Kyle Field (College Station, Texas)

The Horns enter this game with a four-game winning streak and ranked 18th. But it turns out to be a nice 42nd birthday present for Aggies Coach Jackie Sherrill, as QB Kevin Murray leads the way in the most lopsided victory for A&M in a rivalry consisting of 92 games. The Horns help by turning the ball over six times. The kicking game is about all UT has, with Ward getting his 19th field goal of the season and John Teltschik averaging 51 yards on five punts. The Aggies will win in the Cotton Bowl, while Texas will fall to Air Force in the Bluebonnet Bowl. Rumors circulate about Akers' job security, as the Longhorns are about to begin a four-season swoon.

Texas 27, SMU 24 / October 25, 1986 / Memorial Stadium (Austin, Texas)

Having lost their first two home games of the 1986 season (to Stanford and Arkansas), the Horns appear to be blowing out SMU. Then, lo and behold, the Mustangs come back. The game is tied at 24, and just 16 seconds are on the clock when Akers turns to Jeff Ward. Calm as ever, he goes out and hits a 40-yard field goal. The 5' 10", 180-pound captain is hoisted by his brawnier teammates. Not lacking in confidence, he tells reporters after the game, "Give me a chance to beat you, and I will. That I promise you."

Texas Tech 23, Texas 21 / November 1, 1986 / Jones Stadium (Lubbock, Texas)

It's a foggy day on the South Plains. David McWilliams, a Longhorn since 1960, has traded in his orange and white for black and red. With 44,820 fans looking on, his Red Raiders are up by 16 points with seven minutes to go. Then scoring passes from Bret Stafford to Anthony Byerly and Tony Jones make it close. The Horns get the ball back and are driving, hoping to set up Jeff Ward for another last-second field goal. But Tech halts the drive at midfield. Stephen Braggs intercepts three passes, offsetting the two unsportsmanlike-conduct penalties by his defensive backfield mate John Hagy. The bell is tolling for Fred Akers.

Texas 16, Arkansas 14 / October 17, 1987 / War Memorial Stadium (Little Rock, Arkansas)

Coming off a demoralizing 44–9 loss to OU, the Horns need some self-respect. Nearly 55,000 fans at War Memorial Stadium see the Razorbacks on top with less than two minutes to play. Bret Stafford leads UT on an 11-play drive culminating in an 18-yard game-winner to Tony Jones. He holds onto the ball despite absorbing a pair of thunderous hits by Steve Atwater and Anthony Cooney. The little sophomore receiver is mobbed by his teammates in the end zone as Arkansas fans weep and moan. Their team might have won if Coach Ken Hatfield were not so averse to the pass; his Hogs complete one of four attempts for 10 yards.

Texas 24, TCU 21 / November 14, 1987 / Memorial Stadium (Austin, Texas)

The greatest game of Eric Metcalf's season—and there are many—comes at home against TCU. Metcalf has two TDs, gains 206 yards on 36 carries, returns kicks for 66 yards, and catches one pass. It's a one-man show unlike any UT fans have seen in years. Linebacker Lee Brockman returns an interception 43 yards for a touchdown, and the battle in the trenches goes to the Horns. The 21st straight victory in the Texas–TCU series does not come easy against Jim Wacker's Frogs.

Houston 66, Texas 15 / November 5, 1988 / Memorial Stadium (Austin, Texas)

On an otherwise beautiful sun-splashed day in central Texas, the Longhorns have one of the worst games ever. Jack Pardee's run-and-shoot offense registers a Southwest Conference–record seven touchdown passes, but it gets help from a weak UT secondary. Chuck Weatherspoon gains 218 yards on just 11 carries, and Andre Ware looks like the 1988 Heisman Trophy winner, but he will have to wait a year for that. It is the Horns' fourth straight loss, and few of the 69,600 fans remain at the stadium by the end.

Penn State 16, Texas 12 / September 30, 1989 / Memorial Stadium (Austin, Texas)

Joe Paterno brings his Nittany Lions to Austin for the first time. Starting at quarterback for UT is Mark Murdock, who is soon replaced by Peter Gardere, who is in turn replaced by Donovan Forbes. The first two quarterbacks rotate the rest of the way, but none of them look too impressive. And amazingly, the Longhorns are ahead with just over six minutes left. Deep in the UT end of the field, Bobby Lilljedahl is back to punt. Deep snapper Tal Elliott is destroyed by a Penn State defender, another of whom, Andre Collins, breaks through to block the kick. The ball is picked up and run in for a winning touchdown by Leonard Humphries. It is a most disheartening loss for the Horns. The next week, Elliott is dismissed from the team when it is learned that he and 20 teammates have been involved in betting on college and pro games.

Texas 28, Oklahoma 24 / October 14, 1989 / Cotton Bowl (Dallas, Texas)

Peter Gardere has been given the keys to the car, which is something between a Lamborghini and a Yugo. The redshirt freshman is cool, calm and collected in leading Texas to a late winning drive over the Sooners. A sellout crowd is in full-throated roar as he completes five straight passes, the last one a 25-yard scoring shot to Johnny Walker. Some of the UT seniors, who have never beaten OU, are in tears after winning one of the most dramatic games in this storied series. Peter the Great, as some are calling him, is no super athlete but he has the same intangibles as James Street and Robert Brewer. He will win another big one the next week against Arkansas in the hills.

All-Decade Team, Offense

Quarterback   Robert Brewer (1981–1982)
Back   A. J. "Jam" Jones (1978–1981)

193

Back	Eric Metcalf (1985–1988)
Lineman	Terry Tausch (1978–1981)
Lineman	Joe Shearin (1978–1981)
Lineman	Bryan Millard (1980–1982)
Lineman	Doug Dawson (1980–1983)
Lineman	Paul Jetton (1984–1987)
End	Herkie Walls (1979–1982)
End	Tony Jones (1986–1989)
Tight end	Lawrence Sampleton (1978–1981)
Punt/kick returner	Eric Metcalf (1985–1988)
Kicker	Jeff Ward (1983–1986)
Punter	John Teltschik (1982–1985)

All-Decade Team, Defense

Lineman	Kenneth Sims (1978–1981)
Lineman	Kiki DeAyala (1980–1982)
Lineman	Eric Holle (1980–1983)
Lineman	Tony Degrate (1982–1984)
Linebacker	Jeff Leiding (1980–1983)
Linebacker	Ty Allert (1982–1985)
Linebacker	Britt Hager (1984, 1985, 1987, 1988)
Defensive back	Mossy Cade (1980–1983)
Defensive back	Jerry Gray (1981–1984)
Defensive back	Stephen Braggs (1983–1986)
Defensive back	John Hagy (1984–1987)

Q & A

Q. As UT football moved into the 1980s, how did the campus and student body look?

A. There were then 130 buildings on 316 acres, and 46,000 students from every state and 90 countries.

Q. What freshman linebacker got the 1980 Arkansas game off to a rousing start by hurling himself kamikaze-style into the Razorbacks' return man on the opening kickoff?

A. Jeff Leiding, who suffered a severely pinched nerve on that play and had to miss the next several games.

194

Q. This native of Youngstown, Ohio, led the Longhorns in rushing four straight years (1978–1981), but he never made all-conference. Identify him.

A. A. J. "Jam" Jones, so nicknamed to distinguish him from Johnny "Lam" Jones and Johnny "Ham" Jones. In his sophomore season, Jam gained 918 yards and scored 10 touchdowns.

Q. Donnie Little won lasting fame as UT's first black quarterback. How did he do against Rice in 1980?

A. He threw for a school-record 306 yards and had long TD passes to Jam Jones and Lawrence Sampleton.

Q. Who led a late goal-line stand to preserve Texas' victory over Houston in 1980?

A. A couple of Kenneths—Sims and McCune.

Q. What play from the 1980 Bluebonnet Bowl would Herkie Walls like to forget?

A. Probably the time he was run down from behind by North Carolina linebacker Lawrence Taylor.

Q. What UT record does Kenneth Sims still hold?

A. That of most forced fumbles (15).

Q. Fred Akers made a quarterback change prior to the 1981 season. Who did it involve, and why did he make the switch?

A. Donnie Little volunteered to become a receiver, thinking he might better impress pro scouts there. He also knew that Rick McIvor, a strong-armed 6' 4" junior was ready to go. Little never played a down in the NFL, whereas McIvor was a sub with the St. Louis Cardinals for three seasons.

Q. Against what team did McIvor throw for 192 yards in a 14–7 victory in 1981?

A. Miami, which was led by quarterback Jim Kelly. The Hurricanes were on the rise and would win five national titles between 1983 and 2001.

Q. Texas beat OU, 34–14, in 1981. How many passes did the Sooners complete that day in Dallas?

A. They threw eight and completed none.

Q. This Mexican-born kicker had three field goals (one from 52 yards out) in a 9–7 defeat of SMU in 1981. Identify him.

A. Raul Allegre, who went on to a nine-year career with the Baltimore/Indianapolis Colts, New York Giants, and New York Jets. He now works as a broadcaster of Spanish-language NFL games.

Q. McIvor had thrown two interceptions during the first half against Houston at the Astrodome in 1981. With his team trailing by 14, Akers considered moving Little back under center. His assistants urged him to give a former walk-on a chance. Who was he, and how did the game turn out?

A. He was Robert Brewer, son of Charley Brewer, a Longhorns quarterback from the mid-1950s. Brewer directed the team to a tie, and the job was his for the next season and a half.

Q. Three members of the UT secondary were responsible for six interceptions of Baylor's Jay Jeffrey in 1981. Who were they?

A. Jitter Fields, Craig Curry, and Mossy Cade.

Q. Cade later got in some trouble with the law. What was it?

A. In 1986, he was convicted of second-degree rape and served 15 months in prison.

Q. What sophomore running back gained 178 yards as Texas snapped a two-game losing streak to A&M in 1981?

A. John Walker.

Q. He was an all-America offensive lineman in 1981, played seven years with the Minnesota Vikings, and won a Super Bowl with the San Francisco 49ers. Who was he?

A. Terry Tausch.

Q. What kind of receiving numbers did Herkie Walls have in the 1982 season?

A. Walls caught 25 passes, averaging almost 29 yards for each.

Q. The Longhorns had not shut out an opponent in 23 games until early in the 1982 season. Who was the victim?

A. They skunked Missouri, 21–0. Walls had an 80-yard end-around to help declaw the Tigers.

Q. This native of Philadelphia, Mississippi, had been the subject of a huge recruiting war in 1981, eventually choosing to pursue higher education at Oklahoma. He also made noise by charging that UT coaches bought him a pair of fancy cowboy boots during his visit to Austin. Who was he?

A. Marcus Dupree, who had a long touchdown run against the Horns in Dallas in 1982.

Q. What was running back Darryl Clark's best game with the Longhorns?

A. On November 20, 1982, he ran for 202 yards in a defeat of Baylor.

Q. Robert Brewer finished the '82 season with school records for touchdowns (12), passing attempts (193), and yardage (1,415). But he suffered a broken thumb in the week before the Sun Bowl. Who would replace him?

A. Todd Dodge. But he had minimal success against the victorious UNC Tar Heels, hitting 6-of-22 passes. Dodge is now the head coach at North Texas.

Q. Who holds the team record for most sacks, both in a season and in a career?

A. Kiki DeAyala had 22.5 in 1982 and 40.5 for his career.

Q. The 1983 Texas team was loaded with talent. How can that statement be quantified?

A. They lost just one game (by a single point), and they had four all-Americans (Doug Dawson, Jeff Leiding, Jerry Gray, and Mossy Cade) and nine all-SWC players (Dawson, Leiding, Gray, Cade, Fred Acorn, Tony Degrate, Eric Holle, Mike Reuther, and Jeff Ward). No fewer than 21 players off that team reported to NFL camps in the summer of 1983.

Q. How did Doug Dawson do in the pros?

A. He was good enough to last 12 seasons with the Cardinals, Oilers, and Browns.

Q. This freshman tailback stood 6' 4", weighed 228 pounds, and was a mirror image of Eric Dickerson. After a sensational 67-yard run against OU in 1983, Burnt Orange Nation was ready to award him four straight Heismans. Of whom do we speak?

A. Edwin Simmons. But he suffered the first of several injuries the next week against Arkansas and was never the same, although he remained on the team through 1986. Shortly before the Oklahoma game in his senior year, he would be involved in an incident that seems to be remembered more than anything he ever did on a football field. Simmons was arrested by the police, naked and in a daze in the backyard of a north Austin home.

Q. The '83 Horns, undefeated in the regular season, may have lost their focus and momentum in the four weeks before the Cotton Bowl. What are two possible reasons for this?

A. Safety Richard Peavy suffered a knee injury against A&M and underwent surgery. And Akers was strongly rumored to be going to Arkansas, although the job was given to another ex-Razorback, Ken Hatfield.

Q. What players combined on an 84-yard TD pass in a 28–3 defeat of Penn State at the New Jersey Meadowlands in early 1984?

A. Todd Dodge threw it, and tight end William Harris caught it and ran with it.

Q. After tying Oklahoma in the fourth game of the 1984 season, the Long-horns dropped out of the No. 1 spot. When would they be back there?

A. It has not happened again in the ensuing 23 years, even in the national championship season of 2005.

Q. *An extracurricular incident took place late in the 1984 season that alienated team members, alumni, and media. What was it?*

A. Linebacker Tony Edwards and four teammates were involved in a brawl in the wee hours at an Austin nightclub. Edwards was charged with assaulting a police officer, which was later reduced to resisting arrest. There may not be a direct cause-and-effect relationship, but the Horns then proceeded to lose to Baylor, Texas A&M, and Iowa in the Freedom Bowl.

Q. *How in the world did the Hawkeyes beat Texas so badly (55–17) in the Freedom Bowl?*

A. First, it took three votes before the players agreed to participate in that now-defunct bowl game, so there was not much enthusiasm to begin with. QB Chuck Long threw five touchdown passes, and the UT offense and defense were equally inept. The Freedom Bowl loss hurt recruiting efforts and stimulated the fire-Akers crowd.

Q. *He followed in the footsteps of Kenny Sims, winning the 1984 Lombardi Award. Who was this native of Snyder, Texas?*

A. Tony Degrate. Why his pro career fizzled is a mystery. Chosen in the fifth round by the Cincinnati Bengals, he was cut before training camp was over.

Q. *A sophomore quarterback had a 74-yard TD run against Stanford in 1985. Who was he?*

A. Bret Stafford.

Q. *Most people would say he is the finest defensive back UT has ever had. Name him.*

A. Jerry Gray, who had been a quarterback in high school in Lubbock. Equipped with good size and 4.25 speed in the 40, he turned into a two-time all-American. He intercepted 16 passes and made 297 tackles during his time with the Longhorns. A first-round pick by the Los Angeles Rams, he played with them, the Houston Oilers, and the Tampa Bay Bucs. Gray, now an assistant coach with the Washington Redskins, has been mentioned as a some-day replacement for Mack Brown at UT.

Eric Metcalf

Terry Metcalf had been quite a running back and kick returner in the 1970s with the St. Louis Cardinals and Washington Redskins, so when his son started playing football the comparisons were inescapable. Recruited out of a Virginia prep school in 1985, Eric Metcalf surely made his dad proud. In four years with the Longhorns, he was thrice all-conference and compiled 5,705 yards of total offense. As a runner, receiver, and kick returner, he was superlative; he also threw the halfback pass now and then. Not big at 5' 9" and 170 pounds, he was SWC offensive player of the year in 1987, and readers of the *Austin American-Statesman* voted him as UT's offensive player of the decade.

But Metcalf was on some mediocre teams during his four years at Texas. And he had essentially the same problem in the pros. A first-round pick of the Cleveland Browns in 1989, he also played in Atlanta, San Diego, Arizona, Carolina, and Green Bay. During those 14 seasons, his teams made the playoffs just twice. Still, Metcalf put up big numbers, finishing with 17,230 total yards and 55 touchdowns.

Q. How did Edwin Simmons do against Baylor in 1985?

A. He carried 22 times for 94 yards and one touchdown. No longer the spectacular player he was in early 1983, Simmons had become a workhorse.

Q. The Horns had one all-American in 1985. Name him.

A. Center Gene Chilton, known to his teammates as "Gene, Gene, the Coke machine" because of his ample girth.

Q. The 1986 season got off to a bad start as tight end William Harris flunked out, injuries befell linebackers Britt Hager and Bobby Duncum, center Carter Hill, and defensive backs Richard Peavy and Eric Jeffries, and Oklahoma and Texas A&M—among others—beat UT. Players were found to be scalping their complimentary tickets, and most of all the question of whether Fred Akers would be fired dominated the dialogue. How did Austin American-Statesman *writer John Maher characterize that season?*

A. He likened it to the Bataan death march.

Q. What was new at Memorial Stadium in 1986?

A. Neuhaus–Royal Athletic Center was built at the south end, where tennis courts had long stood. This $7 million, 38,000-square-foot facility was first and foremost a modern locker room. But it also had lecture rooms, coaches' offices, a world-class weight-training facility, a large rehabilitation pool, and a laundry area. It originally featured a 70-yard football field on top, but that soon fell into disuse.

Q. He was the third former UT player—behind Clyde Littlefield and Ed Price—to become head coach. Identify him.

A. David McWilliams, a native of Cleburne, who had been a tri-captain on the 1963 national championship team. An assistant under both Royal and Akers from 1970 to 1985, he got the top job at Texas Tech the next year. The Red Raiders had won just four games in 1985, but they won seven in 1986 with McWilliams and played in a minor bowl. The folks in Lubbock loved him, but they were less than pleased when DeLoss Dodds came to town, sweet-talked him, and got him to return to Austin to replace Akers. He would be on the hot seat for five years.

Q. There was an unwritten rule in the Southwest Conference that head coaches did not move from one school to another, as David McWilliams did in leaving Texas Tech for UT. When was the last time that happened?

A. Back in 1928, when Matty Bell left TCU to go to Texas A&M. Francis Schmidt of Arkansas then took Bell's place in Fort Worth.

Q. What then happened to Akers?

A. He was in the unemployment line for just 10 days. Purdue was in need of a coach, and he got the job. Akers strove to succeed with the Boilermakers, but they were 12–31–1 in four seasons. Thus ended his coaching career, although he continued to apply at schools like TCU, Baylor, and Rice.

Q. There was euphoria among the Longhorns and their fans at McWilliams' hiring. How long did it last?

A. Until the first game of the 1987 season, a 31–3 loss to Auburn.

Q. The Horns lost to Houston, 60–40, in the Dome on November 7, 1987. What dubious record did Stafford and his backup Shannon Kelley set in the process?

A. The two quarterbacks combined to have four interceptions returned for touchdowns—something no other major college team had ever done before.

Q. Who led the '87 Longhorns in tackles?

A. Linebacker Britt Hager, with 187. He also had a key stop on Craig "Ironhead" Hayward in Texas' defeat of Pittsburgh in the Bluebonnet Bowl.

Q. The 1988 season opener was even worse than the year before. What happened?

A. Favorites to win the SWC, the Horns traveled to Provo, Utah, and suffered a 47–6 defeat at the hands of BYU. They were missing Eric Metcalf, who had to sit out after having committed an NCAA violation; in the summer, he enjoyed room and board at Jester Dormitory but did not attend school.

Q. SMU was playing football again in 1989 after the NCAA administered the death penalty. How did the Longhorns do against them at tiny Ownby Stadium?

A. It was close at the half, but Texas pulled away to a 45–13 win.

Q. What was the rather controversial, conclusive play of the 1989 Rice game?

A. The Owls were ahead with just over four minutes left. On fourth down from the Rice 4 yard line, Peter Gardere sprinted right, took hits from two Rice defenders and—according to the officials—managed to touch the ball to the pylon for the TD. Rice Coach Fred Goldsmith was gentlemanly about it, but Texas seemed to have benefited from "home cooking."

Q. A 50–7 loss to Baylor at home on November 25, 1989, was pretty awful. How did cornerback Mark Berry describe it?

A. "An old-fashioned butt-whipping." McWilliams conceded his team essentially gave up in this loss to the Bears, which left a lot of people concerned about the direction of the program.

CHAPTER 11
1990–1999

Ricky Williams sings "The Eyes of Texas" along
with 83,687 fans after breaking Tony Dorsett's
career rushing record. The Longhorns beat Texas
A&M that day, 26–24.
(Photo courtesy of the University of Texas.)

The problems with the Southwest Conference had been growing and festering for years. Its main weakness, according to some, was geographical limitation, eight of its nine members being located within Texas. The SWC's defenders, of whom there were many, insisted that Texas was not a typical state and that the conference would eventually return to a position of preeminence.

Such loyalty and optimism were admirable, but they would not carry the day. The smaller and weaker schools could only stand by and watch what the big boys—Texas and Texas A&M—would do. If a breakup were to happen, there would be a lot of hurt feelings and yet it was coming. Arkansas left for the Southeastern Conference after the 1992 season, and some observers thought the Razorbacks were being used as bait to bring UT and A&M there as well. It was a bewildering time, as rumors raged about every conceivable realignment possibility. One thing was certain: The Longhorns and Aggies were in demand.

Where would they go? The SEC, the Big Eight, the Big 10, and the Pac-10 were all possibilities and each had its drawbacks. Finally, the deal came down in 1993 when Texas, Texas A&M, Texas Tech, and Baylor merged with the Big Eight, thus creating the Big 12 Conference (beginning in 1996). Some pundits wondered why Baylor was in and TCU was out, especially given the Horned Frogs' subsequent success as a mid-major football power. It may be pertinent that Texas Governor Ann Richards and Lieutenant Governor Bob Bullock were Baylor grads, and the political damage would be limited by including the Bears. The lesser schools of the former SWC scattered to various leagues such as Conference USA, the Western Athletic Conference, and Mountain West Conference. The shifting and struggling for survival are still going on.

UT athletic director DeLoss Dodds was a key player in the formation of the Big 12. Among other things, he insisted on adherence to higher academic standards than that to which some of the former Big Eight schools were accustomed. Headquarters of the Big 12 were to be in Dallas, which some people in Norman, Boulder, Lincoln, and elsewhere considered indicative. Kansas basketball coach Roy Williams once muttered, "Why don't we just call it the Big Texas and be done with it?" But the fact remains that the SWC had jettisoned its four weak sisters, whereas the Big Eight remained intact. Texas, with the largest endowment of any Big 12 school, also had the most students and alumni, and the largest athletic budget. As in the old SWC, it was first among equals.

The aforementioned issues proved, once again, the old adage that nothing stays the same. The 1990s saw plenty of changes at the Longhorns' home field. First, Dodds was commencing a huge fundraising campaign and he chose that time to rename the stadium. The Athletics Council, President Robert Berdahl, and the Board of Regents were also in favor of honoring Darrell Royal in this way. It mattered not that a similar effort to honor Dana X. Bible had been vetoed less than a decade earlier or that the military veterans to whom the stadium had been dedicated thrice would be forgotten or that the university had a rule that only persons deceased more than five years could be so honored or—most of all—that the proposal was overwhelmingly unpopular. Some people of a socially conscious inclination viewed Royal as undeserving because he had moved with the speed of a turtle in integrating the football program. The decision and the process by which it was made touched a lot of nerves. But it was presented as a *fait accompli* just before the 1996 season began.

There was more naming to be done. Joe Jamail had earned a bachelor's degree from UT in 1950 and a law degree three years later. A brilliant and effective attorney, Jamail was known as the "king of torts." Most famously, he had represented Pennzoil in a case against Texaco in 1985, winning and earning a contingency fee of $335 million. Jamail had been generous to his alma mater and was already recognized by having his name on the UT swim center and the law school library. Far more prominent, though, was Dodds' decision to name the football field after him. Since 1997, the Longhorns have played at Joe Jamail Field at Darrell K Royal-Texas Memorial Stadium. Seven years later, eight-foot-tall bronze statues of Royal and Jamail were erected at the southeast corner of the stadium. Finally, East Campus Drive, which ran between the stadium and the LBJ Library, became Robert Dedman Drive, to honor another of the university's big donors.

In the final years of the 1990s, other tangible changes were made. The stadium's artificial turf was pulled up and replaced with natural grass; a big scoreboard (known as the "Jumbotron") was erected in the south end; 14 luxury boxes were built under the west-side upper deck; the underside of virtually the entire stadium was remodeled; a new visitors' locker room was built; a 5,000-seat east-side upper deck was built, which included 52 luxury boxes and a 13,000-square-foot private club; the track was removed and 20,000-seat Mike Myers Track and Soccer Stadium was built to the east; and the field was lowered seven feet to accommodate new front-row and field-level seats on the east and west sides. Seating capacity was raised to 80,092, although crowds in excess of that are not uncommon. The price tag was roughly $90 million.

By the Numbers

3 Interceptions by UT linebacker Aaron Humphrey against Rutgers in 1997.

4 Game losing streak (Missouri, Colorado, Baylor, and Texas Tech) in the 1997 season.

5 Years added to the coaching contract of David McWilliams after Texas' successful 1990 season.

$10 Scalpers' price for 50-yard line seats half an hour before the 1994 UT–Houston game at Memorial Stadium.

19 Tackles by linebacker Winfred Tubbs against TCU in 1993.

31 Straight games A&M had won at home until a 16–6 loss to Texas in 1995.

34 Years separating Texas' losses to TCU in Fort Worth (1958–1992).

44 Carries by Ricky Williams against Texas A&M in 1998.

90 Games between shutouts of other teams (TCU in 1991, Baylor in 1999).

317 Yards given up to Colorado running back Rashaan Salaam in 1994.

397 Yards passing by James Brown against Texas Tech in 1997, a school record.

678 Yards in consecutive games (Rice and Iowa State) for Ricky Williams in 1998.

6,279 Yards gained in Williams' UT career.

$3 million Contract awarded to John Mackovic to cover the 1996–2000 seasons.

Archive

Home games in **bold**

1990 Record: 10–2 (Southwest Conference champions)
Coach: David McWilliams

Texas 17, Penn State 13

Colorado 29, Texas 22

Texas 26, Rice 10

Texas 14, Oklahoma 13 (in Dallas)

Texas 49, Arkansas 17

Texas 52, SMU 3

Texas 41, Texas Tech 22
Texas 45, Houston 24
Texas 38, TCU 10
Texas 23, Baylor 13
Texas 28, Texas A&M 27
Miami 46, Texas 3 (Cotton Bowl in Dallas)

1991 Record: 5–6 Coach: David McWilliams
Mississippi State 13, Texas 6
Auburn 14, Texas 10
Texas 28, Rice 7
Texas 10, Oklahoma 7 (in Dallas)
Arkansas 14, Texas 13
Texas 34, SMU 0
Texas 23, Texas Tech 14
Houston 23, Texas 14
Texas 32, TCU 0
Baylor 21, Texas 11
Texas A&M 31, Texas 14

1992 Record: 6–5 Coach: John Mackovic
Mississippi State 28, Texas 10
Syracuse 31, Texas 21
Texas 33, North Texas 15
Texas 23, Rice 21
Texas 34, Oklahoma 24 (in Dallas)
Texas 45, Houston 38
Texas 44, Texas Tech 33
TCU 23, Texas 14
Texas 35, SMU 14
Baylor 21, Texas 20
Texas A&M 34, Texas 13

1993 Record: 5–5–1 Coach: John Mackovic
Colorado 36, Texas 14
Texas 21, Syracuse 21
Louisville 41, Texas 10

207

Texas 55, Rice 38
Oklahoma 38, Texas 17 (in Dallas)
Texas 37, SMU 10 (in San Antonio)
Texas Tech 31, Texas 22
Texas 34, Houston 16
Texas 24, TCU 3
Texas 38, Baylor 17
Texas A&M 18, Texas 9

1994 Record: 8–4 (Southwest Conference co-champions)
Coach: John Mackovic

Texas 30, Pittsburgh 28
Texas 30, Louisville 16
Texas 34, TCU 18
Colorado 34, Texas 31
Texas 17, Oklahoma 10 (in Dallas)
Rice 19, Texas 17
Texas 42, SMU 20
Texas Tech 33, Texas 9
Texas A&M 34, Texas 10
Texas 48, Houston 13
Texas 63, Baylor 35
Texas 35, North Carolina 31 (Sun Bowl in El Paso)

1995 Record: 10–2–1 (Southwest Conference champions)
Coach: John Mackovic

Texas 38, Hawaii 17
Texas 38, Pittsburgh 27
Notre Dame 55, Texas 27
Texas 35, SMU 10
Texas 37, Rice 13
Texas 24, Oklahoma 24 (in Dallas)
Texas 17, Virginia 16
Texas 48, Texas Tech 7
Texas 52, Houston 20
Texas 27, TCU 19
Texas 21, Baylor 13

Texas 16, Texas A&M 6
Virginia Tech 28, Texas 10 (Sugar Bowl in New Orleans, Louisiana)

1996 Record: 8–5 (Big 12 champions)
Coach: John Mackovic
Texas 40, Missouri 10
Texas 41, New Mexico State 7
Notre Dame 27, Texas 24
Virginia 37, Texas 13
Texas 71, Oklahoma State 14
Oklahoma 30, Texas 27 (in Dallas)
Colorado 28, Texas 24
Texas 28, Baylor 23
Texas 38, Texas Tech 32
Texas 38, Kansas 17
Texas 51, Texas A&M 15
Texas 37, Nebraska 27 (Big 12 championship game in St. Louis, Missouri)
Penn State 38, Texas 15 (Fiesta Bowl in Tempe, Arizona)

1997 Record: 4–7 Coach: John Mackovic
Texas 48, Rutgers 14
UCLA 66, Texas 3
Texas 38, Rice 31
Oklahoma State 42, Texas 16
Texas 27, Oklahoma 24 (in Dallas)
Missouri 37, Texas 29
Colorado 47, Texas 30
Baylor 23, Texas 21
Texas Tech 24, Texas 10
Texas 45, Kansas 31
Texas A&M 27, Texas 16

1998 Record: 9–3 Coach: Mack Brown
Texas 66, New Mexico State 36
UCLA 49, Texas 31
Kansas State 48, Texas 7
Texas 59, Rice 21

209

John Mackovic

Like a lot of ambitious coaches, John Mackovic had a nomadic career. He grew up in Ohio and despite weighing just 160 pounds, won a football scholarship at Wake Forest. A quarterback there, Mackovic graduated in 1964 and then coached at Miami of Ohio, Army, San Jose State, Arizona, and Purdue. His first head coaching job was back at his alma mater, where he stayed for three years. He helped Tom Landry with the Dallas Cowboys for a couple of seasons before getting hired to run the Kansas City Chiefs from 1983 to 1986. Fired after four years, he then took the job at the University of Illinois, serving also as athletic director.

That's where he was when DeLoss Dodds found himself in need of a man to replace David McWilliams. Mackovic was an innovator of the passing game and a brilliant tactician who would recruit on a national level. Given his vast experience in college and pro ball, hopes were high when he was presented in Austin and gave his first "Hook 'em, Horns" sign. Mackovic's six-year stint at UT was marked by both success and failure. Some locals considered him aloof and condescending, and his taste for fine wine became the subject of mockery. Mackovic lost his job after the 1997 season, but he soon found another one, at the University of Arizona. His experience in Tucson was nothing short of disastrous as the players organized a revolt. Mackovic apologized for his imperfections and vowed to try harder to get along. Early in the 2003 season, however, he was cut loose.

Texas 54, Iowa State 33
Texas 34, Oklahoma 3 (in Dallas)
Texas 30, Baylor 20
Texas 20, Nebraska 16
Texas 37, Oklahoma State 34
Texas Tech 42, Texas 35
Texas 26, Texas A&M 24
Texas 38, Mississippi State 11 (Cotton Bowl in Dallas)

1999   Record: 9–5 (Big 12 South champions) Coach: Mack Brown

North Carolina State 23, Texas 20
Texas 69, Stanford 17
Texas 38, Rutgers 21
Texas 18, Rice 13
Texas 62, Baylor 0
Kansas State 35, Texas 17
Texas 38, Oklahoma 28 (in Dallas)
Texas 24, Nebraska 20
Texas 44, Iowa State 41
Texas 34, Oklahoma State 21
Texas 58, Texas Tech 7
Texas A&M 20, Texas 16
Nebraska 22, Texas 6 (Big 12 championship game in San Antonio)
Arkansas 27, Texas 6 (Cotton Bowl in Dallas)

20 Big Games

Texas 45, Houston 24 / November 10, 1990 / Memorial Stadium (Austin, Texas)

Thirteen losses in the past two seasons have done considerable damage to UT's proud football legacy. And no team has been rougher on the Longhorns than Houston. The third-ranked Cougars have a coach, John Jenkins, who boasts that his offense is "unstoppable." Texas fans fear yet another trip to the woodshed, but not on this night. More than 82,000 of them see the Texas defense blitz UH quarterback David Klingler (four interceptions) repeatedly and hold running back Chuck Weatherspoon to 50 yards rushing. Peter Gardere completes 20-of-28 passes and looks more like a Heisman candidate than Klingler. After the game, Jenkins strikes an unaccustomed humble pose, saying he feels like Jim Bowie and Davy Crockett at the Alamo.

Miami 46, Texas 3 / January 1, 1991 / Cotton Bowl (Cotton Bowl in Dallas, Texas)

The Cotton Bowl Classic once seemed like a birthright for the Longhorns, but they have not been in the venerable stadium on New Year's Day for seven years. Ranked third, they are facing defending national champ Miami. Dennis Erickson's team has lost two games and is not happy to be playing in a "minor" bowl. The tone is set on the opening kickoff when Chris Samuels is knocked woozy and the UM players taunt him and dance. Texas quarterbacks are sacked eight times. The Hurricanes have too much speed and attitude for the Longhorns, who by halftime look like they want it to be over with. Miami, playing its outlaw image to the hilt, has 202 yards in penalties, and its players issue not a word of apology after the game. Writers from both Dallas newspapers blister Miami for its behavior.

Texas 10, Oklahoma 7 / October 12, 1991 / Cotton Bowl (Dallas, Texas)

In a maddening up-and-down year, the biggest "up" comes against Gary Gibbs' sixth-ranked Sooners in Big D. Texas trails in the fourth quarter until James Patton hits OU running back Mike McKinley. He fumbles, and Bubba Jacques scoops it up and races 30 yards for the winning score. Texas fans on one end of the Cotton Bowl have Red River bragging rights for the third straight year, and their counterparts on the other end are somber and stunned. The ecstasy doesn't last long because UT falls the next week to the Arkansas Razorbacks before they head to the Southeastern Conference.

Texas A&M 31, Texas 14 / November 28, 1991 / Kyle Field (College Station, Texas)

The Longhorns, losers of two of their last three games, renew their ancient rivalry with the 10th-ranked Ags. But it gets off to a sour start when, on the first play from scrimmage, Gardere throws a screen pass that A&M linebacker Marcus Buckley takes back for a TD. The game is iced in the third quarter when Kelly McClanahan punts to Kevin Smith, who breezes through UT defenders for a 73-yard score. Texas, which had spoken of this game as an opportunity to salvage a disappointing season, has no choice but to concede that the better team won. The Aggies are off to the Cotton Bowl, whereas the Horns can only lick their wounds. Five days later comes the news that McWilliams has resigned under pressure.

Syracuse 31, Texas 21 / September 12, 1992 / Carrier Dome (Syracuse, New York)

The 100th season of Texas football has begun poorly. A loss to Mississippi State at home is followed by another to No. 9 Syracuse in the din of the Carrier Dome. Peter Gardere connects with freshman Lovell Pinkney on a 73-yard strike to put the Horns up in the third quarter. The Orangemen are unfazed, however. Quarterback Marvin Graves, operating superbly as both an option specialist and a dropback passer, leads his team to two touchdowns and a field goal to ice the victory. Syracuse's most explosive weapon, Qadry Ismail, makes a diving 58-yard grab in the late minutes to help overcome a stubborn Texas defense.

Texas 34, Oklahoma 24 / October 10, 1992 / Cotton Bowl (Dallas, Texas)

Peter Gardere, often criticized for his limitations, is nevertheless the only Texas quarterback to have beaten OU three times. He has a chance to make it four against the No. 16 Sooners before a sellout crowd at the Cotton Bowl. The key play happens in the second quarter when Gardere avoids a blitz, gets a block from Adrian Walker, and throws a 31-yard touchdown pass to tight end Jason Burleson. After the game is over, Coach Gary Gibbs is doused with beer thrown by OU fans sick of losing to the Longhorns.

Texas 21, Syracuse 21 / September 18, 1993 / Memorial Stadium (Austin, Texas)

Marvin Graves, a Heisman Trophy hopeful for 1993, should have known better. In the week before No. 6 Syracuse is to face UT in Austin, he is seen on local television saying the Orangemen need to blow out the Longhorns in order to move up in the polls. He hears about it often from Tony Brackens, Winfred Tubbs, and other Texas defenders in a tie that feels more like a victory to the 65,897 fans who watch in 95° heat. Mike Adams has one of the finest days of his career—a 54-yard punt-return touchdown and an 80-yard kickoff return to set up another score. With eight seconds left, Syracuse can still win the game but Pat O'Neill's 33-yard field goal attempt is wide right.

Louisville 41, Texas 10 / September 25, 1993 / Cardinal Stadium (Louisville, Kentucky)

The Longhorns journey to the Bluegrass State for an intersectional game that turns into a defeat of surprising proportions. On a soggy afternoon at Cardinal Stadium, Jeff Brohm hits Ralph Dawkins for an 80-yard TD on the second play from scrimmage. The Cards are up, 24–0, at the half and the game is as good as over. Neither Shea Morenz nor Chad Lucas can get much done at quarterback. UT's high-strung receivers, Lovell Pinkney and Mike Adams, grumble about not getting enough balls thrown their way. In a season that has started with one tie and two losses, John Mackovic philosophizes in the locker room and vows to right the ship.

Texas 30, Pittsburgh 28 / September 3, 1994 / Pitt Stadium (Pittsburgh, Pennsylvania)

The 1994 season begins far from home, in a cavernous stadium that has seen better days. The dominant player is without doubt Pittsburgh running back Curtis Martin, who carries 28 times for 251 yards—the most UT has ever given up. From 50 yards out, freshman kicker Phil Dawson boots the first of many field goals in his career. The game has a dramatic finish as the Panthers score with 36 seconds left. Texas puts eight defenders on the line of scrimmage, daring Pitt to run Martin again for a two-point conversion that will tie it. Coach Johnny Majors chooses to use him as a decoy, QB Sean Fitzgerald misfires, and the Horns escape with a close win.

Colorado 34, Texas 31 / October 1, 1994 / Memorial Stadium (Austin, Texas)

A sellout crowd witnesses a memorable game between future members of the Big 12. The Buffaloes' Rashaan Salaam solidifies his claim on the 1994 Heisman Trophy by running for 317 yards on 35 carries. CU leads by 10 in the fourth quarter before Shea Morenz and Eric Jackson combine on a 67-yard TD pass, and Dawson hits from 47 yards out. Colorado quarterback Kordell Stewart leads an 83-yard drive capped by Neil Voskeritchian's field goal with just four seconds left. Coaching can be a dangerous profession, as John Mackovic finds out early in the second half. Two of his players are pursuing Salaam when they crash into him on the sidelines. Mackovic goes flying, gets a gash on his chin, and suffers a concussion. He will later assert that the sideline collision against CU gave him some kind of mental clarity that he lacked before, making him a better coach.

Texas 38, Hawaii 17 / September 2, 1995 / Aloha Stadium (Honolulu, Hawaii)

The Longhorns, with an influx of offensive and defensive talent, are trying to resurrect their standing as a national power, which has been dormant for most of a decade. And what better place to start than in the land of sand and surf? The game is well in hand midway through the third quarter when a husky freshman running back, wearing No. 11, takes a handoff from QB James Brown, stumbles slightly at the line of scrimmage, eludes three Hawaii defenders, and sprints 65 yards to the end zone. It is the first of 75 touchdowns for Ricky Williams in his illustrious UT career.

Texas 17, Virginia 16 / October 21, 1995 / Memorial Stadium (Austin, Texas)

A crowd of 70,427—including Governor George Bush—is on hand as Texas wins for the 700th time in its history. Actually, it appears that the No. 14 Cavaliers will take a two-point victory back to Charlottesville largely because UT kicker Phil Dawson has missed two field goals. James Brown puts together a 47-yard drive that includes two critical fourth-down plays, giving Dawson a chance to redeem himself. A 20-mph wind is blowing in his face when he puts instep to ball, which obediently splits the goalposts 50 yards away as time expires. Tiki Barber gains 123 yards on the ground for UVa, and Williams has 139 for Texas.

Virginia Tech 28, Texas 10 / December 31, 1995 / Superdome (Sugar Bowl in New Orleans, Louisiana)

The Sugar Bowl is a big-time bowl game, but one would not know it by the number of fans inside the Superdome on New Year's Eve for this match-up of No. 9 Texas and No. 13 Virginia Tech. It's not even close to a sellout. The Horns are ahead by 10 late in the first half when safety Chris Carter lets an easy interception—and presumably a stroll into the end zone—slip through his hands and into those of a Hokie. James Brown, harried all night long, throws three interceptions. Not only does Virginia Tech pull away to a decisive victory, but the final touchdown sparks a temper tantrum by Stonie Clark, who is ejected from the game. UT fans litter the field with toilet paper rolls, bottles, and various other projectiles. The school's final game as a member of the Southwest Conference is awful, except for the $1.5 million payout.

Notre Dame 27, Texas 24 / September 21, 1996 / Darrell K Royal-Texas Memorial Stadium (Austin, Texas)

If the newly renamed stadium were twice as large, it would still be full on this much-awaited day. As it is, a record crowd of 83,312 is there to see No. 6 Texas and No. 9 Notre Dame, playing in Austin for the first time since 1952. The Longhorns are clinging to a seven-point lead late in the fourth quarter when James Brown inexplicably attempts to sidearm a pass to tight end Pat Fitzgerald. The ball is intercepted, and the Irish tie the game eight plays later. With "mighty mo" (momentum) now in their favor, they regain possession. Five seconds are on the clock when Lou Holtz sends in a fresh-man kicker, Jim Sanson, who coolly hits a 39-yard shot.

Texas 37, Nebraska 27 / December 7, 1996 / Trans World Dome (St. Louis, Missouri)

In the first year of the Big 12's existence, Texas wins the South Division, setting up a title game with the Cornhuskers, champs of the north. The un-ranked Longhorns are 20-point underdogs to Tom Osborne's team, which is No. 3 and thinking in terms of another national title. James Brown makes pre-game comments about winning by three touchdowns. That gets plenty of media attention and has the effect of making his teammates think they can play with mighty Nebraska. John Mackovic, that riverboat gambler, is determined not to be cautious, which is seen in the game's most famous play. Texas leads by three points and has fourth-and-inches at its 28 with just under three minutes left. A punt would seem to be in order or at the very least, a quarterback sneak. But Brown hits tight end Derek Lewis with a short pass, and he motors 61 yards down the left sideline. On the very next play, Priest Holmes takes it in for the clinching TD. This stunning victory before a pro-Nebraska crowd in St. Louis sends Texas to the Fiesta Bowl to meet Penn State.

UCLA 66, Texas 3 / September 13, 1997 / Darrell K Royal-Texas Memorial Stadium (Austin, Texas)

Barely 10 months separate UT's glorious win over Nebraska in the Big 12 title game and one of the worst showings in the history of the program. Given that UCLA has played twice and lost both times, perhaps the Texas coaches and players have reason to expect they, too, will beat the Bruins—even without the injured James Brown at quarterback. If so, their expectations are off by a few light-years. The Longhorns have a nightmare of a game, turning the ball over eight times, giving up seven sacks, gaining just 53 yards on the ground, and missing too many tackles in a 66–3 loss. The boos start at 24–0, and the only reason they do not get any louder is that the fans are leaving the stadium as fast as the Bruins are scoring. Mackovic claims to have no inkling as to what has gone wrong. *Austin American-Statesman* writer Kirk Bohls suggests that the coach, who got a $150,000 bonus for winning the 1996 Big 12 championship, should offer a rebate.

Texas 20, Nebraska 16 / October 31, 1998 / Memorial Stadium (Lincoln, Nebraska)

Nebraska has won 47 straight home games, not losing since September 1991. During that time, they have won two national championships and come close a couple other times. Opponents enter their Memorial Stadium with some trepidation, but Mack Brown has a red-haired freshman quarterback named Major Applewhite, so what's to fear? On a raw afternoon in the Midwest, he throws two touchdown passes. The second occurs with just under three minutes left when he reads the defense correctly and hits Wane McGarity on a 2-yarder. Applewhite pays the price, absorbing a violent hit by Cornhuskers defensive end Mike Reuther that leaves him with a concussion and momentarily blinded. Ricky Williams gets 150 tough yards. The Nebraska fans, disappointed though they may be, applaud the victorious Longhorns.

Texas 26, Texas A&M 24 / November 27, 1998 / Darrell K Royal-Texas Memorial Stadium (Austin, Texas)

He has not yet won the Heisman Trophy, but that is just a formality for Ricky Williams. One by one, he has overtaken the most prolific running backs in college football history: Art Luppino of Arizona, Mercury Morris of West Texas State, Steve Owens of Oklahoma, Ed Marinaro of Cornell, and Archie Griffin of Ohio State. That leaves only Pittsburgh's Tony Dorsett, whose mark of 6,082 yards has stood since his own Heisman year of 1976. Tony D. is in Austin to see history made, and it comes late in the first quarter. Williams takes Major Applewhite's handoff, slips two Texas A&M tacklers, and rumbles 60 yards for a touchdown that gives him the record. The day is made more special by the showing of kicker Kris Stockton. He connects on field goals of 22, 24, 49, and 24 yards. The last one wins it, going through with five seconds on the clock. A crowd of 83,687 fans has witnessed history and a suspenseful, exhilarating game.

Texas 24, Nebraska 20 / October 23, 1999 / Darrell K Royal-Texas Memorial Stadium (Austin, Texas)

It's a full house in Austin. Those lucky enough to get into the stadium see a heart-throbbing victory over No. 3 Nebraska. With speedy quarterback Eric Crouch employing the option offense, Nebraska jumps to a 10-point halftime lead. The Longhorns keep pounding away and go ahead in the third period, then back comes Nebraska. The game-winning drive features two big passes by the right arm of Major Applewhite: 39 yards to Ryan Nuñez and then 17 to tight end Mike Jones. He fights off Huskers defender Kyle Vanden Bosch to get across the goal line. UT's nickel-and-dime offense looks like a million dollars on this day. Shaun Rogers has nine tackles (five for minus yardage), and Ahmad Brooks causes a key fumble toward the end. For the second straight year, Mack Brown gets a lift from his players after beating Nebraska. Going toe-to-toe with Big Red and prevailing is indicative of the program he is building, although Texas has backslid after big wins in recent years. Time will tell.

Arkansas 27, Texas 6 / January 1, 2000 / Cotton Bowl (Cotton Bowl in Dallas, Texas)

A great year becomes merely good with a regular season finale loss to A&M and another to an angry bunch of Cornhuskers in the Big 12 title game in San Antonio. Even worse is this defeat by Arkansas on the first day of a new millennium. Four Longhorns—including defensive end Aaron Humphrey and receiver Kwame Cavil—have been suspended for unspecified rules violations in the week before the Cotton Bowl, but it's a 3–3 game at halftime. Houston Nutt's Razorbacks twice barely avoid safeties and then go all the way down the field. Thus begins the scoring parade. Big 12 player of the year Major Applewhite suffers a knee injury early in the fourth quarter; freshman Chris Simms shows moments of promise but is not ready for prime time. In this, the 14th game of the season, the Horns look tired on a warm day in Dallas.

All-Decade Team, Offense

Quarterback	James Brown (1994–1997)
Back	Shon Mitchell (1995, 1996)
Back	Ricky Williams (1995–1998)
Lineman	Stan Thomas (1987–1990)
Lineman	John Elmore (1993–1995)
Lineman	Blake Brockermeyer (1992–1994)
Lineman	Dan Neil (1993–1996)
Lineman	Jay Humphrey (1995–1998)
End	Mike Adams (1992, 1993, 1995, 1996)
End	Kwame Cavil (1997–1999)
Tight end	Pat Fitzgerald (1994–1996)
Punt/kick returner	Mike Adams (1992, 1993, 1995, 1996)
Kicker	Phil Dawson (1994–1997)
Punter	Duane Vacek (1992–1995)

All-Decade Team, Defense

Lineman	Shane Dronett (1989–1991)
Lineman	Bo Robinson (1989–1992)
Lineman	Tony Brackens (1993–1995)
Lineman	Chris Akins (1994–1997)
Linebacker	Brian Jones (1989, 1990)
Linebacker	Winfred Tubbs (1989, 1990, 1992, 1993)
Linebacker	Anthony Curl (1989–1992)
Defensive back	Stanley Richard (1987–1990)
Defensive back	Lance Gunn (1989–1992)
Defensive back	Bryant Westbrook (1993–1996)
Defensive back	Chris Carter (1993–1996)

Q & A

Q. Intoxicated with joy after winning the 1990 season opener against Penn State up in Happy Valley before a crowd of almost 86,000, what was the refrain of safety Lance Gunn and his teammates?

A. "We've shocked the nation!"

Q. He was a walk-on kicker. For four seasons, he had mostly sat and watched while Jeff Ward and Wayne Clements played. Then in 1990, he got his chance and connected on more field goals than any other kicker in UT history. Name him.

A. Michael Pollak, who had a 56-yard boot that year against Baylor.

Q. One might say the Longhorns "Cashed in" when they beat OU, 14–13, in 1990. How so?

A. Twin brothers Kerry and Keith Cash both caught TD passes from Peter Gardere.

Q. When, in the 1990 season, was the old "nah-nah-nah-hey-hey-goodbye" chant was put to use?

A. After the Longhorns' 49–17 defeat of Arkansas. It was the Hogs' last visit to Austin as a member of the SWC.

Q. What was the climactic play of the 1990 UT–A&M game?

A. With just under four minutes left, the Aggies had scored to close to within one point. Coach R. C. Slocum chose to go for a two-point conversion, but almost as soon as Darren Lewis took a pitchout from Bucky Richardson, there was defensive back Mark Berry to bring him down.

Ricky Williams

Assistant coach Steve Bernstein deserves credit for having persuaded Ricky Williams of San Diego's Patrick Henry High School to become a Longhorn in 1995. Williams agreed, but with the understanding that he would also play minor league baseball in the summers, and he did—with the Batavia Muckdogs in upstate New York.

Williams, a rare combination of speed, power, and endurance, was not just a star but *the* star the moment he got to Austin. When his four years were up, he held or shared 20 NCAA records. Most significantly, he was the career rushing leader, although his record would be broken the next season by Ron Dayne of Wisconsin. In late 1998, Williams was in New York to accept the Downtown Athletic Club's 64th Heisman Trophy. Smiling and wearing his now-famous dreadlocks, Williams joined Earl Campbell as the only UT players to have won it.

He was chosen in the first round by the New Orleans Saints, who had traded all of their other draft picks to get him. But Williams hired an agent with virtually no experience in negotiating NFL contracts, so he ended up with a foolish, incentive-laden deal that would lose him countless millions of dollars. After three years with the Saints, he was shipped to the Miami Dolphins for two first-round picks. In his first season there, Williams led the NFL in rushing with 1,853 yards.

Always known for being quiet and gentle off the field, he was diagnosed with depression and social anxiety disorder, treating it with medication, therapy, yoga, and—most of all—marijuana. He tested positive, and was fined and suspended numerous times. Williams retired and traveled to India and Australia, to the consternation of pro football fans. But he soon found out he could not afford to do so. Back with the Dolphins, he was no longer the dynamo of old. After flunking yet another drug test, he was allowed to play for the Toronto Argonauts of the CFL. Even in that league, his showing was nothing special. Ricky Williams, arguably the greatest running back in college football history, has been lionized and criticized in equal measure. He is an enigma, no doubt about that.

Q. What lineman blocked two field goals against Auburn in 1991?

A. Shane Dronett. An all-American that year, he was chosen in the second round of the NFL draft by Denver. Dronett had a nine-year career with the Broncos, Falcons, and Lions.

Q. In a 32–0 defeat of TCU in 1991, Peter Gardere became the most prolific passer (in terms of throws completed) in UT history. Who did he surpass?

A. Bret Stafford. And the next season, Gardere would go by Bobby Layne for the most scoring passes thrown.

Q. This son of a former Texas great was on the team in the early 1990s, moving around from quarterback to running back to kick returner, but he could not replicate his dad's magic. Who was he?

A. Jimmy Saxton.

Q. DeLoss Dodds had chosen David McWilliams as his new football coach in 1987 largely because he was a well-loved and avuncular figure, a true orangeblood. After five years (and a 31–26 record), Dodds was determined not to let that happen again, so what did he do differently in 1992?

A. Of course, Dodds made the final call, but he employed a professional search firm in zeroing in on John Mackovic.

Q. According to the Austin American-Statesman, *who were the front-runners to succeed McWilliams?*

A. Dennis Erickson of Miami, Bobby Ross of Georgia Tech, Howard Schnellenberger of Louisville, Dick Sheridan of North Carolina State, and Dennis Green of Stanford. Mackovic was listed among "others to consider."

Q. And what became of David McWilliams?

A. He took a job as an associate AD in the athletic department, working primarily with the T Association, which maintains contact with lettermen in all sports.

Q. What did Mississippi State Coach Jackie Sherrill do to help get his team ready for its game with Texas to open the 1992 season?

A. He had a bull—representing Bevo—castrated in front of his team on a practice field in Starkville. News of the incident got out, and the MSU president called Sherrill on the carpet. He apologized but insisted the procedure had been done for educational and motivational purposes.

Q. What do Gardere and Bill Bradley have in common?

A. Both played quarterback for the Longhorns, and both punted—although in the case of Gardere, it did not happen often.

Q. Name the defensive end who intercepted a pass and returned it 24 yards for a game-winning TD against Houston in 1992.

A. Norman Watkins.

Q. UT fans felt there was something odd about Baylor's 21–20 defeat of Texas on a cold and rainy day in Waco in 1992. What was it?

A. Grant Teaff was retiring after 21 years as BU's coach, and his team benefited from some dubious officiating. The accusation was that the refs got caught up in the feel-good moment and intentionally helped the Bears win. Perhaps, but the Horns were their own worst enemies: Lovell Pinkney dropped three passes, the deep snapper twice sent the ball over punter Kelly McClanahan's head, and UT had 129 yards in penalties.

Q. How did Peter Gardere do in his final game as a Longhorn?

A. On November 26, 1992, Gardere was 13-of-32 passing (including one interception returned 95 yards for a score) but he caught a short TD pass from Darrick Duke against Texas A&M. The Aggies won, 34–13, and finished the regular season undefeated.

Q. Who constituted one of the Longhorns' few bright spots against OU in 1993?

A. Mike Adams, who caught seven passes for 117 yards and two TDs.

Q. Texas played in the first-ever college football game in San Antonio's Alamodome. When was it, and who was the opponent?

A. On October 23, 1993, the Horns took a 37–10 win over SMU in front of 42,787 fans. It was technically a home game for Tom Rossley's Mustangs.

Q. In the 1993 Houston game at the Astrodome, who booted a 56-yard field goal—the longest in the SWC that year?

A. Scott Szeredy.

Q. Starting quarterback Shea Morenz had an injured knee, so who was tossed into the fire against OU in 1994?

A. Redshirt freshman James Brown, who completed 17-of-22 passes in leading UT to a defeat of the Sooners. Brown, who was blessed with a quick delivery, ran well, had a knack for turning bad plays into good ones, and was cock-sure of his ability to win games. He soon wrested the job from Morenz.

Q. With a nice financial incentive from ESPN, Dodds agreed to have the 1994 game with Rice played on a Sunday night. How did it turn out?

A. A national audience got to see Texas fall to the Owls, 19–17, at Rice Stadium. As Mackovic put it, "Our offense was not hitting on all cylinders."

Q. This defensive back had played 19 games for UT and never snagged an interception until a 38–27 defeat of Pittsburgh in 1995, when he had three. Name him.

A. Tre Thomas.

Q. The 380-member Longhorn Band played eight minutes at halftime of the 1995 UT–Notre Dame game in South Bend. What did it cost them to make that trip?

A. More than $100,000.

Q. There were a few days when Ricky Williams was outshone by other UT running backs. Name one of them.

A. In the 1995 SMU game in Dallas, Shon Mitchell gained 180 yards and scored two touchdowns.

Q. Texas jumped to a 21–0 lead in the first nine minutes of the 1995 Oklahoma game but did not win. What happened?

A. There were crucial penalties and turnovers, and the Horns may have relaxed a bit. OU's Jerald Moore had 174 yards and scored twice.

Q. James Brown put on a memorable performance against the Ags in 1995. What did he do that night in College Station?

A. He wore an ankle brace, was heavily taped, and was limping noticeably but he led the Horns to a methodical 16–6 victory. In the locker room, the players savored possession of the final Southwest Conference championship trophy.

Q. Three days before the Longhorns were to play Virginia Tech in the 1996 Sugar Bowl, some fairly amazing news broke. What was it?

A. A special teams player and substitute defensive back, "Ron McKelvey" was revealed to be an impostor. His actual name was Ron Weaver. He was 30 years old and had played six or possibly seven years of college football in California. Weaver, who had borrowed another man's name and Social Security number to make the ruse work, left New Orleans in a rush. Dodds, Mackovic, and the entire UT athletic department were surprised and embarrassed. Weaver's later explanation was that he just loved college football too much to stop playing.

Q. What was the first game in the history of the Big 12 Conference?

A. On August 31, 1996, Texas beat Missouri, 40–10, in Austin. Maybe the football gods were upset about the demise of the Southwest Conference because the game was interrupted in the third quarter by a torrential downpour with copious lightning. After 45 minutes, play was resumed.

Q. Even the best ones have bad games, and James Brown had one in Charlottesville in 1996. How bad was it?

A. By the opening minutes of the second quarter, he had thrown three interceptions and fumbled once in a 37–13 loss to Virginia. He was benched in favor of sophomore Richard Walton.

Q. *Texas led winless OU by 11 points with less than 10 minutes to play in 1996. What then happened?*

A. John Blake's Sooners tied the game, sent it into overtime, and won it. Although UT had suffered a huge collapse, the season would be salvaged.

Q. *In the 1996 UT–Kansas game in Lawrence, the Horns won handily. Ricky Williams gained 190 yards, but one of the Jayhawks bested him. Who was it?*

A. June Henley, who carried 44 times for 209 yards.

Q. *The Longhorns, winners of the Big 12 title game in St. Louis, won a trip to the Fiesta Bowl to play Penn State. How did it go?*

A. James Brown threw an interception on the game's first play, leading to a Nittany Lions TD. The Texas defense yielded far too much ground in the second half as Joe Paterno's team took a 38–15 decision.

Q. *Who became UT's all-time leading scorer early in the 1997 season?*

A. Kicker Phil Dawson. He would soon be replaced atop the scoring list by Ricky Williams.

Q. *Oklahoma State got a little payback for its 71–14 loss to Texas in 1996. In what form did it come?*

A. The next year, the Cowboys rode the Longhorns out of Stillwater by a score of 42–16.

Q. *On a muddy and gloomy day in College Station in which Texas lost for the seventh time in the 1997 season, what record did Ricky Williams break?*

A. Earl Campbell's single-season rushing mark of 1,744 yards, which Williams topped with 1,893. A few days after that game, the announcement was made that Coach John Mackovic was being "reassigned."

Q. *This man appeared to be the next UT coach until a last-minute change of direction took place. Who was he?*

A. Gary Barnett of Northwestern. A few days later, North Carolina's Mack Brown was in Austin, gripping and grinning with Darrell Royal.

Q. *When did Williams set the UT career rushing mark?*

A. In the second game of the 1998 season, a 49–31 loss to UCLA at the Rose Bowl. The Longhorns would be back at that venue six years later, under very different circumstances.

Q. *Identify the SWC superstar from an earlier age with whom Williams bonded during his senior year.*

A. Doak Walker of SMU. They met when Williams won the Doak Walker Award as the nation's top running back the previous season. When Walker died in September 1998, Williams got permission to wear his No. 37 in the Oklahoma game, which was played in "the stadium Doak built."

Q. *In 1998, Texas and Oklahoma State were tied at 34 with three seconds left. In came kicker Kris Stockton to attempt a 29-yard field goal. Did he make it?*

A. After getting iced by three OSU timeouts, he got his foot into the ball, which caromed off the goalpost and through.

Q. *What wide receiver set a UT record by catching four touchdown passes in a 42–35 loss to the Red Raiders in Lubbock in 1998?*

A. Wane McGarity.

Q. *How did Williams (recent winner of the Heisman Trophy) do in his final game with the Longhorns?*

A. Williams gained 203 yards and scored twice in a defeat of Mississippi State in the Cotton Bowl as Mack Brown got an obligatory Gatorade bath.

Q. *How or why did the Horns lose to North Carolina State (23–20) in the 1999 season opener?*

A. Three blocked punts had a lot to do with it.

Q. *How did Baylor Coach Kevin Steele respond after suffering a 62–0 loss to UT in Waco in '99?*

A. In the postgame handshake, he laid his head on Mack Brown's shoulder, listened to consoling words, and wept.

Mack Brown

From childhood on, Mack Brown had football in his veins; both his father and grandfather coached the sport. He attended Vanderbilt in his native Tennessee before transferring to Florida State. An injury ended Brown's playing career prematurely, so he began coaching. Not unlike Mackovic, he moved around although his career path had a somewhat clearer trajectory. He coached wide receivers at FSU, Southern Mississippi (where he also earned a master's degree), Memphis State, and Iowa State. After one year at LSU, he got his first head coaching gig, at Appalachian State. Brown was offensive coordinator at OU in 1984, then head coach at Tulane. He resuscitated that program before moving to North Carolina. He faced a tough job in Chapel Hill, winning just one game in each of his first two seasons there. Things got better—much better. Brown's 1996 and 1997 teams won 10 games apiece, and the Tar Heels had a top-five program.

Brown was a hot commodity, although critics said he was a better recruiter than football coach. The people at UNC did all they could to keep him. But the offer of a larger contract from Texas and, with it, a better chance to win, brought Brown his next and presumably last job. In nine seasons at UT, he has never won fewer than nine games and has been in that many bowl games, including, of course, a pair of Rose Bowls. He convinced Ricky Williams to stick around for his senior year and recruited a very promising quarterback out of Houston by the name of Vince Young. When his team won the 2005 national crown, he was voted coach of the year. As the stadium has gotten bigger, so has the athletic department's budget and Brown's salary. Winning begets money, and he is in the highest echelon of college coaches, raking in about $2.5 million per annum.

Q. What was the worst game of Major Applewhite's best year?

A. In 1999, Kansas State took full advantage of his three fumbles and three interceptions in a 35–17 win. Applewhite was also sacked thrice.

Q. Kris Stockton won another game at the end, this time in 1999. Who was the victim?

A. Iowa State, up in Ames. The Cyclones were ahead with just over three minutes to play when Applewhite and running back Hodges Mitchell put together a 65-yard drive that set up Stockton's short but pressure-filled field goal.

Q. Who ran 80 yards for a touchdown on the first play of the UT–Oklahoma State game in 1999?

A. Mitchell. The Longhorns won it, 34–21.

Q. Texas was ahead of A&M by 10 points with less than 20 minutes left in the game in College Station in 1999. Did the Horns get the victory?

A. No. Quarterback Randy McCown led the Ags' victorious comeback. It was a game full of emotion because a week earlier 12 students had died in the annual bonfire held on the A&M campus each year for decades. It had always been indicative of the Aggies' "burning desire to beat UT."

Texas' incomparable quarterback, Vince Young,
scampers across the USC goal line late in the Rose
Bowl, securing the 2005 national championship.
(Photo courtesy of the University of Texas.)

As a new century dawned, University of Texas football was in very good shape. It was among the three top programs in terms of both wins (809 through the 2006 season) and winning percentage—trailing just Michigan and Notre Dame. Oh, there were problems, challenges, a few players getting in trouble with the law, and painful losses such as those to Oklahoma in 2000 and 2003. An upset by Colorado in the 2001 Big 12 championship game was an unpleasant surprise, too. Those who made the most demands simply did not understand how difficult it was to reach the top in a hyper-competitive endeavor like college football and to do so in a remotely ethical way. But there was clearly an upward trend. The budget in the athletic department overseen by DeLoss Dodds continued to grow, closing in on $100 million per year. Attendance was better than ever. Gone were the days of the early 1990s when it was possible to buy a $5 ticket from a local grocery store and sit with room to spare in the north-end horseshoe. Darrell K Royal-Texas Memorial Stadium, bigger and more commodious than before, began to be sold out even for games against such weaklings as Louisiana–Lafayette, New Mexico State, Rice, and Sam Houston State.

Most of all, the Longhorns were winning, with no fewer than 10 victories each season between 2001 and 2006. It is hard to say whether they would have won a national crown if not for the signing of a 6' 5", 220-pound quarterback out of Houston named Vince Young. He voluntarily redshirted in the 2002 season, won the job by the middle of 2003, and did things of legend over the next two years. Bobby Layne, Tommy Nobis, Earl Campbell, and Ricky Williams all had done their part in building the Texas football legacy, but perhaps none match VY in terms of leadership and sheer athletic ability. As we will see, Young's dazzling Rose Bowl performances against Michigan and Southern California led some football cognoscenti to proclaim that never before had there been such a player.

Changes were afoot at the stadium, beginning with the erection of an $8 million scoreboard in the south end, known as the "Godzillatron." This 7,370-square-foot piece of high-tech equipment certainly changes the dynamics of watching a UT home football game. It is a video screen that effectively shows replays, snippets of player info, and—most annoying—advertisements, some of them played quite loudly. There have been times when the music of the Longhorn Band was drowned out by the omnipresent ads. When first put to use in 2006, it drew a mixture of applause and horror.

After years of planning, the athletic department announced that the horseshoe, built eight decades earlier, had to go. In fact, because the stadium originally contained a track, those 13,000 seats were far from the action, which only served to dilute home-field advantage. The Board of Regents approved a $150 million expansion plan, due for completion in 2008, that will entail new seating much closer to the north end zone and an upper deck that will wrap around from that now on the east side. A plaza at the northwest corner will be a memorial to military veterans—an item first promised 10 years earlier when the stadium was renamed for DKR. A pair of 115-foot towers, club space, 44 luxury boxes, offices for a severely overcrowded athletic department, and a new academic center will all be part of the complex. Seating capacity will be just over 90,000.

There is no time frame for expansion in the south end, but contingency plans have already been drawn up. Dodds won't say when it will happen or give it a price tag, but a project similar to that now being built in the north end is sure to be started in the south. At some time in the future, UT's stadium will have 200 luxury boxes and room for a staggering 115,000 football fans. As Dodds once said, "We don't try to keep up with the Joneses. We *are* the Joneses."

By the Numbers

0 Touchdowns for Roy Williams against Oklahoma in four games.

4 Chris Simms interceptions returned for touchdowns in 2000.

8 Sacks suffered by Houston quarterback Jason McKinley in a 48–0 loss to Texas in 2000.

14 Points scored by Baylor against Texas from 2002 to 2005; the Horns had 203.

15 Times Chris Simms started and won at Royal-Texas Memorial Stadium.

17 Returning starters in 2001.

20 Game home winning streak, busted by Arkansas in 2003.

23 Years since a UT quarterback had rushed for 100 yards until Vince Young did it against Oklahoma in 2003.

29 TD passes by Colt McCoy in 2006, tying a national record for freshmen.

35 Years since Texas sat at the top of the college football world (1970–2005).

40 Wins in four years for Texas' 2002 seniors like Chris Simms, Cory Redding, Derrick Dockery, and Rod Babers.

80 Percentage of revenue the UT athletic department derives from football.

282 Straight games between shutouts (Baylor in 1980, Oklahoma in 2004).

652 Points scored in the 2005 season, an NCAA record.

42,500 Attendance at the Orange–White game on March 31, 2007.

89,422 Fans at the UT–Ohio State game on September 9, 2006. It was the largest crowd ever to watch a football game in the state of Texas.

Archive

Home games in **bold**

2000 Record: 9–3 Coach: Mack Brown
Texas 52, Louisiana–Lafayette 10
Stanford 27, Texas 24
Texas 48, Houston 0
Texas 42, Oklahoma State 7
Oklahoma 63, Texas 14 (in Dallas)
Texas 28, Colorado 14
Texas 46, Missouri 12
Texas 48, Baylor 14
Texas 29, Texas Tech 17
Texas 51, Kansas 16
Texas 43, Texas A&M 17
Oregon 35, Texas 30 (Holiday Bowl in San Diego, California)

2001 Record: 11–2 (Big 12 South champions) Coach: Mack Brown
Texas 41, New Mexico State 7
Texas 44, North Carolina 14
Texas 53, Houston 26
Texas 42, Texas Tech 7
Oklahoma 14, Texas 3 (in Dallas)
Texas 45, Oklahoma State 17
Texas 41, Colorado 7
Texas 35, Missouri 16
Texas 49, Baylor 10
Texas 59, Kansas 0
Texas 21, Texas A&M 7
Colorado 39, Texas 37 (Big 12 championship game in Irving)
Texas 47, Washington 43 (Holiday Bowl in San Diego, California)

2002 Record: 11–2 Coach: Mack Brown

Texas 27, North Texas 0
Texas 52, North Carolina 21
Texas 41, Houston 11
Texas 49, Tulane 0
Texas 17, Oklahoma State 15
Oklahoma 35, Texas 24 (in Dallas)
Texas 17, Kansas State 14
Texas 21, Iowa State 10
Texas 27, Nebraska 24
Texas 41, Baylor 0
Texas Tech 42, Texas 38
Texas 50, Texas A&M 20
Texas 35, LSU 20 (Cotton Bowl in Dallas)

2003 Record: 10–3 Coach: Mack Brown

Texas 66, New Mexico State 7
Arkansas 38, Texas 28
Texas 48, Rice 7
Texas 63, Tulane 18
Texas 24, Kansas State 20
Oklahoma 65, Texas 13 (in Dallas)
Texas 40, Iowa State 19
Texas 56, Baylor 0
Texas 31, Nebraska 7
Texas 55, Oklahoma State 16
Texas 43, Texas Tech 40
Texas 46, Texas A&M 15
Washington State 28, Texas 20 (Holiday Bowl in San Diego, California)

2004 Record: 11–1 Coach: Mack Brown

Texas 65, North Texas 0
Texas 22, Arkansas 20
Texas 35, Rice 13
Texas 44, Baylor 14
Oklahoma 12, Texas 0 (in Dallas)
Texas 28, Missouri 20

Texas 51, Texas Tech 21

Texas 31, Colorado 7

Texas 56, Oklahoma State 35

Texas 27, Kansas 23

Texas 26, Texas A&M 13

Texas 38, Michigan 37 (Rose Bowl in Pasadena, California)

2005 Record: 13–0 (Big 12 champions, national champions) Coach: Mack Brown

Texas 60, Louisiana–Lafayette 3

Texas 25, Ohio State 22

Texas 51, Rice 10

Texas 51, Missouri 20

Texas 45, Oklahoma 12 (in Dallas)

Texas 42, Colorado 17

Texas 52, Texas Tech 17

Texas 47, Oklahoma State 28

Texas 62, Baylor 0

Texas 66, Kansas 14

Texas 40, Texas A&M 29

Texas 70, Colorado 3 (Big 12 championship game in Houston)

Texas 41, Southern California 38 (Rose Bowl in Pasadena, California)

2006 Record: 10–3 Coach: Mack Brown

Texas 56, North Texas 7

Ohio State 24, Texas 7

Texas 52, Rice 7

Texas 37, Iowa State 14

Texas 56, Sam Houston State 3

Texas 28, Oklahoma 10

Texas 63, Baylor 31

Texas 22, Nebraska 20

Texas 35, Texas Tech 31

Texas 36, Oklahoma State 10

Kansas State 45, Texas 42

Texas A&M 12, Texas 7

Texas 26, Iowa 24 (Alamo Bowl in San Antonio)

20 Big Games

Stanford 27, Texas 24 / September 16, 2000 / Stanford Stadium (Palo Alto, California)

A night game at Stanford Stadium draws 43,970 fans, some of whom may fear a repeat of the 69–17 drubbing the Cardinal got last year in Austin. No need to worry, though, because they lead by 11 points entering the fourth quarter. In quick succession, Major Applewhite throws touchdown passes to B. J. Johnson and Victor Ike. But Stanford's backup quarterback, Chris Lewis, soon hits DeRonnie Pitts for a go-ahead score with just over a minute left. The Longhorns, who run the ball 28 times for just 13 yards, have dropped four of their last five games.

Texas 42, Oklahoma State 7 / September 30, 2000 / Darrell K Royal-Texas Memorial Stadium (Austin, Texas)

A pre-game ceremony honors Ricky Williams, now in his second year with the New Orleans Saints. The visiting Cowboys of Oklahoma State score an early touchdown and have notions of upsetting No. 13 Texas. Applewhite comes off the bench for the third time in four games—his many supporters castigate Mack Brown for starting Chris Simms—to throw for 291 yards and three touchdowns. The most dazzling is a 96-yard game-breaker to freshman Roy Williams during the third quarter. Sophomore Kenny Hayter makes a name for himself by running for 122 yards. The Horns better enjoy the feeling, because they will get mauled by OU the next week in Dallas.

Oregon 35, Texas 30 / December 29, 2000 / Holiday Bowl (Qualcomm Stadium in San Diego, California)

The Horns have finished the regular season strong, with wins over Colorado, Missouri, Baylor, Texas Tech, Kansas, and Texas A&M. None of those games are really close, but the five-week layoff plays havoc with conditioning and timing. The Holiday Bowl, against No. 8 Oregon, features a wild second half but one that goes the Ducks' way. Chris Simms throws three interceptions, while his counterpart in green, Joey Harrington, leads the game-winning drive.

Texas 44, North Carolina 14 / September 8, 2001 / Darrell K Royal-Texas Memorial Stadium (Austin, Texas)

This is a memorable game for several reasons. North Carolina, the school Mack Brown left for UT, is at the stadium to meet his fourth-ranked Longhorns. But

233

Cedric Benson

He had an unparalleled schoolboy career in Midland, gaining 8,423 yards and leading his team to three state championships. In those three games, Cedric Benson scored 15 touchdowns. When he signed with UT in 2001, the comparisons with Ricky Williams were inevitable. Both wore dreadlocked hair, both dabbled in minor league baseball, both were big—although Williams was bigger as well as faster—and both young men could really carry the rock. A four-year starter, Benson won the Doak Walker Award (as did Williams, twice) in 2004 and finished with 5,540 yards, the sixth most in NCAA Division I-A history. His best day as a Longhorn came against Texas A&M in 2003 when he carried 35 times for 283 yards and scored 4 TDs.

Although he was not an especially adept receiver or pass blocker, Benson was chosen in the first round by the Chicago Bears. He missed 36 days of training camp before signing a five-year deal. In Benson's first two seasons in the Windy City, he has dealt with injuries and struggled to get playing time under Coach Lovie Smith. In the 2006 NFC championship game against the New Orleans Saints, he scored a touchdown and gained 60 yards. Two weeks later in the Super Bowl, however, he fumbled, had minus 1 yard rushing, and was injured in Chicago's 29–17 loss to the Indianapolis Colts.

Nathan Vasher returns eight punts for a school-record 153 yards and Chris Simms sparkles at quarterback as the Horns roll. Julius Peppers, the Tar Heels' great defensive end, has no impact whatsoever on the game. Texas scores a final touchdown with 36 seconds to play, and Applewhite takes a knee to preserve the score as a way of honoring Cole Pittman (who wore No. 44), a player who died in a car wreck the previous February. Less than three days later, terrorists will strike in New York, Washington, and Pennsylvania.

Colorado 39, Texas 37 / December 1, 2001 / Texas Stadium (Irving, Texas)

Having hammered Colorado in Austin six weeks earlier, the No. 3 Horns are solid favorites to win the Big 12 championship game and possibly advance to the Rose Bowl, where they would face Miami. Mack Brown reminds his players of it shortly before this game at Texas Stadium, where the audience has an unmistakable burnt orange hue. But Chris Simms throws three interceptions (one of which is taken back all the way and another of which is taken back 73 yards before Chris Brown scores soon thereafter) and fumbles once before getting injured late in the first half. He is booed mercilessly. Applewhite throws a 79-yard TD pass to B. J. Johnson on his second play and nearly brings the Longhorns a victory. Other players have bad games, but none like Simms. It is a sweet victory for Gary Barnett, once Texas' would-be coach.

Texas 47, Washington 43 / December 28, 2001 / Holiday Bowl (Qualcomm Stadium in San Diego, California)

The surprise loss to CU, a second straight trip to the Holiday Bowl, and an injury to star freshman running back Cedric Benson might be reason enough to sulk, but the Horns won't do it. Still, they trail Washington by 19 points in the fourth quarter. Applewhite leads a miracle comeback that ends with Ivan Williams scoring in the final minute. Applewhite is serenaded by fans chanting his name, and UW Coach Rick Neuheisel says, "Major Applewhite had a fitting end to his unbelievable career." He doesn't do it alone, of course. Roy Williams catches 11 passes, and freshman linebacker Derrick Johnson has an interception, a sack, and a bunch of tackles. This is Texas' first 11-win season since 1983.

Texas 17, Kansas State 14 / October 19, 2002 / KSU Stadium (Manhattan, Kansas)

Texas and K-State are tied with less than two minutes left when Simms calls an audible, goes back to pass and is hit by a trio of Wildcats as he releases the ball. It falls into the hands of B. J. Johnson for a 32-yard gain, setting up Dusty Mangum's go-ahead field goal. The Horns avoid overtime when Marcus Tubbs blocks Jared Brite's 36-yard attempt. UT has three blocks in the game—an extra point, a punt, and now this potential game-tying field goal. Simms, who wins the 21st game of his college career, shows plenty of moxie against a determined team in Manhattan.

Texas 27, Nebraska 24 / November 2, 2002 / Memorial Stadium (Lincoln, Nebraska)

It's a freezing day. The biggest crowd yet at Memorial Stadium—78,268—is on hand to see whether the Cornhuskers can beat their visitors from down Texas way. Quarterback Jamaal Lord does his part, rushing for 234 yards. The 6' 5" Simms is no runner, but he throws for 419. Roy Williams has 13 receptions, and Nathan Vasher preserves the win by intercepting Lord's pass on the 1-yard line with 10 seconds to go. Of Nebraska's last 75 home games, just 2 have been defeats, both of them administered by the Longhorns.

Texas 35, LSU 20 / January 1, 2003 / Cotton Bowl (Cotton Bowl in Dallas, Texas)

A late-season loss to Texas Tech has sent the Horns to Dallas, although they had planned on being in Tempe, Arizona, site of the Fiesta Bowl. And playing an unranked LSU team in a stadium where they have lost their last four games is not an inspiring recipe. Chris Simms, one of the most scrutinized quarterbacks in college football, hits Roy Williams with 57- and 75-yard bombs. End Cory Redding and linebacker Reed Boyd lead a stout defense that frustrates Tigers QB Marcus Randall from the get-go.

Oklahoma 65, Texas 13 / October 11, 2003 / Cotton Bowl (Dallas, Texas)

The players have talked about extra-tough practice sessions and a willingness to pay the price for football success, but one would not know it from their showing at the Cotton Bowl. The domination begins early for Bob Stoops' team. Cornerback Derrick Strait (an Austin native) intercepts a Chance Mock pass and sets up the first of OU's many scores. He also recovers two fumbles. Redshirt freshman Vince Young replaces Mock before the first quarter is out, and although he gets 127 yards rushing, he makes a plethora of mistakes. It is a huge defeat, such a complete meltdown that some scribes wonder whether it might signal the beginning of the end for Brown, as had the 1997 loss to UCLA for John Mackovic. To his credit, Brown takes full blame.

Texas 43, Texas Tech 40 / November 15, 2003 / Darrell K Royal-Texas Memorial Stadium (Austin, Texas)

Ever since losing his starting job to Vince Young in the OU game, Chance Mock has been the consummate teammate. He has supported Young, advised him, and been willing to go in for mop-up duty against lowly and beaten teams. But he has his moment against Texas Tech on this night in Austin. The Red Raiders are up by five with less than two minutes to play when Brown tells Mock to warm up. Starting at the 14-yard line, he hits Roy Williams for a big gainer and then it goes to B. J. Johnson in the corner of the end zone to cap a dramatic and unique comeback. Mock, who was born in Lubbock and whose father played and coached for the Raiders, is likely to long remember 11/15/03.

Texas 22, Arkansas 20 / September 11, 2004 / Razorback Stadium (Fayetteville, Arkansas)

One year after the Razorbacks won in Austin and rubbed it in with the upside-down Hook 'em signs, it is time for a little payback in the Ozarks. Sophomore QB Vince Young is not a finished product, but he puts together a masterful third-quarter drive that gives UT a lead it will never surrender.

Not that Arkansas will quit, not with the biggest crowd (75,671) ever at Razorback Stadium. Houston Nutt will have plenty of questions to answer about his move toward the end of the game. The Hogs have the ball at the Texas 13-yard line, and an easy field goal will put them on top, possibly winning it. He calls a sprintout pass for quarterback Matt Jones, but before he can throw he is hit by Michael Huff and Larry Dibbles. Jones' fumble is recovered by Michael Griffin. Cedric Benson gains 188 yards, topping 4,000 for his career.

Texas 56, Oklahoma State 35 / November 6, 2004 / Darrell K Royal-Texas Memorial Stadium (Austin, Texas)
With impressive wins over Missouri, Texas Tech, and Colorado, the Long-horns appear to be moving with the speed and force of a freight train. Then, they somehow fall behind Oklahoma State by 28 points in the second quar-ter. A 5-yard pass from Young to tight end Bo Scaife just before intermis-sion seems meaningless—or is it? Brown sees that his team is positive and energetic, the fans are not booing, and most of all he has Young, whose high school coach once said of him, "He will not let his team lose." Be-fore 13 minutes of the third quarter have elapsed, the score is tied, and the Longhorns keep on going in one of the more amazing comebacks in college football history. Young is 18-of-21 through the air, Benson has five TDs, and 83,181 enthralled fans will be able to say they were there to see it. The Cowboys are stunned, to say the least.

Texas 38, Michigan 37 / January 1, 2005 / Rose Bowl (Rose Bowl in Pasadena, California)
Lots of controversy is hanging over this game. Some pundits are upset that Brown had campaigned for his team to be put in a BCS bowl—as if other coaches haven't done the same. And parochial natives of the West Coast don't like it that the Pac-10/Big 10 rivalry is no longer locked in for the Rose Bowl. As it is, the No. 13 Wolverines have far weaker credentials than Texas, whose fans have not always been the most dedicated about traveling to away games. But some 45,000 have made it to Pasadena to see the Horns in the granddaddy of them all, the Rose Bowl. Young, showing boldness and bravado like no other quarterback before, is simply spectacular. He runs for 192 yards, passes for 180, and scores four times. In the last quarter, in particular, Young dashes through the Wolverines' defense repeatedly; they

know he's coming, but they can't stop him. He sets up Dusty Mangum for a wobbly game-winning 37-yard field goal as time expires. Linebacker Derrick Johnson and running back Cedric Benson, a couple of great ones, conclude their UT careers.

Texas 25, Ohio State 22 / September 10, 2005 / Ohio Stadium (Columbus, Ohio)

"Hey y'all! Rose Bowl's over!" Vince Young hollers at the first team meeting of the 2005 season. As the Longhorns' undisputed leader, he sets the tone in every way and they turn their attention to the tasks at hand. The biggest game on the schedule is part of a home-and-home series that fans have been anticipating since it was first scheduled a decade earlier: Ohio State in Columbus. The eyes of the college football world are focused there, given that the Longhorns are No. 2 and the Buckeyes No. 4. Both teams have national title aspirations. The famous old horseshoe on the banks of the Olentangy River holds a frothing crowd of 105,565, and it is loud in the final minutes. OSU's high-powered offense has been limited to 255 yards and one TD, but they are ahead. Young silences the crowd with a seven-play drive that finishes with a 24-yard scoring pass to Limas Sweed, who has to stretch over defensive back Nate Salley to make the grab.

Texas 45, Oklahoma 12 / October 8, 2005 / Cotton Bowl (Dallas, Texas)

This is the 100th meeting of the Sooners and Longhorns. The last five seasons, OU has been Mack Brown's primary nemesis, winning by margins that range from 11 to 42 points. On a bright, sunny day in Dallas, a tight game early on changes with one big play: Young hands off to Jamaal Charles, who breaks three tackles and heads for the house, 80 yards away. The high-stepping freshman from Port Arthur will gain 116 yards on nine carries before leaving in the third quarter with an injured ankle. By that time, the game is well in hand. Billy Pittman catches two TD passes, and Cedric Griffin and Aaron Harris help limit Oklahoma to 171 yards of total offense. The players have a wild celebration in the locker room. His gray hair and bowed legs notwithstanding, Brown shimmies to Young's favorite rap music.

Texas 41, Southern California 38 / January 4, 2006 / Rose Bowl (Rose Bowl in Pasadena, California)

Undefeated in 12 games, the Horns have only been challenged once—by Ohio State. They are coming off a 70–3 humiliation of Colorado in the Big

12 title game. UT is back in Pasadena for the second straight year, but this time no local yokels dare say they don't belong. The stakes are high: No. 1 USC is the defending national champ, owner of a 34-game winning streak, with two Heisman Trophy winners (quarterback Matt Leinart from 2004 and running back Reggie Bush in 2005) in the backfield. Young, who came in second to Bush, wanted the trophy so he uses that as extra motivation on a night that won't soon be forgotten. The Trojans have been hyped as some kind of super-team, but they have never seen a player like VY. He has a dip in his hip and a glide in his stride from start to finish. He passes for 267 yards and rushes for 200 more, including an 8-yard scramble into the end zone that wins it with 19 seconds left. Against a very worthy foe, the Horns have grabbed their fourth national championship as 93,986 fans look on. Multicolored confetti flutters down on all of them, none more than No. 10. In the days after this game, sports fans and writers just cannot rave enough about Vince Young. The greatest player in UT history? That's saying a lot, but it appears to be the consensus opinion. Young is a splendid athlete, an iron-willed and unstoppable magician with a football in his hand.

Ohio State 24, Texas 7 / September 9, 2006 / Darrell K Royal-Texas Memorial Stadium (Austin, Texas)

It is time for the second half of that home-and-home with Ohio State, and a record crowd is at the stadium to bear witness. Jim Tressel's Buckeyes come to Austin ranked first, and their hosts are just one spot back. Vince Young is learning the ropes with the Tennessee Titans, so it is a very different team. UT's 21-game winning streak ends as QB Troy Smith (soon to be the 2006 Heisman Trophy winner) passes for 269 yards and a pair of touchdowns. When his counterpart, freshman Colt McCoy, throws a costly interception early in the second half, the Bucks start to pull away. They will go on to play in the national championship game, losing to Florida. Texas, meanwhile, recovers nicely and wins its next eight before some late season struggles.

Texas 22, Nebraska 20 / October 21, 2006 / Memorial Stadium (Lincoln, Nebraska)

The snow is coming down late in the fourth quarter of this wild and serendipitous game in Lincoln. The Cornhuskers have gone ahead for the first time with a 25-yard pass from Marlon Lucky to Nate Swift. They regain possession and appear likely to win until Marcus Griffin recovers a fumble with 2:17 to go. Colt McCoy then leads his team on an eight-play, game-winning drive. It includes Quan Cosby gaining 14 yards on a reception and fumbling, only to have offensive lineman Kasey Studdard come along and claim it. UT advances to the Nebraska 5-yard line, at which time Mack Brown turns to walk-on place-kicker Ryan Bailey. It would have been Greg Johnson, but the latter is injured and has had an extra point blocked and has missed two short field goals. Bailey's kick rings true, and the Longhorns escape with a surprising victory.

Texas 35, Texas Tech 31 / October 28, 2006 / Jones AT&T Stadium (Lubbock, Texas)

From a UT perspective, this game gets off to a terrible start. Texas Tech's Graham Harrell has thrown two touchdown passes, and Colt McCoy has had a pass taken back 19 yards for a score. But Texas' budding star quarterback has scoring strikes to Nate Jones, Jordan Shipley, and Limas Sweed, so halftime finds the Horns down by just 10. A raucous bunch of fans are screaming for more, but they will get no more on this night. The decisive moment comes early in the fourth quarter when McCoy hits Cosby on an out pattern. Two Tech defenders gamble for the interception and fail, leaving Cosby an uncontested trip into the end zone for a 28-yard TD. Red Raiders Coach Mike Leach is beside himself after the game, practically accusing all the refs of having orange blood.

All-Decade Team, Offense

Quarterback	Vince Young (2003–2005)
Back	Hodges Mitchell (1997–2000)
Back	Cedric Benson (2001–2004)
Lineman	Leonard Davis (1997–2000)
Lineman	Mike Williams (1998–2001)
Lineman	Derrick Dockery (1999–2002)
Lineman	Justin Blalock (2003–2006)
Lineman	Kasey Studdard (2004–2006)
Tight end	David Thomas (2002–2005)
End	Roy Williams (2000–2003)
End	Limas Sweed (2004–2007)
Punt/kick returner	Nathan Vasher (2000–2003)
Kicker	Kris Stockton (1996, 1998–2000)
Punter	Richmond McGee (2003–2005)

All-Decade Team, Defense

Lineman	Casey Hampton (1996, 1998–2000)
Lineman	Shaun Rogers (1997–2000)
Lineman	Cory Redding (1999–2002)
Lineman	Marcus Tubbs (2000–2003)
Linebacker	Derrick Johnson (2001–2004)
Linebacker	D. D. Lewis (1998–2001)
Linebacker	Aaron Harris (2002–2005)
Defensive back	Quentin Jammer (1997, 1998, 2000, 2001)
Defensive back	Michael Huff (2002–2005)
Defensive back	Nathan Vasher (2003–2005)
Defensive back	Aaron Ross (2003–2006)

Q & A

Q. In the first game of the 2000 season, Louisiana–Lafayette jumped to a 10–0 first-quarter lead. The Cajuns, not accustomed to playing in front of 80,000-plus fans, had notions of winning. Did they?

A. No. Major Applewhite took over from Chris Simms at quarterback, and UT scored the next 52 points.

Q. On a cold and wet day at the Cotton Bowl in 2000, Oklahoma gave the Longhorns a severe 63–14 beating. After the game, what did the Sooners' band do to pour salt in the gaping wound?

A. They stopped in front of the UT locker room and played "Boomer Sooner" five times.

Q. He was the littlest Longhorn, but he had 279 all-purpose yards in a 46–12 trouncing of Mizzou in 2000. Identify him.

A. Hodges Mitchell. He gained 151 yards rushing, 47 on pass receptions, and 81 on punt returns that day against the Tigers. He was even better three weeks later against Kansas with a Big 12–record 375 yards.

Q. Although Baylor fell to UT, 48–14, in 2000, the Bears were not too unhappy. Why?

A. At least they scored. They were coming off shutouts by Texas Tech, Texas A&M, and Nebraska.

Q. What linebacker set a school record five fumble recoveries in 2000?

A. D. D. Lewis.

Q. He transferred from Duke and caught a few balls for the 2001 and 2002 UT teams. Who was he? Hint: His father serves as head coach of the Denver Broncos.

A. Kyle Shanahan, who is now the Houston Texans' quarterbacks coach. His father, of course, is Mike Shanahan, owner of two Super Bowl rings.

Q. What was the behind-the-scenes tussle over the 2001 Texas–Houston game?

A. It would be played in the Bayou City, but where? UT officials wanted it to be held at the Astrodome or Rice Stadium, which were bigger than the Cougars' Robertson Stadium. Built as a high school facility in 1941 by the Works Progress Administration, it had been spruced up as much as possible. UH insisted that the game be played there, although it meant a considerable sacrifice in terms of ticket sales. At any rate, Texas won by a score of 53–26.

Q. Freshman linebacker Derrick Johnson got his first start against Texas Tech in 2001. How did he do?

A. He had nine tackles and one sack, bringing extra speed to the linebacking corps.

Q. What play settled the game in a gut-wrenching 14–3 loss to defending national champion OU?

A. The Horns were on their 3-yard line in the late minutes, trailing by four points. Sooners safety Roy Williams leaped over a lineman and hit Simms' arm just as he threw. The ball fluttered to Williams' teammate, Teddy Lehman, who waltzed into the end zone. Simms, who was sacked five times and gave up four picks against Oklahoma, did much better the next week against O-State: five touchdown passes.

Q. Identify UT's honorary captain for the 2002 season opener versus North Texas, joining the football-playing captains at midfield for the coin-toss.

A. Lance Armstrong, fresh off winning his fourth straight Tour de France.

242

Q. In Chapel Hill, North Carolina, where fans still viewed Brown as the Benedict Arnold of football coaches, Texas was struggling to put away the Tar Heels early in the fourth quarter. How did it turn out?

A. Chris Simms hit Roy Williams for a 58-yard TD strike, and a 31-point rout was on.

Q. The Horns beat Tulane, 49–0, at the Superdome in 2002. What was unusual about that game?

A. It was unusual in that it was not unusual for UT to shut out the Green Wave, having done so for the 10th time in 18 meetings that date back to 1894.

Q. After winning their first five games of the 2002 season, the Long-horns were No. 3, Simms was more in command and less prone to mistakes in the pocket, and Brown was ready to turn the tables on his OU counterpart, Bob Stoops. Did he?

A. No. The third-ranked Sooners got 248 yards from diminutive running back Cedric Griffin and pulled away to a 35–24 win. Simms had three picks. It made the cover of *Sports Illustrated*.

Vince Young

Like Benson, Vince Young enjoyed a splendid high school athletic career. He started at quarterback for three years at Houston's Madison High School, compiling 7,624 yards of total offense. As a basketball player for the Marlins, he averaged 25 points per game. He ran track and was twice a member of the school's district champion 400-meter relay squad. Young somehow found time to play two seasons of baseball, pitching and playing in the outfield.

As a redshirt freshman at UT in 2003, Young sent Chance Mock to the bench after five games (although Mock did come on and save the day against Texas Tech). The coaches adapted their offensive schemes according to the unique talents of Young, using the shotgun formation with three wide receivers. He had a growing reputation as a dual-threat quarterback, able to inflict serious damage by running or throwing.

In his final two seasons, he led Texas to 24 victories, losing just once—to OU in 2004. Two-time Rose Bowl MVP, Young performed on such a high plane as to have an endless number of superlatives rain down upon him. After leading Texas to the national championship, he went back to his hometown of Houston where January 10, 2006, was dubbed "Vince Young Day." Taken third overall by the Tennessee Titans, he had commandeered the starting job by early October. Young led his team to dramatic comeback victories over the New York Giants, Indianapolis Colts (that year's Super Bowl winners), Houston Texans, and Buffalo Bills. The first rookie quarterback named to the NFL Pro Bowl, Young has already been on the cover of *Sports Illustrated* six times.

Q. UT won four more games and had hopes of playing in a BCS bowl before losing on a chilly evening in Lubbock. Who was the culprit?

A. Quarterback Kliff Kingsbury, who threw for six touchdowns in a 42–38 victory. About 20,000 Tech fans stormed the field when it was over.

Q. When did Vince Young make his UT debut?

A. In the 2003 season opener against New Mexico State (a 66–7 slaughter), he entered the game in the fourth quarter. Young had two TD runs and lobbed a 60-yard pass to Sloan Thomas to set up another score. A crowd of 83,096 was rather pleased to see what the rookie could do.

Q. What did Arkansas Coach Houston Nutt do after his team beat UT in Austin in 2003?

A. He climbed atop the band director's podium and led a victory chorus or two.

Q. It was the fourth quarter of the 2003 K-State game, and the Horns trailed by four. What key play helped them win it?

A. Defensive back Phillip Geiggar stripped Wildcats QB Eli Roberson and fell on the ball. Second-team (not for long) quarterback Vince Young then led an 88-yard scoring drive.

Q. In the third quarter of UT's 46–15 defeat of A&M at Kyle Field in 2003, Nathan Vasher intercepted one of Reggie McNeal's passes. What was the historical significance of that catch?

A. Vasher tied Noble Doss' career interception mark of 17, which had stood since 1941.

Q. Following the 2003 season, Texas was back in the Holiday Bowl for the third time in four years. Surely the Horns would have no trouble with Washington State, right?

A. Wrong—the Cougars pulled a 28–20 upset. Brown chose to start Mock, and the UT offense was sloppy and uneven, whoever was at quarterback.

Q. A couple of heavyweights, the No. 5 Longhorns and the No. 2 Sooners, went mano-a-mano in Dallas in 2004. Who prevailed?

A. OU, which was blessed with a most impressive freshman running back named Adrian Peterson. He gained 44 yards on his first carry and finished with 240. Young was 8-of-23 passing. But Cedric Benson was right to remind reporters, "We still have plenty of games left. The season's not over."

Q. Why did many Texas Tech fans started heading to the parking lot in the third quarter of their team's game with UT in 2004?

A. Young (10-of-15 through the air, 158 yards rushing, and 4 touchdowns) and his mates were putting a collective knot on the heads of the Red Raiders, 51–21.

Q. In a fairly easy victory over Colorado at Folsom Field in 2004, what career mark did Cedric Benson achieve?

A. He became the 10th player in college football history to gain more than 5,000 yards. Benson had 141 that chilly day against the Buffs.

Q. Benson ascended to the sixth spot two weeks later against Kansas, but it was his teammate, Vince Young, who again made the headlines. What did he do this time?

A. Texas trailed the Jayhawks by three points with just over a minute to play. Facing fourth-and-18, he scrambled 22 yards to keep hope alive. That led to a 21-yard scoring strike to Tony Jeffery for a very dramatic win. In a postgame press conference, KU Coach Mark Mangino was irate, accusing the referees of favoritism. Within a day, he had apologized and made plans to pay the $5,000 fine incurred.

Q. How did Texas' tight ends do in the Rose Bowl against Michigan?

A. David Thomas and Bo Scaife combined to catch nine of Young's passes for 122 yards and one TD.

Q. The Horns wore throwback uniforms (circa mid-1960s) for their 2005 season opener against Louisiana–Lafayette. What was different about them?

A. Each player's number appeared on his helmet, there were no numbers on the shoulder pads, no names on the backs of the jerseys, and no "Texas" on the front. The ever-present Nike "swoosh," however, remained.

Q. What issue was the subject of widespread discussion in the days after UT's big win over Ohio State in Columbus in 2005?

A. The rude, crass, and disrespectful behavior allegedly shown by Buckeyes fans to anyone wearing orange. It was a late game, and it seemed that many

245

people had been boozing all day long. OSU President Karen Holbrook wrote a letter of apology on behalf of her institution.

Q. What made Texas' 45–12 defeat of OU so special for Rodrigue Wright?

A. The 315-pound tackle picked up a fumble and hotfooted it 67 yards for a TD.

Q. Many people had doubts about Young's passing accuracy, especially given his somewhat unorthodox throwing motion. When did those doubts disappear?

A. Perhaps on October 15, 2005, when he completed 25-of-29 passes, to seven different receivers, for 336 yards and two touchdowns in a 42–17 defeat of Colorado.

Q. Young once again displayed poise under pressure in the 2005 Oklahoma State game in Stillwater. What did he do?

A. His team was down by 19 points, but Young never panicked. He gained 267 yards rushing, scored two touchdowns, and threw for another two as the Longhorns won, 47–28.

Q. Name the sophomore running back who scored four TDs in Texas' 62–0 defeat of Baylor in Waco that year.

A. Ramonce Taylor.

Q. What victory was necessary for the Longhorns to go back to Cali for a second straight year?

A. They had to beat Colorado in the Big 12 title game in Houston. A lopsided 70–3 victory was more than enough to have them smelling roses again.

Q. After vanquishing the mighty Trojans in the Rose Bowl, what did Young do?

A. He took off his pads and jersey, and put on a "2005 National Champions" T-shirt and cap—cocked sideways. He then took the Waterford crystal football that topped the trophy and struck a Heisman pose.

Q. The Tower was lit orange, with a big "1" on all four sides after Texas' titanic win over Southern Cal. So what issue was on the minds of most UT fans?

A. Whether Vince (in Austin and other Texas cities, his first name had come to suffice) would stay for his senior year or head to the NFL. Four days later, he announced he was leaving and few dared complain after what he had done.

Q. Winning a football championship is unlike anything else, but UT had some other winners in the early part of this decade. What were they?

A. Both men's and women's basketball teams reached the Final Four in 2003, and the baseball team won a pair of national titles. Besides Vince Young, there were stars such as Sanya Richards (track), Huston Street (baseball), Cat Osterman (softball), and T. J. Ford and Kevin Durant (men's hoops).

Q. Young took his considerable talents to Tennessee, but before he did so he spoke highly of the freshman who would be taking his place. Who was he, and where did he come from?

A. Colt McCoy, from the small west Texas town of Tuscola, had his doubters but he seemed quite capable in the 2006 season opener against North Texas. McCoy completed 12-of-19 passes for three touchdowns.

Q. A nine-foot statue was unveiled at the southwest corner of Royal-Texas Memorial Stadium when the Horns hosted Ohio State on September 9, 2006. Who was featured?

A. Earl Campbell. The bronze sculpture, entitled "The Tyler Rose," was the brainchild of James Nixon, a San Antonio oilman, and was created by Ken Bjorge.

Q. The Horns' 37–14 defeat of Iowa State was made memorable because of what meteorological event?

A. A series of lightning strikes moved through central Texas, causing the fourth quarter to be delayed for more than an hour.

Q. What were the keys to UT's 28–10 defeat of Oklahoma?

A. Two touchdown passes by McCoy and the defense holding Sooners running back Adrian Peterson to 38 yards in the second half.

247

Q. McCoy set a school record the next week against Baylor. What was it?

A. Six touchdown passes. James Brown and Chris Simms had held the previous record of five.

Q. Fourth-ranked Texas went to Manhattan fully expecting to get a ninth straight victory. And that may well have happened, except for what unfortunate event?

A. Halfway through the first quarter, Colt McCoy was trying a quarterback sneak at the KSU goal line. He suffered a shoulder injury and was unable to return. His replacement, freshman Jevan Snead, could not get it done and the Horns lost an anguishing game, 45–42.

Q. McCoy was able to play two weeks later in the regular season finale, a 12–7 loss to the Ags. How did he do?

A. With an ailing shoulder, he threw three interceptions. He also got some very rough treatment from the boys in maroon toward the end of the game. Kellen Heard made a late hit on McCoy and got ejected. Then with 20 seconds left in the game, Michael Bennett gave him a nasty blow to the jaw although no penalty flag was thrown. McCoy lay dazed on the grass for almost 10 minutes, and was put on a stretcher and taken to a local hospital.

Q. What UT offensive lineman set a school record of 50 career starts with that game against A&M?

A. Justin Blalock.

Q. The Longhorns trailed Iowa by four at halftime of the 2006 Alamo Bowl but came back to win. How did they do it?

A. Not by the running game, which got just 70 yards on 21 carries. Ryan Bailey had a 43-yard field goal, McCoy and Jamaal Charles combined on a 72-yard TD pass, and Selvin Young's 2-yard run capped a long drive in the fourth quarter.

Q: Not so long ago, the University of Texas had a reputation as a school that produced few NFL players. That is no longer the case. Name some of the Longhorns who are making it in the pros as of 2007.

A: No star shines brighter than Vince Young, quarterback for the Tennessee Titans. But let's not forget receiver Roy Williams (Detroit Lions); defensive linemen Casey Hampton (Pittsburgh Steelers), Shaun Rogers (Detroit Lions), Marcus Tubbs (Seattle Seahawks), and Cory Redding (Detroit Lions); offensive linemen Derrick Dockery (Buffalo Bills) and Leonard Davis (Dallas Cowboys); tight ends Bo Scaife (Tennessee Titans) and David Thomas (New England Patriots); linebacker Derrick Johnson (Kansas City Chiefs); running backs Cedric Benson (Chicago Bears) and Ahmard Hall (Tennessee Titans); quarterback Chris Simms (Tampa Bay Buccaneers); kicker Phil Dawson (Cleveland Browns); and defensive backs Nathan Vasher (Chicago Bears), Michael Huff (Oakland Raiders), Cedric Griffin (Minnesota Vikings), and Quentin Jammer (San Diego Chargers).

Index